OVERCOMING BIAS

A JOURNALIST'S GUIDE TO
culture & context

Sue Ellen Christian
WESTERN MICHIGAN UNIVERSITY

Holcomb Hathaway, Publishers
Scottsdale, Arizona

Library of Congress Cataloging-in-Publication Data

Christian, Sue Ellen.
  Overcoming bias : a journalist's guide to culture & context / Sue Ellen
Christian.
     p. cm.
  ISBN 978-1-934432-20-4 (print version) -- ISBN 978-1-934432-36-5
(ebook version)
  1. Journalism—Objectivity—Handbooks, manuals, etc.   2. Reporters
and reporting.   I. Title.
  PN4784.O24.C47 2012
  070.4--dc23

                                                    2011044756

To the home team—
Bob,
Robert, Daniel & Amelia—
with love

Copyright © 2012 by Holcomb Hathaway, Publishers, Inc.

Holcomb Hathaway, Publishers, Inc.
8700 E. Via de Ventura Blvd., Suite 265
Scottsdale, Arizona 85258
480-991-7881
www.hh-pub.com

10   9   8   7   6   5   4   3   2   1

ISBN PRINT: 978-1-934432-20-4
ISBN EBOOK: 978-1-934432-36-5

Printed in the United States of America.

CONTENTS

Context, Culture and Cognition   1
Making the case for reflective practice in journalism

Habits of Thought   17
How cognitive processes influence journalistic practice

Encountering the News   33
How the mind organizes and interprets information—
and how story ideas get lost in the process

Story Without Stereotype   51

*How stereotypes may influence reporting in stealthy ways—
and what to do about it*

Understanding Culture,
Understanding Sources   73

How social groups serve as lenses for looking at the world

Training the Reporter's Eye   95

*What gets journalists' attention can influence how they
portray events and explain behaviors*

Critical Decisions Before Deadline   115
*Why even experienced journalists neglect certain facts
and what to do about it*

The Power of Words and Tone   133
When words suggest unintended meanings

Attribution and Editing Without Bias   153
When to include data and how to determine cause

Journalism and Reflective Practice   171
Cultivating an open mind

APPENDICES

 Story Excerpts   189

Surveys and Questionnaires   196

by Jonathan Blakley

When I first arrived in Iraq as a producer for National Public Radio in 2007, I had my own cultural biases to deal with. I'd never been to the Middle East and I didn't speak a word of Arabic. I saw the images of the Middle East on television just like everyone else in America. The people didn't dress like us. They were usually either protesting or praying. They were described as terrorists and anti-American. I didn't know what I was getting into.

In Iraq, I found myself managing a staff of more than a dozen Iraqis. And they had their own biases about me. They admitted to me that they only knew about African Americans through television, or from their occasional contacts with the military, not all of which were pleasant.

But for security reasons, we all had to live together in the same house in central Baghdad, outside of the Green Zone. And we got to know each other, because we talked to each other. I met many of their families. I trusted them with my life.

Interviewed on the public television program "Bill Moyer's Journal" in September 2008, National Association of Black Journalists founder Les Payne said it takes reporters on the ground in situations like the war in Iraq to report the truth and cut through the potential bias: "We need reporters on the ground to go, sit, observe, listen, watch body language and to begin to use the b.s. detector to know when someone is spinning them, when someone is telling them an untruth or when someone is lying. I think that the further you get away from a source, with people who kind of filter out the information, I think the further you get away from credible collection of facts."

Journalists need to know the community that they're covering and the biases that might be part of that community—whether it's an ethnic community or a religious community or some other community of people bound by important commonalities.

Journalists need to carefully examine their own cultural biases. Can a journalist, who is aware of his or her own biases, be a fair and objective reporter? Of course. Does everyone have a bias towards something? Yes. No one is free of bias. To suggest otherwise would be farcical. But, the public craves *real* news and analysis, not flashy gimmicks that are purported to be "fair and balanced." Our democracy depends on journalists being able to report accurately *what* happened, to *whom*, *where* and *why* it happened and *how* it affects communities.

The key for journalists is being aware of what contributes to one's own biases. Learning about one's own biases is essential to truly accurate journalism; that's why this book, *Overcoming Bias: A Journalist's Guide to Culture & Context,* is so important. Journalists need to be aware of their own perceptions of news events and understand how distortions in judgment can affect news stories. Take me, for example. I am an African-American male, born in the late 1960s and raised in Detroit, Michigan. So as a journalist, I obviously come from a specific culture and background, with my own set of assumptions. Excellent journalism happens when we are able to set aside our own viewpoints and allow ourselves to better grasp the world of our sources and the communities we cover.

Striving to be a good journalist and, just as importantly, a respected journalist, is a daily struggle. Excellent journalism happens when we are able to set aside our own viewpoints, and allow ourselves to better grasp the world of our sources and the communities we cover.

At the end of the day, every journalist must take the steps to be as free of bias as possible, and to understand that much of that bias begins internally. But the struggle is worthwhile, and necessary in a free and open democratic society. As writers, reporters, producers and editors, we are all a part of a valuable, essential tool of democracy: fair, critical, open-minded and accurate journalism.

Jonathan Blakley is a foreign desk producer for NPR and a 2011–12 Nieman Fellow at Harvard University, with study concentrations in history, politics and social media in sub-Saharan Africa, and the domestic media environment in the United States.

PREFACE

Journalists *are* biased. . . . Just not in the way that most American news consumers think they are.

Media bias, or a *purposeful* slanting of the news, is the most common charge against journalists today. I believe the charge is overblown, and that the majority of journalists go out of their way to be neutral and independent in their coverage of people and events. Instead, the biases that this book explores are far more real and pervasive. They are biases in the way that humans think, the way that we naturally and instinctively categorize people, filter information, ration our attention, rely on cultural norms and default to rehearsed ways of thinking. These biases affect journalism at every stage of the reporting and writing process.

Overcoming Bias shows journalists how they can examine and know their habits of thought, allowing them to engage in more accurate reporting and coverage of the cultures in their communities and the world. Journalists need to know the biases they bring to a reporting situation in order to avoid distorting news accounts and to better serve their increasingly diversified audiences. This book provides specific advice, strategies and examples to help journalists embrace a more inclusive and open-minded approach to covering a multicultural society.

I wrote this book after nearly a decade of reporting with my students on diversity issues in our Midwest community. I needed a concise, practical resource to explain to a student why even if his quotes are right the story may still be wrong; to teach a student how to step outside herself to examine ways in which the preconceptions she brings to a story may skew her account into an inaccurate version of events; to invite these new journalists to challenge their well-worn ways of processing the world around them. I wrote this book for my students, after seeing them struggle to figure out how to understand and capture the truth of lives very different from their own.

My goal was to create a book for journalism students and working journalists that is easy to use and highly applicable. To that end, I sought to draw from the most relevant aspects of cognitive psychology and the related field of social cognition as well as intercultural communication. Cognitive psychology examines how people acquire, process and store information. A related field is social cognition, which examines how people think about themselves and others. Particularly exciting in this age of global journalism is considering how cultures affect our brains' workings. The research I drew upon comments on everyday thinking patterns and is not specific to how people think when in a professional mode, when on the job. This is in part purposeful, because journalists often spend time with sources in everyday life situations rather than in formal work settings. Journalists interact with people as social beings and strive to encourage sources to feel comfortable and to relate to them. This book draws from various theories and schools of thought, unaligned with any single research paradigm except the findings that may best service journalism.

In addition to scholarly research, this book draws on advice from working journalists. I was a journalist at large urban daily newspapers for more than a dozen years, and so I approached this book as a reporter. I interviewed journalists who are working in various roles throughout the United States. These journalists were forthright about their experiences as they grappled with cultural assumptions, attempted accurate judgments and felt discomfort in covering people unlike themselves. Their insights show readers how this book's theories apply in real life and, on occasion, they provide a dose of humor.

AUDIENCE

This book is appropriate for undergraduate and graduate journalism courses focusing on journalism practice or journalism ethics; it will also be useful for professional newsroom training. Educators and trainers will find that the book adapts to their purposes, because each chapter can stand independently if needed.

THE BOOK'S FORMAT AND FEATURES

Chapters 1 and 2 of this book provide an overall framework for open-minded thinking that I hope will become a career-long foundation for doing journalism. The following seven chapters focus on specific journalistic practices: story ideas and focus (Chapter 3); understanding sources (Chapter 4); source selection and interviewing (Chapter 5); observation, attention and framing stories (Chapter 6); journalistic decision-making (Chapter 7); word choice (Chapter 8); and editing (Chapter 9). The final chapter summarizes and sets forth numerous specific strategies for overcoming bias and increasing the accuracy of one's thinking.

I begin each chapter with an example that illustrates a habit of thinking, such as stereotyping, and how that habit affects information processing in the brain. Chapters also include the following features:

- **Learning Objectives** preview the chapter's content for readers.
- **Pause & Consider** segments throughout the text prompt reflection and discussion on substantive material.
- **Exploration Exercises** allow readers to put the chapter concepts into practice as well as observe them in others' work.
- **For Review** sections provide a recap of each chapter's key points.
- **Article excerpts** throughout the chapters and in Appendix A complement the in-depth discussions provided about the reporters' thinking processes.

Throughout this book I have also included anecdotes and advice from many reporters working in various facets of news media and in a variety of positions, from staff at mainstream media outlets to editors and independent entrepreneurs. In written responses and personal interviews, these journalists offered their wealth of experience. Their relevant comments provide firsthand knowledge that supports the scholarly research underpinning this book. Their contributions are called "On Assignment" and are indicated by this symbol:

Here is a sample of what these professionals encourage journalists to do:

- Treat all people as your equal discovered Conner Boals, a producer for Reuters, while covering a story about an elderly Montana couple. He relates lessons from his reporting in Chapter 2.

- Delve below superficial assumptions about other cultures, as Kerry Luft, now a senior editor at the Chicago *Tribune,* learned to do in a story about children in poverty. He tells about his experience in Chapter 4.

- Know your prejudices, as Teresa Puente of *Latina Voices* did when covering an anti-immigration rally as a Mexican American. She shares her experience in Chapter 4.

- Think critically about events to avoid imposing motives on others, especially those from cultures unlike your own. In Chapter 5, M.E. Sprengelmeyer, reporter and publisher of the Guadalupe County *Communicator*, describes a story about Mexican business owners in the U.S. that didn't fit his original hypothesis.

- Be prepared to be uncomfortable as you seek out the truth behind events. Finding the truth may take some time, as public radio journalist Annie Shreffler discovered in reporting about a fatal shooting in a Brooklyn neighborhood. She shares her advice in Chapter 5.

- Appreciate the influence that the tone of a story can have in communicating bias or balance. Christina Samuels has written about students with disabilities as a staff writer for *The Washington Post* and now for *Education Week*. She discusses the importance of tone in Chapter 8.

- Emphasize evidence over assumption and anecdote, advises Benjy Hamm, the editorial director for Landmark Community Newspapers, a company with over 50 papers in 15 states. In Chapter 9, Hamm tells about editing a story about teen pregnancies for which he had to deal with this principle.

- Actively consider all reasons for someone's behavior before deciding the cause of his or her actions. In Chapter 9, ESPN.com journalist Wayne Drehs describes how he practiced this advice in a profile of a devout Christian and NFL quarterback.

- Strive to make the unfamiliar familiar, as Thomas Curwen of the *Los Angeles Times* did while writing a story about a woman with a severe facial disfigurement. His conclusion about one of the greatest services that a news organization can provide is in Chapter 10.

I welcome any feedback you may have about the book. Please feel free to share your comments, ideas and your own experiences by emailing me at: info@hh-pub.com.

I wrote this book because my students needed it. When I was a daily journalist, I would have benefited greatly from the information and advice in this book. I hope that others will find it useful and even essential.

ACKNOWLEDGMENTS

I am grateful to the Western Michigan University College of Arts and Sciences for a Faculty Research and Creative Activities Support award to begin early research into the concepts that resulted in this book. Thank you to Leigh Ford, director of the School of Communication, for her support of this project. Current and former graduate students Scott Richmond, Amanda Torrens, Catherine VanDerMaas and Raquel Hellenga provided valuable research assistance. I am also grateful for the work of Siobhan Keenan, the school's administrative assistant, and of Patricia VanderMeer, our librarian liaison at Waldo Library. My students throughout the past decade inspired this book. I am thankful for their honesty and their trust as we learned together.

The initial framing of this book was influenced by two conversations with Frank Conner, professor of psychology at Grand Rapids Community College. I am humbled by the work of many fine researchers in the field of psychology, notably Susan T. Fiske and Shelley E. Taylor, whose clear, authoritative prose often guided me. I sought to simplify the complex theories and excellent research primarily from the field of cognitive psychology and to select the most relevant conclusions for use by journalists. Any misapplication of research and concepts in this interdisciplinary approach is unintentional, and solely my responsibility.

I thank Mary B. Cohen and Louise Kiernan, both of whom read portions or all of the manuscript in various stages. Thanks also to Bob Hegel for proofreading assistance. I am indebted to Brian Carroll of Berry College, whose thorough and incisive review comments helped shaped the final manuscript. I also gratefully acknowledge the constructive comments of the other manuscript reviewers: Tom Dickson, Missouri State University; Cecile S. Holmes, University of South Carolina; Tim McGuire, Arizona State University; Bill Minutaglio, The University of Texas at Austin; Aaron Quinn, California State University, Chico; Earnest L. Perry, University of Missouri; Kimmerly Piper-Aiken, Wayne State University; and Ernest L. Wiggins, University of South Carolina. Their help is sincerely appreciated. In addition, my heartfelt appreciation goes to an anonymous reviewer who showed the way with supportive, critical and far-reaching suggestions.

My sincere gratitude goes to the many journalists included in this book who took time to share their experiences from the field: I appreciate your honesty and ethics, and know others will too. I also wish to thank the Holcomb Hathaway professionals with whom I had the pleasure of working: Colette Kelly, Lauren Salas, Gay Pauley, Sally Scott and Kari Helseth. Thank you for your dedication to quality.

On a personal note: To Andrea Boucher; thank you for support on the home front. I am inspired and grateful for the example of my parents, Dan and Jill Christian, both WMU alumni, who have demonstrated a lifelong devotion to justice and an acceptance of all people. I have felt guided throughout this process by my personal faith, and give praise to God for His gifts.

This book is dedicated with love to my family: To my husband Bob Isacksen, for his rock-solid support, and to our children, Robert Christian, Daniel Louis and Amelia Kathryn. Thank you for being so patient when you heard the words, "I can't right now; I'm working on the book." May each of you always have an open mind and an open heart.

An accompanying website for readers, **www.hhpcommunities.com/ overcomingbias,** is available to provide dynamic application of the principles outlined in *Overcoming Bias*. The site includes:

- relevant news and updates on the topics covered in the book
- links to scholarly articles for those who want to find out more about the science and studies discussed throughout the book
- interactive exercises to explore individual thinking patterns
- additional interviews with working journalists
- additional real-world activities that will allow readers to put the skills they've learned into immediate practice

ABOUT THE EBOOK

This book is available as an ebook. The ebook version can be purchased on the Holcomb Hathaway website, **www.hh-pub.com.** The electronic version of the book offers a colorful layout and matches the print book page for page. In addition, those reading the ebook will find the following interactive features:

- Direct links to URLs and additional resources on the book's website, www.hhpcommunities.com/overcomingbias.
- Instant access to cross-reference links between chapters.
- Digital note-taking and unlimited bookmarking.

SUE ELLEN CHRISTIAN is an associate professor of journalism at Western Michigan University in Kalamazoo, Michigan. Christian was a reporter for the *Chicago Tribune* for a decade and has also served on the reporting staffs of the *Detroit News* and the *Los Angeles Times*. Her beats at the *Tribune* included government, politics and public health. She is the recipient of news writing and reporting awards as well as honors for her scholarship and teaching, including a College of Arts and Sciences Faculty Achievement in Teaching award. Christian teaches news writing and reporting, and organizes community-reporting projects around issues of diversity with a focus on multimedia storytelling. Christian's scholarly work focuses on multicultural and cross-cultural communication, service learning and journalism pedagogy.

Photo by Zolton Cohen

1

Context, Culture and Cognition

Making the case for reflective practice in journalism

LEARNING OBJECTIVES

- *To understand the elements of effective multicultural reporting.*
- *To recognize that a journalist's own culture may affect how he or she interprets and understands news events.*
- *To know the journalistic principles that support inclusive journalism.*

FOCUSING ON DIVERSITY

I stood in a bunkhouse on a sod farm on the outskirts of metropolitan Chicago. The wooden structure was shared by seven workers, all men from the same village in the south of Mexico. They came here to work, earning in eight months what their families could live on in Mexico for a year. The bunkhouse kitchen was crowded with three stoves and four refrigerators, one held shut with a rubber trash can fastener. The rich scents of their dinner of beans, rice and meat wrapped in soft white bread instead of tortillas clung to the unmoving air of the summer night. At the time, I covered suburban issues as a reporter for

1

the *Chicago Tribune* and was writing a story about migrant workers in the fields of the far suburbs of Chicago. I was trying to get it right.

I had enough sense to know I needed to tell the story of the area's migrant workers by actually trying to talk to them, afterhours, away from their bosses, and away from government agriculture officials. I had gotten myself there, among the workers, and was attempting to converse with them through an interpreter about their lives away from home: the hours, the working conditions, their often poor health, the struggle for higher wages, the skimping here in the U.S. so that more cash could be sent back to their families in Mexico. I had enough sense to ask good questions, questions about adequate housing, fair wages and accessible healthcare.

Still, it was tough going.

Age, gender, language and culture made for a gap in understanding between journalist and source. A journalist needs to be able to jump that divide, to see the situation from another's vantage point. Jumping the divide happens when you've done background research into the issues at hand. When you have a basic understanding of the ways that people in a culture communicate. When you select words that build trust and not distance. When you're honestly interested. When you set aside your own ideas about how things and people should work.

I sought to ask questions that would lead to revealing answers and not just adequate responses. I searched the place for clues that would help me portray how these men felt about their temporary lives there. I think they struggled to explain to me and to show me, to tell me the truth, but not so much truth that their jobs were jeopardized.

I am white, middle-class, English-speaking, Protestant and college-educated. My sources were Mexican, lower-income, Spanish-speaking, Catholic and had limited formal education. As I interviewed, I was constantly aware of all these labels—all the ways in which journalist and source were different. I tried not to thrust my values on their situation. They had their own view of what their problems and joys were.

I wrote the story, approximately 2,000 words long, and it ran on the front page of the metropolitan section to about a million readers, the Sunday circulation at the time. (You can read part of the story in Appendix A.) I heard through the local organization that advocated for the welfare of the migrant workers that the workers thought the story was fair. They sent copies home to their families.

Yet this story is one that stays with me. It captivates me nearly 20 years later because of its many layers: The practical matter of getting and keeping a job that pays a living wage; the emotional issues of distance and longing for family; the different standards of health care in the two countries the men shuttled between; the large-scale bureaucracy of immigration and the small-scale lives of a band of men who were not in the military or on some survival adventure but on a survival excursion of a different kind. Even the uncertain rhythms of the growing season.

It also stays with me because of what this book seeks to explore: What we as journalists bring to the story because of who *we* are, and how our thinking about the world affects accuracy and fairness.

To do a story like the one on the migrant workers well requires understanding that there are many ways to look at the world, each valid in its own right. I know now, after many more years of reporting, writing and editing, what I didn't fully know then: That none of those labels for journalist and source mattered, and that those labels mattered terribly. This book is about how journalists acquire, filter and judge information, and how we must do our utmost to provide information as free from preconceptions and assumptions as possible. We must engage in label-free thinking.

Part of the job of a journalist is to figure out which of the labels matter and *why*. We have to know the *why* in order to tell the right story, the truest story at that moment.

pause & *consider* Read the excerpt of my story[1] in Appendix A. Use your university or newsroom library database to access the entire story or visit www.hhpcommunities.com/overcomingbias to access the link from the Chapter 1 page. Talk with a peer about something you learned about the men's culture from reading the excerpt. Reflect on how your own culture differs from that of the migrant workers and whether that matters.

JOURNALISM WITH AN OPEN MIND

Journalists work in a multicultural, multiethnic, multifaceted world. Communicating information about the world—without systematically excluding any group of people from news coverage—

requires being conversant in diversity. Journalists need to be aware of and knowledgeable about the differences around them. This diversity includes but is not limited to diversity of race, ethnicity, gender, sexual orientation, religion, geography, physical ability and socioeconomic standing.

Journalists also need to understand how their own thinking processes can influence a news account. To give a fair account of a person or situation requires monitoring one's assumptions, biases and prejudices, and favoritism. Only then can we be as accurate as possible and portray news events with relevant context. After all, excellent journalism is founded on seeking and telling the truth. Truth relies on context and on accuracy, which is influenced by our perceptions, interpretations and conclusions about people and events.

Understanding Your Mind

An important step to achieving a journalistic standard of accuracy and fairness is to understand how, as an individual journalist, you encounter the world. What preconceptions do you bring to different situations? What do you notice? What don't you notice? How do you categorize people and events? How does your upbringing affect your ability to interact with people unlike you? Is your mind able to tolerate some ambiguity in a situation, or do you need things to be concrete and quickly defined? Knowing your own mind allows you to better navigate the mental processes that unfairly bias your thinking. News audiences need journalists who view the world with an open mind.

Journalists benefit from looking inward in order to better report on the outer world. To better understand how your culture has shaped your thinking about others, take the Social Attitude Survey in Appendix B. Figure your score using the system provided.

To think further about your results on the Social Attitude Survey, see item 1 in the Exploration Exercises at the end of this chapter.

Reporting with an Awareness of Culture and Context

News reporting requires that a journalist cross into cultures unlike his or her own. Says Rick Hirsch, managing editor at the *Miami Herald:* "The biggest mistakes you can make are to make assumptions about what is going to matter to people who aren't like you."[2]

Culture has many meanings. This book uses the broad definition of a group of people organized around important commonalities. **Culture** is a "learned set of shared interpretations about beliefs, values, and norms, which affect the behaviors of a relatively large group of people."[3] What's more critical than the particular commonality is its effect on those in the group, because *a culture provides its members with a shared system of knowledge*—knowledge about how to communicate with others, and about group values, attitudes and behaviors. Culture for our purposes is a fairly stable presence in someone's life, such as race or gender, as opposed to a transient group membership, such as affiliation with a college culture or a sport such as skateboarding.

Context describes the interrelated conditions in which something exists or occurs. It is the circumstances that create the environment for an action, statement or idea. A contemporary dispute over Native American land

Practicing inclusive journalism means acknowledging the influence of a source's culture while also seeing the source as an individual in his or her own right.

rights needs to be seen within a historical context of their removal from native lands by U.S. government policies, for example. News doesn't happen in a vacuum.

A journalist's own culture may affect what she notices, how she interviews sources, what she remembers as important about an interview, the words she chooses when writing the story and the approach to editing it, too. The meaning and significance of events are distorted when a journalist applies *her* culture to a news event. Doing so in the case of land rights for American Indians might mean adopting a modern day, pro-development approach to land use, discounting ideas about native tribal rights and holdings that are not prevalent in her own culture. Relevant cultural context is essential for a complete news account.

"Accuracy plus context equals truth. Accuracy is about facts, but context is about getting the right facts."

AL TOMPKINS, POYNTER INSTITUTE[4]

EFFECTIVE MULTICULTURAL REPORTING

Journalists are frequently reporting about people and issues different from themselves. So it's worth noting some important lessons from research that focus on skills for communicating across different cultures. Exhibit 1.1 is a basic formula for multi-cultural reporting that is based on various models of what's called "intercultural competence."[5] The goal is to develop portable skills that will serve journalists as they cross cultural borders.

I'll apply these elements to my reporting on the migrant workers and their families: My attitude was in pretty good shape; I had pitched the story and was curious to discover more about the world of migrant workers. My knowledge was decent about the migrant culture due to extensive interviews with experts. But my skills were limited, specifically my ability to identify how significantly my own preconceptions influenced my judgment about the story's focus.

What could I do about that while in the midst of the story? I could have considered what assumptions I had before entering my field reporting, including my assumption that the mens' lives had to be miserable, with such cramped lodgings, difficult jobs and families thousands of miles away. While those three things were true, it was also true the men loved one another's company, had encyclopedic knowledge of the growing cycles and saw their jobs as a means to an all-important end: Feeding their families. From that vantage point, they were proud, not miserable.

I could have also recognized my own surprise at something new to me: the wrinkly photos of the Virgin Mary taped to the warped wood

exhibit 1.1   ELEMENTS OF EFFECTIVE MULTICULTURAL REPORTING

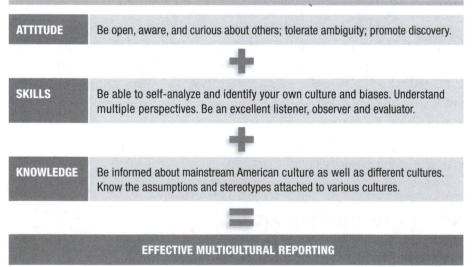

ATTITUDE	Be open, aware, and curious about others; tolerate ambiguity; promote discovery.

SKILLS	Be able to self-analyze and identify your own culture and biases. Understand multiple perspectives. Be an excellent listener, observer and evaluator.

KNOWLEDGE	Be informed about mainstream American culture as well as different cultures. Know the assumptions and stereotypes attached to various cultures.

EFFECTIVE MULTICULTURAL REPORTING

paneling and on dressers and over mirrors in the bunkhouse. I wasn't used to the sight, and the images captivated me. Such self-discovery doesn't mean the detail doesn't get mentioned, but rather how it gets mentioned: detail not as spectacle but as setting.

Multicultural Reporting in Action

Only when journalists acknowledge their biases in thinking toward a subject can they can begin to lessen the impact of those biases on news coverage. Reporters who strive to be open to new meanings will quickly dilute their preconceptions. Attitude is a powerful tool, so enter news stories with the expectation of discovery.

Teresa Wiltz, senior editor at *The Root* and former style/culture writer for *The Washington Post,* put many of the elements of effective multicultural reporting into action when she traveled to Afghanistan after an American-backed invasion led to the overthrow of the Taliban in 2001. Wiltz went with the intention of writing about women and life in Kabul, the country's capital, where Islam is the dominant religion. As part of her reporting, she shadowed a doctor in a maternity ward. Wiltz describes her mindset as she began reporting as being patronizing in her assumptions about why women wore the burqa, the outer garment associated with some Islamic traditions. The burqa cloaks the entire body and face except for the eyes. Wiltz shares her reporting experience:

The bias I had was thinking these women were victims. I had these preconceived notions that the women were going to be all happy because we've freed them from the burqas. I found it was much more complicated than that.

I had to go in and listen to what they had to say. Honestly, the burqa is the least of their issues. They are victimized but they are not victims. They are strong, smart, funny women.

I learned by hanging out at the clinic, the maternity ward. I spent about 24 or 36 hours there. I watched the doctor seeing patients. I saw she was prescribing birth control pills. Also, I saw how the women handled the burqa; one young woman climbed up on the examining table and gently pushed the burqa to the side over her shoulder, like it was a curtain of long hair. It was part of them. Not everyone liked it . . . but for them it was a protection and part of their culture.

I had a very patronizing view about that. We think they are not being educated. These women were really smart and they found their own ways to rebel.[6]

ON ASSIGNMENT

pause&consider Wiltz says she began her reporting thinking the women were victims. How does she say she overcame that bias about women in Kabul? What aspects of effective multicultural reporting did she put into practice?

An excerpt of Wiltz's story is in Appendix A. Note how she describes perceptions of the burqa. Wiltz's attitude of curiosity, her skills of observation and her knowledge of her assumptions enabled her to write a gripping story that set aside her preconceptions.

Inclusive journalism seeks to tell the stories of diverse, marginalized and unheard voices in society.

THE ETHICS OF INCLUSION

The Society of Professional Journalists' (SPJ) *Code of Ethics*[7] in many ways speaks to the mindset of journalists as they go about their work. Cultivating that mindset includes developing a multicultural and inclusive approach to journalism. The SPJ code states that journalists should:

- Tell the story of the diversity and magnitude of the human experience boldly, even when it is unpopular to do so.
- Examine their own cultural values and avoid imposing those values on others.
- Avoid stereotyping by race, gender, age, religion, ethnicity, geography, sexual orientation, disability, physical appearance or social status.
- Give voice to the voiceless; official and unofficial sources of information can be equally valid.

The National Press Photographers Association has a code of ethics that promotes similar principles, including: "Be complete and provide context when photographing or recording subjects. Avoid stereotyping individuals and groups. Recognize and work to avoid presenting one's own biases in the work."[8]

In addition, the Project for Excellence in Journalism (PEJ) reminds news people of the guiding principles of their craft:

Journalism is a form of cartography: it creates a map for citizens to navigate society. Inflating events for sensation, neglecting others, stereotyping or being disproportionately negative all make for a less reliable map. The map also should include news of all our communities, not just those with attractive demographics. This is best achieved by newsrooms with a diversity of backgrounds and perspectives.[9]

pause&*consider* As a journalist, what do you stand for? No matter the latest technology or the current industry trends—what are and will remain your core values?[10] How do they compare with the ethics statements offered by SPJ and PEJ?

DEVELOPING AN INCLUSIVE MINDSET

Practicing journalism should include examining the stereotypes that one holds, the culture in which one has lived and one's perspective on the world in order to more easily set them aside as limiting factors. Doing so allows for new ways of seeing the world. Knowing your own mind is an opportunity to gain better vision. You'll see things not seen before. You'll see beyond the stereotypes and unfair associations that you've previously made that your own background and popular culture conspired to create and reinforce. To get started on this path, here are two tips for developing an inclusive mindset:

• Be aware that who you are influences how you interpret events and sources. You have several relatively fixed positions in your life, such as your age, hometown, religious beliefs, gender, ethnicity or race, education level, income level and sexual orientation. You view people and events from these fixed positions. They combine to make up your standpoint on the world. They influence your view of and attitude toward happenings in the world. Take a moment and make a list of these positions as you hold them now.

• Be aware of an "us vs. them" approach when forming conclusions about others, especially those unlike you. This framework implies a right and a wrong way of behaving. It describes a world of people you belong with and relate to—and then everyone else. Take a moment and list some of the social or cultural groups you feel most positively toward and most a part of and those you feel most negatively toward and distant from.

Going Beyond Both Sides

Understanding how your own mind works can help you identify where it isn't working fairly or reasonably when it comes to others. As a journalist, this understanding can help you go beyond reporting both sides of the story to seeing multiple viewpoints.

Fairness, balance and objectivity are basic goals of ethical journalism—it is simply good journalism and good business to create and present news in this way. The following are guidelines for fairness, balance and objectivity.

Fairness means including all relevant perspectives in a news account, and working hard to ensure that the various perspectives are represented clearly and accurately. Though multiple views should be considered, not all views will always be mentioned in a story. Journalists need to be able to reliably consider various perspectives on an issue and identify those that are uninformed or not credible. Take time to inquire into various perspectives so as to avoid excluding valuable ones out of ignorance. When it comes to fairness, a journalist's loyalty should be not to sources, but to a solid understanding of the facts; this understanding is then communicated to the audience.

Balance requires presenting multiple voices, but it does not mean that each viewpoint must be allotted identical coverage. Journalists must work to discern the most informed, relevant and factual perspectives on issues and offer those to audiences without distortion.

Objectivity, according to Michael Bugeja, means "seeing the world as it is, not as the reporter would like it to be." Bugeja encourages reporters to "discern whether they have any biases that might taint a story and, if so, how they might adjust for that when filing a report."[11] In a way, objectivity can be seen as a foundation for fairness and balance, because only when we gather and interpret information objectively can we create a fair and balanced story.

The definitions above are not comprehensive, and they raise important points: Fairness includes critical thinking, so that journalists provide harried, hurried news audiences with the most valid and factual perspectives on issues and events. In addition, balance demands testing and investigation of perspectives. Including a point of view for the sheer sake of giving "both sides" of the story at times would mean giving exposure to ludicrous ideas, assertions with no evidence or faulty evidence or even hateful speech. Objectivity traditionally implied that journalists delivered the news without opinion or emotion. The concept has since been modernized to allow for the fact that humans do the news, not robots. Objectivity calls on journalists to know their biases so as to avoid letting those biases taint their work.

Fault Lines

Cultures are social groups. Humans create them and give them distinctive meaning. In their work, journalists are constantly crossing the borders of one culture and entering another. When journalists recognize that they have crossed a cultural border, they can appreciate the potential role of the culture's ideas, beliefs, values and knowledge on news events.

The Robert C. Maynard Institute for Journalism Education created the Fault Lines as a tool to help journalists be more aware of the cultural borders they cross. The Fault Lines, shown in Exhibit 1.2, are based on social categories that humans create, since the human mind naturally categorizes people. The Fault Lines of race/ethnicity, gender, generation, class and geography are depicted as the most enduring forces shaping lives, experiences and social tensions. The lines shape journalists' perceptions of themselves, others and news events. There is often more than one fault line at play in a given situation (a Native American issue may have as much to do with class and geography as race or ethnicity). The system helps highlight one's blind spots based on personal experiences and serves as a reminder of different viewpoints.[12]

For example, consider the viewpoint of the working poor when a devastating tornado or flood hits town and paralyzes daily activities for a few days. For the working poor, the natural disaster is more than an inconvenience, which is a middle-class way of considering the effects of schools closing, grocery stores running out of fresh food or gasoline being hard to come by. For low-income workers, the disaster goes beyond a few days of inconvenience. Each day of missed work due to a flood means a day of lost wages. Every dollar is needed to make the rent bill, to pay for daycare, to buy food; there's not that much cushion.[13]

In another example of the Fault Lines, the South Florida *Sun-Sentinel* news and business staffs engaged in an exercise designed to

exhibit 1.2 THE FIVE FAULT LINES[14]

1. RACE/ETHNICITY	Black, Asian, Hispanic/Latino, Native America, mixed race, white.
2. GENDER	Male, female, gay, lesbian, bisexual, transgender.
3. GENERATION	Youth (0–19), 20s, 30s, 40s, 50s, 60s+ • baby boomer (born 1946–1964) • Generation X (born 1965–1976) • Generation Y or Millennials (born 1977–2002). While age and personal life experience can alter a point of view, that same point of view often is defined by generational experiences. For instance, Generation X didn't watch Richard Nixon resign as president. The baby boomers did not live through the Great Depression.
4. CLASS	Rich, upper middle class/wealthy, middle class, working class, poor.
5. GEOGRAPHY	Urban, suburban, rural; plus region.

Source: The Maynard Institute for Journalism Education. Reprinted with permission.

help them see events from the viewpoint of sources and not the perspective of journalists. They went to visit a South Florida area largely populated by immigrants from Haiti and Jamaica. The staff wanted to ask residents how the paper could better cover the community. The residents essentially told the reporters: "Stop using your middle-class point of view to describe us. You keep calling us poor. You see two families living in one house, sharing one car, and you call us poor. Now we say we have a house and we have a car. We are not poor."[15]

Other cultural divisions, such as religion or political ideology, might also be a significant Fault Line for any given community and could be added to the above list. In addition, "social fissures" such as politics, religion or disability (seen or unseen) may create divisions.

These boundaries also apply to both journalists' and sources' perspectives on people and events, as shown in Exhibit 1.3. Awareness of where you as a journalist are situated on the Fault Lines chart better enables you to see the world through someone else's eyes.[16]

exhibit 1.3   THE FIVE FAULT LINES—YOUR AND YOUR SOURCES' PERSPECTIVES

1. RACE/ETHNICITY	Your race or your ethnicity influences your view of events.
2. GENDER	Your gender or sexual orientation affects your view of events.
3. GENERATION	When you grew up affects your view of events.
4. CLASS	Financial circumstances influence perspectives.
5. GEOGRAPHY	Where you're from can shape how you see events.

Source: The Maynard Institute for Journalism Education. Reprinted with permission.

MOVING FORWARD

A theme throughout this book is growing awareness of one's outward journalistic practices and inward thought processes, and how they interrelate. The following chapters discuss specific habits of thought that may distort accuracy and fairness in news accounts. Each chapter offers ways that journalists who honestly consider their own thinking can counter those habits. This book is an invitation to do even better journalism by starting with one's own mind and personal history.

exploration EXERCISES

1. After you have taken the Social Attitude Survey in Appendix B and figured your score using the system provided, respond to these items:
   a. Identify at least one question that was particularly uncomfortable for you because your answer didn't seem socially acceptable or "politically correct."
   b. React to your score and to the question you singled out in a blog posting.

   c. Pair up with a peer to compare your attitudes about the issues raised in the survey.

   d. Write a story pitch that would allow you to further explore this attitude with people on the street.

2. Use your newsroom library or university library to access *The Washington Post* archives to read Teresa Wiltz's story of Feb. 24, 2002, titled "A Woman's Place: At a Kabul Clinic, Childbirth Means a Cold Table and a Tireless Doctor." After reading Wiltz's story, respond to these questions:

   a. Note the places in the story where Wiltz refers to the burqa. Decide if the tone is neutral or not.

   b. Research the role of the burqa in Islamic tradition. Identify at least two local sources to comment on the burqa and how women feel about wearing it.

   c. Develop a list of questions for sources about the burqa's use and significance, and seek out a source for comment.

   d. Write a statement about your attitudes toward the burqa.

3. As a class or newsroom staff, brainstorm specific ways that journalists can be more inclusive in their reporting and writing. Post the list on a discussion board or on a Facebook group for all to see and use. Add or edit the list as you move through this book.

4. Download a free news app such as CNN Mobile to your mobile phone or bookmark a local news source on your laptop. One app, Newsy, provides video from multiple news sources, allowing users to compare differences in reporting choices between outlets. However you check the news each day, make it a habit to scan a story a day for Fault Lines. Then, select one story by you or someone else for this Exploration Exercise.

   a. Review the selected story with the Fault Lines in mind; then answer these questions to yourself or in a small group:

   b. Which Fault Lines are represented in the work?

   c. Are any of the Fault Lines missing that could be realistically included in the coverage?

   d. How do you or members of your group feel about the way that different perspectives are presented and played in the coverage? Is it fair and complete?

FOR review

- Recreate the diagram for Effective Multicultural Reporting and post it near your workspace.

- Explain to a peer what the following ethical mandate means: "Give voice to the voiceless; official and unofficial sources of information can be equally valid."

- Select a story to report for which you try apply the five Fault Lines in your sourcing.

- Paraphrase the definitions of fairness, balance and objectivity included in this chapter.

notes

1. Sue Ellen Christian, "Harvesting a Dream: Migrant Workers Sow Sweat, Reap Survival," *Chicago Tribune,* June 13 1993.

2. Rick Hirsch, Interview with author, August, 2010.

3. Myron W. Lustig and Jolene Koester, *Intercultural Competence: Interpersonal Communication across Cultures,* 3rd ed. (New York: Longman, 1999), p. 30.

4. Al Tompkins, "Teachapalooza!," in *Let's Get Critical* presentation (St. Petersburg, Fla.: Poynter Institute, 2011).

5. Darla K. Deardorff, "Identification and Assessment of Intercultural Competence as a Student Outcome of Internationalization," *Journal of Studies in Intercultural Education 10* (2006); Mary F. Howard-Hamilton, Brenda J. Richardson, and Bettina Shuford, "Promoting Multicultural Education: A Holistic Approach," *College Student Affairs Journal 18,* no. 1 (1998); Brian H. Spitzberg and Gabrielle Changnon, "Conceptualizing Intercultural Competence," in *The Sage Handbook of Intercultural Competence,* ed. Darla K. Deardorff (Thousand Oaks, Calif.: Sage, 2009).

6. Teresa Wiltz, Interview with author, 2009.

7. Society of Professional Journalists, "Code of Ethics" (1996), http://www.spj.org/ethicscode.asp, retrieved August 7, 2010.

8. National Press Photographers Association, "NPPA Code of Ethics," (2011), http://www.nppa.org/about_us/governance/bylaws.html, retrieved July 9, 2011.

9. Project for Excellence in Journalism, "Principles of Journalism," Pew Research Center (1997), www.journalism.org/resources/principles, Principle 8, retrieved August 7, 2010.

10. Kenneth Irby, "Diversity across the Curriculum Seminar" (St. Petersburg, Fla.: Poynter Institute, 2009).

11. Michael Bugeja, "Think Like a Journalist: A News Literacy Guide from *NewsTrust*," *NewsTrust*, Point 3: Discern, http://newstrust.net/guides/think-like-a-journalist, retrieved July 7, 2011.

12. Maynard Institute, "Fault Lines: Cultural Diversity Training in the Workplace" (2011), http://www.maynardije.org/faultlines, retrieved June 14, 2011.

13. Maynard Institute, "Chapters 3 and 4: Diversity Is in the Details." (Oakland, Calif.: Maynard Institute, 2011), http://mije.org/chapter-3-diversity-details, retrieved July 7, 2011.

14. Maynard Institute, "Fault Lines: What Is Diversity? (Part I)" (Oakland, Calif., 2010), http://www.maynardije.org/part-i-what-diversity, retrieved June 2, 2011.

15. Maynard Institute, "Chapter 6, Getting Past Our Frustrations: Let the Conversation Begin." In *How We See Our Sources, How They See Themselves.* (Oakland, Calif.: Maynard Institute, 2011), http://mije.org/chapters-v-and-vi, retrieved July 7, 2011.

16. Maynard Institute, "Fault Lines: What Is Diversity?"

2

Habits of Thought

How cognitive processes influence journalistic practice

LEARNING OBJECTIVES

- *To understand what habits of thought are and how they affect a journalist's work.*
- *To be able to explain the difference between cognitive bias and media bias.*
- *To recognize how reflective practice in journalism promotes excellence.*

CATEGORIZING OUR WORLD

At age 20, Connor Boals, now a producer at Reuters, had a reporting experience that prompted him to rethink some of his preconceptions about how "old" people lived. He felt better prepared than most college grads to interact with elderly sources, given his two independent grandparents and a 103-year-old great-grandma who drove a car well into her 90s. The summer after graduating from journalism school, he landed a journalism fellowship. On the following page, Boals shares how his multimedia reporting assignment during the fellowship challenged his ideas about age and abilities. After reading his account, visit this book's website, **hhpcommunities.com/overcomingbias,** to watch Boals' video of the Cushmans.

OA

The fellowship had an expansive budget, including travel. There was, however, one catch: We were to cover old people. Boring, smelly and hard of hearing. My reporting partner and I were given a profile assignment about an elderly couple that lived in a remote area of Montana. The home of Bob and Sue Cushman, both almost 60 years my senior, was filled with feats of engineering that Bob, a former nuclear engineer, had pulled off in designing their cabin. Nestled in 60 acres of Montana forest, the Cushmans' house was powered by solar panels, had a wood-fired sauna and bay windows that let in a sunlight more pure than anything I had seen while living in New York City. We followed Sue through her daily chore of felling 30-foot pine trees with a chainsaw, cutting them into logs that the couple burned for heat in the winter.

Never for a second did we consider them frail.

But the challenge for us came when we sat down to talk. With the camera on, we were suddenly tongue-tied because of our upbringing. The thing about being a 20-something reporter and dealing with elderly people is that, well, you feel really young. And when I feel really young, I revert to a childhood state of mind. The biggest thing I remembered from my childhood was that you always respected your elders.

The Cushmans seemed so focused on self-reliance that I was worried that asking questions that highlighted their vulnerabilities would shut them down in the interview. But Bob's health had seriously deteriorated. Sue had fallen off the roof and broken her hip. Our editor expected us to ask the Cushmans if they were happy in old age, and if they actually felt old. We danced around this topic of aging and de-generating health and dependence on others. I had all these ideas in my head about how aging would make a person feel depressed and helpless. So my colleague and I asked the Cushmans all sorts of fluffy questions about the beauty of nature, their kids and their neighbors.

But the wonder of journalism, if you do it well, is that your take on a piece of the world can be flipped by the time you've finished the story. Eventually, we started asking the questions about aging and growing old and what that feels like. And they answered every single question. Sue was moved to tears when asked to think about a life without Bob, a possibility they have both had to recently consider after his health started to worsen. Bob was so candid in his reflections that after the interview, Sue thanked us and asked us for a copy of the entire interview so their family could have it as a keepsake. I think the piece came out wonderfully. The Cushmans liked it too. It was a highlight of my still-budding journalism career.

During the visit, I realized that I was there to tell the Cushmans' story—their whole story, because that was the most respectful thing to do. The Cushmans had opened their home to us, treated us like equals. Now, it was our turn to return the favor. I learned this: Treat sources as equals—even when there are 60 years and a world of differences between you and them.[1]

pause&*consider* When reporting on a person unlike yourself, imagine your source giving this advice: "Recognize my differences but treat me the same."[2] In what way does Connor Boals offer this same advice? Briefly discuss with a peer how you would implement that advice in an interview with someone unlike you.

Connor Boals' reflection focuses on his thinking while approaching the story, his opinion on the assigned topic, his take on the Cushmans themselves and his own ideas about aging. Notice he also addresses how his interviewing approach was influenced by the values of his own cultural background regarding respect for one's elders. In small ways, Boals' reporting experience showcases much larger themes. A journalist's thinking, influenced by one's culture, upbringing and the mind's own natural processes, may influence the news product.

HABITS OF THOUGHT

People generally process information in common ways. For purposes of this book, these common ways of mental processing are described by the phrase **habits of thought.** Everyone's minds—journalist or not—follow some basic approaches to gathering, sorting, deciphering, interpreting and assessing information. They aren't hard and fast rules of thinking, and they aren't always bad, but they do describe tendencies in the way all people naturally think. Understanding our habits of thought helps us see our way to better journalism.

Cognitive Biases

The habits of thought discussed in this book generally fall into two categories: cognitive biases and mental frameworks. **Cognitive biases,** and cognitive errors, are the errors and distortions in human thinking that can occur automatically, meaning spontaneously and involuntarily, and without conscious intention to distort. A person doesn't have to harbor a negative attitude or prejudice to be cognitively biased.

Knowing how the mind works and what can be done to control the cognitive biases that most impact journalism can help news people produce more inclusive coverage. To know your own mind is also to know how wonderfully efficient it is, how speedily it can process a good deal of information throughout a day! It is also to know how flawed some perceptions and reasoning can be. A consequence of this efficiency is that people naturally process information in ways that include a host of mental distortions. Some of these cognitive biases take the form of shortcuts in thinking that are extremely useful in everyday living because they allow people to make decisions efficiently. Other cognitive biases result in negative stereotypes and faulty reasoning.

Cognitive errors are at work especially when we are emotionally stressed (as with a looming deadline) or dealing with large amounts of information (such as a breaking news story). Research[3] shows that time pressure reduces people's openness to new information and their motivation to be accurate, and increases tendencies toward confirming initial hunches or story lines.

Journalists' cognitive biases can infect:

- *Story ideas*—permitting preconceptions to dictate what they perceive as news.
- *Reporting*—seeing what they expect to see at a reporting scene.
- *Interviewing*—asking questions in a way that elicits the responses anticipated.
- *Story focus*—allowing assumptions about what happened to shape news accounts.
- *Writing*—using words, especially when on deadline, that further stereotypes, not question them.
- *Editing*—missing errors in judgment because of a lack of awareness of a judgment's affect on a story.

Cognitive errors are mistakes in thinking, or deviations from a normal, "correct" thinking process.

Cognitive biases are systematic distortions of otherwise correct thinking processes, such as underusing or overusing a particular useful mental function. An example would be categorizing people (a normal, useful thinking process) too much and too often so that it led to stereotyping and prejudice.

Source: Fiske and Taylor, *Social Cognition*, 1984.

Mental Frameworks

The other habits of thought discussed in this book are not cognitive biases but what can be considered different kinds of mental frameworks. These **mental frameworks** describe the perspective from which a person views the world and his or her viewpoint on what is normal or accepted practice and behavior. A person's background and culture shapes his or her mental framework.

Significant research explores the concept of **standpoint,** or the position from which people and things are considered or judged; a point of view or outlook. Our perspective determines what we focus on and what we miss in the world around us. It influences our knowledge of the world.

For example, consider how individuals can have differing standpoints regarding the concept of "family." One may see family as a traditional and limited hub consisting of mother, father, and siblings. Another, having grown up with extended family, may view family as a web that includes nontraditional elements and people beyond blood relatives. For yet another, family might be more about good friends who have your back and help you pay your bills rather than your biological relatives.[4]

Journalists' standpoints on family and on all topics affect their point of view. These standpoints may come into play, for example while interviewing sources and considering who counts as family. An awareness of standpoint is useful for journalists seeking to understand their own and their sources' point of views.

Metacognition

Thinking about the ways that we think is called **metacognition.** To do journalism with a standard of excellence, journalists need to understand their brains' mechanics, noting how their minds sort ideas and people, and what gets labeled and how. The goal of metacognition with the practice of journalism in mind requires installing mental filters that help scrub stories of distortions and accentuate truth-telling. For example, when Connor Boals hears from an editor that he is going to interview an elderly couple for a profile, he might not even be aware that his automatic response is stereotypical (they are "old, smelly, boring") until invited to think about his

This is a test. This is only a test.

Attention: We interrupt the regularly scheduled text of this chapter for an important (and blunt) note. No one is free from biases and prejudices and judgments. No one. So, if you happen to be a member of a group often misunderstood or inaccurately portrayed by the media—even if you fit into a category of people who may seem to be typically victims and not perpetrators of assumptions and stereotypes—you are not exempt from these biases. We are all human, with the same wiring in our brains. The mental processing that goes on inside our heads isn't as different as our exterior appearances might suggest.

And now, back to the chapter.

initial reaction to the assignment. Evaluating one's thinking about the world requires acknowledgement of an important truth.

MEDIA BIAS

Cognitive bias is not the same as media bias. While both terms share the word *bias*, that's where the overlap essentially ends. **Media bias** has many interpretations but in general, it describes an intentional and purposeful slanting of the news to a specific viewpoint or ideology. Ideological bias, the type practiced by some cable news hosts or opinion blogs is popular, welcomed and doing fine in ratings, page views and retweets. While such commentary might play well, it's not news. It's opinion. In contrast, **cognitive bias** is typically not intentional and it is not directed toward any specific ideology. Cognitive bias refers to the mental processing that influences our perceptions and our reasoning.

Part of a journalist's job is to report so thoroughly that members of the news audience can make informed conclusions about people and events in the world. The difference between informed reporting and purposeful bias is the order of action. Informed reporting digs out relevant detail and critical facts to draw a conclusion. Purposeful bias starts with a conclusion and finds facts and detail to support it. As journalists, the goal is to ensure that one's cognitive biases do not create a practice of starting with a conclusion and then seeking facts to support it.

Biases in Professional Journalism

The practice of journalism in mainstream news organizations in the United States has developed a roster of biases, or slants, toward coverage. These are not individual cognitive biases, but generalized practices that have become routine in the industry. They have little to do with an individual reporter and much more to do with professional norms. Sometimes, but not always, these biases result in news stories that are unfair, incomplete or inaccurate. Media biases are most often in the minds of news audiences when they criticize news coverage.

Some examples of biases embedded in the very structure of the profession as it's practiced today in the U.S. include:

- A bias toward conflict and dramatic events (these play well on television).
- A bias toward whatever is new or shocking (consumers like this, so that means advertisers do too).
- A bias toward a narrative structure with lead characters, heroes and villains and a beginning, middle and end, and clear outcomes (although many people's lives are non-linear and without such pure characterizations).
- A bias toward including quotes from an opposing side (even when there really isn't a vocal, distinct opposition).
- A bias toward expediency (publish first, publish fast).

pause & *consider*   Find a news story online that is representative of one of the biases listed above. Share it in a small group and explain how the story demonstrates the bias.

Expediency, the last bias on the above list, is so powerful in digital news media that it is worth further exploration. This bias describes how, in a competitive industry ruled by deadlines, the most easily reachable information and people can dictate a story's direction. Popular culture commentator Chuck Klosterman writes:

Everybody seems to be concerned that journalists are constantly trying to slip their own political and philosophical beliefs into what they
cover. This virtually never happens. . . . The single most important impact of any story is far less sinister: Mostly, it all comes down to (a)
who the journalist has called, and (b) which of those people happens
to call back first.

And even when everyone else does call back before deadline, the
template has already been set by whoever got there first; from now
on, every question the reporter asks will be colored by whatever was
learned from the initial source. Is this bad? Yes. Does it sometimes lead
to a twisted version of what really happened? Yes. But it's not an agenda. It's timing.[5]

Klosterman's wry conclusion rightly points to a real bias toward
a rush to upload content by going with the first sources who respond. Responsive sources can get undue authority to shape a story
simply by being accessible. A reporter isn't following some biased
agenda; he or she is feverishly working to get a decent story upload-
ed. The rush to publish isn't going away. So journalists are wise to be
aware of this undue influence by "first responders" and remember,
amid the relief that sources have called back, to challenge sources'
opinions. Include in the story what questions remain unanswered.
Be clear about the number of sources informing the story. When possible, follow up with same-day updates that include other opinions
as more sources are reached.

Organizational Biases

Because media bias encompasses such a range of issues involved in
the profession of journalism, it often occurs at the level of a news
organization and without the intention of an individual journalist.
Here's a for-instance: Despite the growing number of independent
news producers, the era of media conglomerates emphasizing share-
holder profits is still in force. News outlets are increasingly owned
by remote publishers focused on giving audiences what they want.

One result of that focus is more celebrity news coverage. Other
news, such as ongoing conflicts in developing countries, historically
don't get much attention anyway from U.S. news outlets, but even
less so in a news organization championing celebrity news. You
might call that a bias toward the rich and famous as opposed to the

poor and disenfranchised. But it's not as if an individual journalist set out to ignore the civil unrest in Ghana. Greater forces at work in the news industry produced that result. And, consumers of the news further the choice of certain topics over others by clicking on celebrity online updates and not registering complaints about a lack of international coverage with their news outlets.

While journalists can and should acknowledge that many forms of media bias are all around them as they work, they can also focus on the aspect of the job they have the most control over: how they think as they do their jobs. A good starting point is making time to reflect on how you work.

THE JOURNALIST AS REFLECTIVE PRACTITIONER

Just as there are habits of thought, there are also habits in how one approaches the craft of journalism. Journalists are just like any other professionals; over time, they develop work habits that help them be more efficient and successful. In the case of journalists, these habits are built around efficiently reporting news events and filing on deadline again and again.

Professional journalists develop a repertoire of reporting and writing techniques that serve them well in the rush of breaking news. They form expectations about how stories roll out. They learn what to look for in a news event and how to respond to what they find. They become less and less subject to surprise. They are so capable and adept at the job that they are seen as specialists.[6] These are all seen as positive and laudable traits that help a journalist file stories that lead the home page schedule and kick off the newscast. When I was a journalist for a large metropolitan daily newspaper, it felt great to reach the point on a beat when I could anticipate sources' viewpoints and I knew whom to call for input on certain topics. Such efficiency allowed me to make deadline consistently. It also allowed me to deliver more complete leads for the mid-afternoon editors' meeting when story placement was decided, which in turn meant a stronger possibility of Page 1 play.

Scholar Donald Schön wrote about how professionals think in action in his book *The Reflective Practitioner*. Schön noted that the negative side to professional specialization is that it can lead to an assumptive approach to the world instead of a curious one. This describes the journalist who is sure of what he's going to encounter before he even gets to the interview and who has learned perhaps too well what to look for and how to respond.

Professional specialization can create a "parochial narrowness of vision."[7] Journalists, like any other professional, can develop a repertoire of expectations because of repetition. As in: "Another case of child neglect? Let me guess: Grandma was taking care of the grandkids and left them alone while she worked a third shift. What's new about this?" Or: "Who are we looking for? A high school drop-out, Asian female, with a rap sheet for selling drugs? Might as well drive straight to the South Side; that neighborhood is filled with kids like that. Someone will know her."

Given such smooth functioning, a journalist may miss opportunities to think about what she is doing. She can overlearn what she knows. She may automatically place events and sources into well-worn categories in her mind to explain motivation and behavior. She is no longer attentive to specific and unique circumstances.[8] What she needs is to adopt a reflective approach to her work.

Reflective Practice

Reflective practice invites professionals to identify and evaluate their automatic perceptions and judgments that have grown up around repeated experience. An automatic perception or judgment is one that takes place without conscious thought or pause for assessment.

Make reflective practice a career-long habit.

To put this in journalistic terms, ask the question: How do I know? What makes me believe this? Why am I so sure? Are there other viewpoints I'm missing? What assumptions lie beneath this judgment?

Reflective practice is immediately applicable for working journalists, and a habit well worth forming for student journalists as they prepare for their careers. It can be done after every published piece or over the course of several months on a beat. It can also be done mid-story, as problems or issues surface that require thoughtful solutions. Schön called the ability to adjust what one is doing while he is doing it in order to achieve a better outcome "reflecting-in-action."

He noted how pitchers adjust mid-game. Jazz musicians improvise on the spot. So should journalists adapt. Reflective practice allows for improvisation in the face of uncertainty and uniqueness.[9]

Experiential Learning

Most reporters love to learn. They are curious people. They stick with the profession in the face of industry turmoil because it is a career of continuous mental growth; there is always something interesting happening. Reflective practice should be a natural habit for journalists, as it involves learning by doing—also called experiential learning. **Experiential learning** means learning and gaining skills and knowledge by doing, not merely by studying. It's what good journalists do everyday on the job. They broaden their repertoire of skills and knowledge with new assignments and different challenges, from how to find tax liens on a property to figuring out how to network their way to the key sources in a corporation. Their learning is done through experience.

As seen in Exhibit 2.1, a model of experiential learning emphasizes having a concrete experience (as in reporting a story) and then reflecting on one's performance from many perspectives, including those of reporter, source, editor, news audience. What worked well? What didn't? What feedback did you get and from whom? What groups aren't commenting that might be if you had included other sources or taken a different angle?

Then, use your observations and others' feedback, or lack of feedback because they weren't included in the story process, to envision a strategy for a specific improvement next time. For example, familiarize yourself with the local slang before another neighborhood-based interview; dress more appropriately for a conservative setting; honestly explore the reasons behind your discomfort with a specific source or group of people you're covering; research the various advocacy groups for people with physical disabilities to better sort out rhetoric from fact; know your geography so you're not lumping the issues of Turkish Americans in with those of Iranian Americans. Put your strategy into action on the next story, ideally with editors or educators playing supporting roles.[10] Through reflective practice, you teach yourself to be a better journalist.

exhibit 2.1 AN EXPERIENTIAL LEARNING MODEL FOR JOURNALISTS[11]

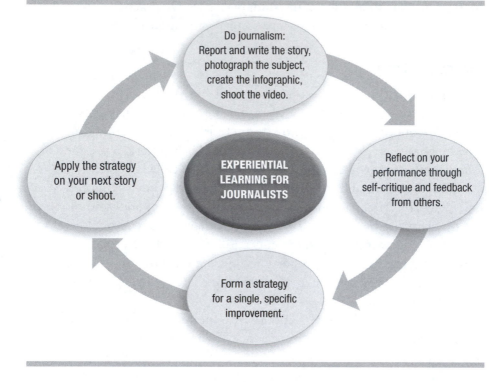

For example, for a story I wrote on grandparents raising their grandchildren, I received positive feedback from the three women I interviewed who were the primary caregivers for their grandchildren. I talked to many experts for the story, including the author of a nationwide study on depression in grandparents raising children. The news feature included women of various incomes and races, including a grandmother in her late 50s raising three grandchildren, ages 4, 3 and 5 months old. Had I applied reflective practice to this story, I hope I would have seen the opportunity to better place readers in the grandmother's position instead of describing her situation at arm's length.

I mentioned telling details, such as gates at the stairs of one couple's contemporary home and decorative walls along the staircase that had been heightened for safety. But I needed a paragraph on living this life: A close-up view detailing the grandmother up at 2 a.m. feeding the baby, or in the morning wiping the toddler's breakfast oatmeal off the floor, or playing catch with the 4-year-old. These details of the sheer physicality of her job would have given a mental picture to support one quote that began: "I get tired and feeling down."

I wouldn't of course be doing the same story again. But my take-home lesson of nailing down specific, vivid details to illustrate a source's quote is applicable in any story. News audiences can better relate to unfamiliar situations when reporters give them enough concrete details to allow them to see themselves in the same position as the story subject.

Feedback

A note on feedback from others, the second step in experiential learning: The Internet provides journalists more feedback than ever before in the form of user comments. To most effectively seek informed feedback, consider setting up a beat blog. A beat blog focuses on a well-defined beat or coverage area. One excellent example of such is *The Sacramento Bee*'s blog The State Worker by Jon Ortiz, a beat blog about state employees.

A blog such as Ortiz's builds community and engages users. This can lead to tips, data, new sources, corrections, story ideas and more accurate coverage. While you want to cultivate a network of people whose input you value, beware of creating an echo chamber in which the only input you get is similar to your own viewpoints and position in the world. Seek input from a variety of sources: members of your news audience, peers, colleagues, editors, valued sources and most importantly, critics. Ortiz, for example, posts polls for users to take on a variety of topics related to the beat. He also has a regular feature called "blog backs" in which he posts corrections, suggestions and criticisms from users. You might choose to keep your "blog backs" private. In that case, log them in a journal.

It can be hard to find time to review your latest work, as you're already rushing toward deadline on the next piece. But pause, if only for the time it takes you to post one comment about something that you did well in the coverage and one thing you'd like to do better. You might choose to ask for feedback on terminology used, to seek out better sources on the subject or to invite feedback on what's missing that people still want to know. News audiences appreciate transparency in coverage.

Improvement and application

Your strategy for improvement may be technical; perhaps you don't speak the language of your sources and needed a translator during the last interview. Or, it may be contextual; you don't understand the unspoken rules of a given cultural group and more background research is a must. Or, it may be knowledge-based; you need to know more about physical disabilities and the rights of individuals who are disabled in order to convey the issues with proportionality. Or, it may be rooted in your own biases about a group of people or a person; in that case, you need to identify your prejudice and figure out how it affects your journalism. Apply your new knowledge or approach during the next reporting experience and note the effect. The learning cycle has begun again.

exploration EXERCISES

1. Review the list of biases in professional journalism (p. 23). Select a news account to evaluate; are any of the biases listed evident in the account? In what way(s)? How might a news outlet alter its process to counteract the bias?

2. Note the role of expediency in online news stories by comparing similar accounts from two or more news outlets.
   a. Compare when the outlets filed a breaking news story down to the minute.
   b. Count the number of sources cited and the focus of the leads.
   c. Decide if your findings support or contradict Chuck Klosterman's statements on page 24 regarding responsive sources dictating story focus. That is, do any of the accounts have just one source? Report back to a small group about your conclusions.

3. Don't wait for the world to come to you to discover its diversity. It's around you. Focus on anything or anybody different from your status quo. So start where you are. The key is to be open-minded. Try to appreciate and understand people who have different backgrounds than your own.

a. To do this, spend an hour or two reporting in your own neighborhood. Look to break out of your comfort zone and meet new people, especially those who are different from you in age, race/ethnicity, gender, physical ability or another significant way.

b. Based on your reporting, write a short personal column aimed at a community audience.

c. Share the column with at least one source you interviewed and solicit feedback via email.

d. Follow the Reflective Practice Model for Journalists (p. 28) to reflect on the story process and your interactions with sources. What did you learn? Was anything surprising to you? Why or why not? What sort of feedback did you receive? What would you do differently next time? State a lesson learned in one sentence.

FOR review

- List the elements of the news reporting process that can be affected by one's cognitive biases.

- Explain the difference between media bias and cognitive bias.

- Develop a system for soliciting feedback on your journalism. If it's not a blog, it might be a private journal or an informal debriefing over coffee with a peer or a community member.

notes

1. Connor Boals, Interview with author, 2010.

2. Keith Woods, "Diversity across the Curriculum Seminar" (St. Petersburg, Fla.: Poynter Institute for Media Studies, 2009).

3. Arie W. Kruglanski and Tallie Freund, "The Freezing and Unfreezing of Lay-Interferences: Effects on Impressional Primacy, Ethnic Stereotyping, and Numerical Anchoring," *Journal of Experimental Social Psychology 19*, no. 5 (1983); Raymond S. Nickerson, "Confirmation Bias: A Ubiquitous Phenomenon in Many Guises," *Review of General Psychology 2*, no. 2 (1998); S. Holly Stocking and Paget H. Gross, *How Do Journalists Think? A Proposal for the Study of Cognitive Bias in Newsmaking* (Bloomington, Ind.: ERIC Clearinghouse on Reading and Communication Skills, 1989).

4. Ruby K. Payne, *A Framework for Understanding Poverty*, 4th ed. (Highlands, Tex.: aha! Process, Inc., 2005).

5. Chuck Klosterman, "All I Know Is What I Read in the Papers," in *Sex, Drugs, and Cocoa Puffs: A Low Culture Manifesto* (New York: Scribner, 2004), pp. 204–06.

6. Donald A. Schön, *The Reflective Practitioner: How Professionals Think in Action* (New York: Basic Books, 1983), Ch. 2.

7. Ibid., p. 60.

8. Ibid.

9. Ibid.

10. David A. Kolb, *Experiential Learning: Experience as the Source of Learning and Development* (Englewood Cliffs, N.J.: Prentice Hall, 1984).

11. Based on the experiential learning model of American social psychologist Kurt Lewin as described in Kolb, *Experiential Learning*.

Encountering the News

*How the mind organizes and interprets information—
and how story ideas get lost in the process*

LEARNING OBJECTIVES

- *To understand how schemas work and how they can affect journalists.*
- *To be able to define the perseverance effect and the self-fulfilling prophecy.*
- *To learn techniques to counter the potentially negative impacts of schemas on news stories.*

PERILOUS ASSUMPTIONS

In March 2006, a woman who was a student at North Carolina Central University was hired to dance at a party held by members of the Duke University lacrosse team. After the party, she told police that three players had sexually assaulted her. The students were charged with first-degree sexual offense, kidnapping and rape. The district attorney handling the case, Mike Nifong, stated that a rape had taken place and prosecuted the three students even as doubts surfaced about the woman's account of the events.

When the news first broke, the coverage was immediate and extensive. Major stories ran in *The New York Times, Newsweek* (one cover story was entitled "Sex, Lies & Duke"), *The New Yorker, Rolling Stone* and *Sports Illustrated*. Thousands of news outlets covered the event. *60 Minutes* devoted five segments to the case.[1] Countless blogs and commentators weighed in. A piece in *Inside Higher Ed*[2] began this way:

Something ugly happened at a party held by members of Duke University's lacrosse team March 13. Whether a gang rape took place, as a woman has charged, isn't clear. But even without that allegation, it would be a disturbing picture:

At a gathering in an off-campus home, some members of the highly ranked team were gathered—and drinking. Lacrosse is a sport largely played by white athletes—46 of the Duke squad's 47 members are white. Those at the party called an escort service to provide two "private dancers," who arrived to put on a show for the students. One of the women was also a college student—at North Carolina Central University, a historically black institution also in Durham, Duke's home.

This woman, a mother of two, was helping to finance her education by working for the service.

According to the woman, she thought she was going to a small gathering, and was shocked to find herself and her fellow dancer surrounded by more than 40 college men, who shouted racial slurs at them. She also says that three members of the team raped her in a bathroom at the house.

pause&*consider* As you read about the Duke lacrosse case, sets of main characters emerge: the male college lacrosse players, the three white players accused of rape, and the victim, a black female student working as an exotic dancer. What personal knowledge or experiences involving each of these categories of people come immediately to your mind? Write down your *expectations* about how these main characters behaved.

DEFINING SCHEMAS

Journalists from throughout the nation were descending upon the town of Durham, North Carolina, and scrambling for information about the Duke case. While the reporters, photographers and videographers were physically going to press conferences, roaming the campus and checking in at the courthouse, something else was going on in their minds. A cognitive phenomenon was at work in the coverage of the lacrosse scandal: schemas.

A **schema** is a category of knowledge that helps people interpret and understand the world. It is a mental structure used to simplify and organize knowledge. The mind can have schemas about people, social roles, specific events and ourselves.[3] When the mind meets new information, it will search for an existing schema about that type of information.

So, a reporter on the Duke story would be taking in new information on the case, and assimilating the information or differentiating it from existing knowledge and experience already in his brain. He might have a set of schemas that relate to many aspects of the case: college rape cases, house parties, exotic dancers, hate crimes. Like all schemas, these would have been acquired through experiences. He may have acquired those schemas directly through his own experiences. Or, he may have acquired the schemas indirectly through television shows, stories, movies and cultural myths. With each specific encounter or experience, he would have accompanying mental processing that involved adding and subtracting information to the organized knowledge he had in his mind—his schema on this subject. As the reporter moves around Durham, he adds new information to his schema about college athletes such that the existing schema now becomes a more specific concept about white male college athletes. He may, based on the amount of new information he's taking in, create a whole new, separate schema for Duke lacrosse players.

Experts have well-developed schema in a subject area, and that helps make their judgments less extreme. To put it in journalistic terms, a longtime beat reporter will notice, recall and use material that varies from or disagrees with established schema more than a news intern will. People who have been exposed to many schema-relevant experiences form more complex schemas that moderate their judgment. Researchers conclude, "The more variety one has encountered, the more complex the issues, and the less clear-cut it all seems, and the less extreme one's judgment."[4]

THE FUNCTIONS OF SCHEMAS

I t is important to learn about schemas because they are foundational in understanding how the mind works. Schemas affect what people (including journalists) notice, think about and remember.[5]

Schemas help individuals know what to expect from other people, oneself, social roles and social events so they can focus energy on the most relevant features of a situation. Schemas guide a person's perceptions, memory and judgments toward consistency with their preexisting expectations.[6]

Schemas are culturally influenced. The culture in which a person lives exerts its influence by instilling schemas that influence the way the person will understand and interpret the world.[7] For instance, a person raised on a crop farm has schemas about the spring planting time and each growing season. Conversely, an urban dweller has schemas about riding the subway and interacting with other riders. Either schema is generated by experiences unique to the geographic setting in which the person lives.

Schemas affect:

- *what people notice*
- *how people remember and interpret things*
- *how people make decisions*

Mental Shortcuts

The good thing about schemas is that they allow a person to take mental shortcuts in interpreting lots of information at once. Schemas help one subconsciously process lots of information throughout the day.

Due to schemas, the journalist covering the prosecution of the Duke lacrosse players doesn't have to spend a lot of mental energy understanding the workings of the court process in the case. That's because he has an existing cognitive framework about the judicial system and its workings. Instead, he can go to an unfamiliar courthouse and know how to behave and generally what to expect in the court proceedings: Rise when the judge enters. Use a quieter voice. No photographs unless given permission. He has a court proceedings "script" in mind that tells him what to expect, and he can use his mental energy on other story-related events.

The bad thing about schemas is that they are just that: shortcuts. So if the reporter's schema about prosecutors is that "the prosecutor always uses accurate facts," then a shortcut in processing information might mean the reporter doesn't pause to closely examine the prosecutor's motives or behavior in the case.

He will tend to exclude pertinent information because it doesn't fit in his mental packet of preexisting beliefs and ideas. Given that, the reporter may not even consider that the county prosecutor *wouldn't* have a load of evidence to convict the accused players. It just isn't a part of the reporter's cognitive framework on prosecutorial conduct.

Or, perhaps the reporter, a veteran of the courts who has a complex schema that allows for discrepancies, can indeed entertain that the prosecutor might be wrong—but he cannot believe that the woman is lying and the players are telling the truth in this case. His schema in these areas may be decidedly at novice level.

Interpreting and Filing New Information

One of the ways that schemas influence how we interpret things is that they are used to fill in gaps in information. So, when the brain encounters information that can be interpreted in a variety of ways, meaning the information is ambiguous, a person uses an existing schema to interpret the new information. Also, when people remember information, they often guide their memory to what's called "schema-consistent" information.

What does that mean for our reporter on the Duke case?

In the case of the accuser, she had various labels ascribed to her—single mother, young black woman, exotic dancer, community college student—that the reporter could use to quickly fit her into an existing schema. Placing the accuser in the "exotic dancer" schema instead of the "community college student" schema means certain information is accentuated, perhaps what she wore, and other information is downplayed, such as her college academic record.

The reporter also has to think about word choice when describing the accuser and how word choice may affect the schemas of his readers. One academic analysis of press coverage of the case tallied how often the accuser was described in one of four ways: mother, single mother, student or stripper/dancer. *The New York Times, USA Today, NBC Nightly News* and the *Raleigh News & Observer* were analyzed. The results were as follows: The accuser was described as a "mother" 29 times; as a "single mother" 19 times; as a "student" 92 times; and as a "stripper" or "dancer" 264 times.[8]

pause & **consider** Why do the descriptive terms for the accuser matter? What effect might the various terms have on a reader's schema? Is there a context in which one term is more appropriate than the others? How do the terms suggest blame or cause?

Here's how the Duke case turned out: A little more than a year after the scandal, in April 2007, North Carolina's attorney general announced at a crowded press conference that the students were innocent. The charges against the players were dropped. Mike Nifong, the district attorney, eventually resigned and was disbarred over ethics violations in his handling of the case. Duke University reached an undisclosed financial settlement with the three former lacrosse players who had been falsely accused. The North Carolina attorney general did not pursue any action against the accuser for making the false accusations. Think about how that fits into your existing schemas.

More Attention to the Inconsistent

It takes more work for people to process an individual's actions when the behavior is especially incongruent with existing mental concepts; when it doesn't fit with existing schemas. People remember those behaviors and other incongruous information *better* presumably because of that extra effort of trying to fit the material into existing sets of ideas and beliefs.[9] Information inconsistent with existing schemas receives more mental attention as people try to explain the inconsistencies. Also, because expected information is effortlessly integrated into a schema, this leaves extra attentional resources for processing and remembering unexpected information.

This extra processing can be a good thing for journalists who are on the lookout for inconsistencies in narratives. It can force a journalist to take note of what seems incongruous. However, it's important to remember that the *reason* something was noticeably inconsistent was because of personal categorizations and stereotypes; it was noticeable because of a journalist's internal view of how things should be, not because of an outside, empirical rule about how things should be. Strive to notice *why* you think what you think. And don't believe everything you think.

TYPES OF SCHEMAS

The way that people think about social groups and social interactions involves various schemas, as Susan T. Fiske and Shelley E. Taylor explain in their text on social cognition.[11] They include the person, event and role schemas.

Person Schema

A **person schema** is a mental file containing your perceptions of the person's traits and goals. You may have a person schema about your editor and what her personality is like. People tend to remember behavior that is relevant to their schema about the person—such as that your editor is always in better shape after a third cup of coffee, so make the morning story meeting a bit later. But you wouldn't necessarily remember or find relevant what kind of car she drives.

Person schema may encourage a reporter to fit new information about a source into an existing schema. But journalists must pause to evaluate whether the new information should instead alter their schema of the person. In other words, allow your ideas about what people are like to change as more information about them comes in, rather than shoving new information into an outdated mold.

Event Schema

An **event schema,** sometimes referred to as a *cognitive script,* describes a person's knowledge of the typical sequence of recurring events as well as for standard social occasions. Like other schemas, event schemas guide the interpretation of ambiguous information toward being in line with existing schemas. Ordering, being served, eating and paying at a restaurant is a standard script, or schema, for eating out. For journalists, an example of an event schema would be a press conference.

A person may also have an event schema that is uniquely ethnically or racially influenced. An example would be a schema for a recurrent event such as being stopped by police for DWB (driving while black), the expression used to describe a traffic stop by police for no apparent reason other than the driver's skin color. Another event schema that is ethnically or racially influenced would be if a woman experiences the recurring event of being trailed by security while shopping in clothing stores because of her appearance. She may then develop a "trailed-while-shopping" schema. Similarly, people of Arab origin who travel may have a schema about airline security checkpoints and the additional scrutiny they encounter that most travelers in the U.S. cannot comprehend.

According to some researchers, such event schemas can create the notion that more experiences are infused with racial components than actually are: "There is no doubt—there is indeed abundant evidence— that conscious and unconscious 'racial profiling' exists; but it may also be that event schemas such as these can generate the interpretation and experience of racial profiling even in marginal or ambiguous situations, thereby further 'racializing' social experience"[12]

Role Schemas

Role schemas organize one's knowledge about appropriate behaviors attached to social positions, such as how a police officer should act on the job, or how a mayor should behave at a city council meeting. Unlike person or event schemas, role schemas can contribute to stereotyping.

Role schemas create expectations about people in socially defined categories. An exotic dancer is likely a role about which people have schemas. Certain behaviors and standards are expected of people based on their age, race, sex, religion, education and so on. For example, a stay-at-home parent may be seen as nurturing and attentive if female, but unmotivated and directionless if male.

When it comes to memory and one's role schemas, the typical case will trump details of a specific instance. People apparently remember the category of information that they put someone into *better* than they remember the person as an individual. They remember the person's role even if they remember nothing about the person. As in: "She was an exotic dancer, but I don't recall her name or what she was studying at college." This lasting power of categorization lays the groundwork for stereotyping, which is examined at length in Chapter 4.

The Perseverance Effect

While not a schema in itself, the **perseverance effect** is a concept that describes how people's beliefs and schemas persist despite contradictory information. For journalists, the perseverance effect was demonstrated in the coverage of rape allegations against the three players on the Duke lacrosse team.

In their analysis of the coverage, two academic researchers wrote, "The case had elements that played into stereotypes and standard scripts about race and class—dynamics that were reinforced by Duke's mostly affluent, mostly white student body and faculty located in Durham, a small city (population approximately 190,000) with a predominately working-class and poor population, forty-four percent of which is African American." Other groups pushing various storylines for the case included faculty, which saw the case as a symbol of race, class and gender injustices. In general, the case played into the cultural schema of athletes misbehaving and administrators looking the other way.[13] In addition, some in the news media saw the story as one of Southern white males exploiting black females, even though the young men involved were not from the South.

Another insightful analysis of the Duke case[14] details how, in the frenzy of early coverage, many news outlets downplayed assertions by team captains and their defense attorneys that the charges were patently false, players were cooperating with police and DNA results would clear them. Instead, story lines clung to the script of lacrosse thugs raping a woman and covering it up.

One critic of the coverage, Kurt Andersen, writing in *New York Magazine,* asserted that the news media coverage was about reinforcing clichés and preconceptions. The lack of regard for finding the truth prompted Andersen to quote a longtime joke around newsrooms that "some juicy fragment of reporting is 'a fact too good to check.'"[15] Andersen's commentary of *The New York Times*' coverage of the Duke lacrosse team in *New York Magazine* began this way:

> As a young writer at *Time,* whenever I'd hear "That story'll write itself," I wanted to reach for my revolver. The line, delivered with bluff cheer, suggests that good material makes good writing easy, which isn't true. Its premise is the very wellspring of hackdom: The more thoroughly some set of facts reinforces the relevant preconceptions, caricatures, clichés and conventional wisdom, the easier it makes life for everyone, journalists as well as their audiences. Most people want to be told what they already know. . . .
>
> Thus the enthralling power of the Duke lacrosse-team story when it broke last spring. As a senior *Times* alumnus recently emailed me, "You couldn't *invent* a story so precisely tuned to the outrage frequency of the modern, metropolitan, *bien pensant* journalist." That is: successful white

men at the Harvard of the South versus a poor single mother enrolled at a local black college, jerky superstar jocks versus $400 out-call strippers, a boozy Animal House party, shouts of "n——r," and a . . . gangbang rape in a bathroom.[16]

pause&consider With peers, talk about what Andersen means when he says that a story will "write itself"? Why is that such a bad thing?

The Self-fulfilling Prophecy

Schemas don't just affect our thinking. They can influence reality in very concrete ways. The **self-fulfilling prophecy** is the tendency for people's expectations to elicit behavior that is consistent with those expectations. It describes the interaction that occurs when a journalist holds an expectation about how a source will behave. The interviewer's treatment of that source can foster the very behavior that was anticipated and so the expectation is confirmed, as illustrated in Exhibit 3.1.

exhibit 3.1 THE SELF-FULFILLING PROPHECY

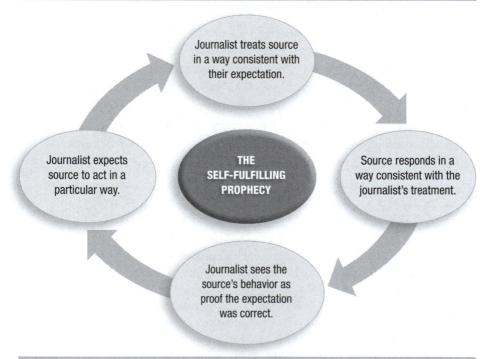

Hypothetical journalist Adarsh Singh anticipates that the female CEO he's interviewing will be pushy and aggressive in her demeanor, because that's his schema for female CEOs. His impressions have been formed by television portrayals of hard-bitten women executives. Singh's expectation impacts the way he acts toward her in the interview; he questions her briskly and unemotionally. Singh frequently interrupts to challenge her on less-than-complete answers, presuming he must be aggressive and confrontational to get information out of her.

In turn, the CEO responds to the way she's being treated by the reporter. She pushes back, delivering some hostile answers to his hostile questions. The reporter's expectation has just come true. "See," Singh says to himself as he exits her corner office after the interview, "she was just like I expected she would be: impersonal, angry, domineering. An ice queen."

COUNTERING THE BIASING POWER OF SCHEMAS

Journalists are storytellers. They love a good tale. But be wary of the easy narrative. If information seems to fit too neatly into a predetermined template, there may be a schema at work. Research shows[17] that when people have trouble remembering, they use schemas to fill in the blanks with what they think should be there. Andersen's comments in this chapter about a story "writing itself" are a reminder that careful journalists will work to dismantle the predictable script, purposely trying to "undo" it.

Combatting the Perseverance Effect

First, let's look at some basic techniques specifically found to combat the perseverance effect:

1. **Counterargue.** Explain to someone why your point of view on the story might be wrong. This act can help you see other ways of thinking about the event and to rewrite the usual scripts.[18] So if the reporter's take on the Duke lacrosse case is that of course the three players are guilty, he would argue their innocence to his editor or colleague, calling on all evidence possible to justify his position.

2. **Think it through.** When people are told to think carefully about how they evaluate information and to pay attention to their

biases as they sift through the data, the perseverance effect is moderated.[19] So the reporter on the Duke lacrosse case might know that he has a negative bias toward college athletes as cocky, privileged and aggressive. Research indicates he could offset that bias by reminding himself to think carefully about *how* he is evaluating the evidence in the case. He could pay attention to his inclination to discount evidence from the players. Making a list of facts and statements by key sources helps lay out evidence clearly.

3. **Have meaningful contact.** When it comes to role schemas, personal interaction between people unlike one another helps undercut the categorization that occurs.[20] So it stands to reason that a journalist on a beat might benefit from actively seeking out conversations with sources about whom she has pre-defined ideas or strong opinions, particularly negative ones. Developing a one-on-one professional relationship with such sources may result in more neutral schemas. In the Duke case, the sources were not accessible to news reporters due to the pending litigation, but reporters did attempt to interview friends, coaches, neighbors and faculty to better understand the key players involved.

Choose Your Thinking Wisely

Schema-driven thinking is pretty easy on the brain. It's spontaneous and unintentional. It's low-effort. It involves quick judgments based on past experiences.[21]

The opposite is **stimulus-driven thinking.** This is high-effort. It's controlled thinking. Intentional. Conscious. Voluntary. With this kind of thinking, different aspects of a person are considered individually. People cannot constantly engage in this type of controlled thinking because it requires more time and mental energy.[22] But journalists need to engage in this type of thinking when trying to figure out a source's motivation for her actions, for example.

Two tools can help encourage stimulus-driven processing and counter the effects of negative schemas on accurate perceptions. The first is **reflective practice,** which was discussed at length in Chapter 2. Recall that reflective practice encourages people to identify and evaluate their perceptions and judgments that have formed due to repeated experience. It simply encourages pause for assessment.

A reporter functioning with schema-driven thinking will automatically believe the district attorney's charges are based on valid evidence due on the dozens of past cases the reporter has covered in which the D.A. was right. Reflective practice allows the reporter to construct a new view of the situation at hand through careful assessment of the information: Is it valid? Why am I so sure? Where's the proof? What information am I missing?

A second tool to help journalists avoid schema-driven processing is to consider multiple perspectives. This technique involves the act of shifting perspectives to improve recall of events or to enrich interview questioning or background research. The **Rashomon effect** refers to how individuals remember events differently, but plausibly, from other's remembrances.[23] This effect got its name from the movie *Rashomon,* directed by Akira Kurosawa. This 1950 Japanese mystery details a crime witnessed by four individuals, who describe the event in four different and contradictory ways. The "truth" for each individual is different because their perspectives are different.

It's useful to think of this effect when reporting a story with many key players. Work to report the story from each source's perspective, and compare and verify information with other sources' interpretations of events. Continue to shift and compare the perspectives. In essence, this is trying on alternative schemas about the event. Where are points of conflicting interpretation?

A hypothetical example of this would be the very different interpretations of why the African American driver of a city bus ordered all Latino riders to get off her bus one afternoon after an altercation. For each party involved, the truth is different. Let's see how:

The driver recalls the incident this way: "These Mexicans were saying racist things about me in Spanish. I can't speak it well, but I know enough words to know they were racist. I'm trying to drive a bus safely. They were speaking loudly and getting all hostile. I have to think about all the passengers' safety. The company says I can kick anyone off the bus for harassment."

Another perspective, of course, is that of the Latino passengers. One of the passengers remembers the episode this way: "No one said anything racist about that woman! We were mad at her, though, because she didn't stop when we asked to be let off at a corner. She ignored us on purpose. She drove two more blocks just to show us

On finding story ideas: look for the non-event

We, as journalists . . . write about events, so we tend not to talk about non-events. Someone shooting a Sikh is an event. People calling their Muslim friends to offer support is not. Bush calling for war is an event. People wanting peace is not. A friend complained recently that from reading the papers you'd think all Americans want to go to war. I think we have to work twice as hard at providing context and multiple perspectives.[24]

Gelareh Asayesh

author, *Saffron Sky: A Life between Iran and America*

who was boss, and then she kicks us off because she can. Black people in this city do that all the time, trying to remind us they were here first and we are second-class to them."

The other two passengers on the bus who were not Latino or African American offer a third perspective. Said one: "Wow, the whole thing just happened in a flash. There was some sort of misunderstanding about when the bus could pull over to let the passengers off. The riders were gesturing and pointing and then started shouting. I don't know what they were saying. That driver got angry really quickly—she seemed sort of scared. But it makes me think of all these tensions in the city lately between blacks and Latinos over who is getting city jobs."

Research has shown that shifting one's perspective based on another person's goals allows one to remember details not easily recalled from the other perspective. "To see the impact of goals on understanding, take a mental tour of a friend's house, with burglary in mind," write researchers Fiske and Taylor. "What details are important? You know that burglary includes looking for expensive, easily disposable items such as color televisions, silver, and stereos, so that is what you will focus on most. To get an idea of the schema's impact, think again of the friend's house with the goal of possible purchase. Suddenly, the leaky basement matters; you remember the sagging stairs and forget the stereo."[25]

Thinking about people's intentions in specific situations can be used effectively in reporting. Shifting perspectives can help a person recall details.[26] For journalists, the Duke lacrosse case had many perspectives to consider. Thinking about each perspective and each source's goals as events unfold can help reporters present the full story.

exploration EXERCISES

1. In the form of a short essay or blog entry, write about whether your ideas and beliefs about the main characters in the Duke case—the accuser, the three players and the county district attorney—changed in light of the case's conclusion.

    a. What, if anything, is surprising to you about the people involved now that you know the outcome of the case?

    b. Compare these notes with your earlier Pause & Consider reaction from page 34, written before you knew the outcome of the case.

    c. If you were familiar with the case before reading this chapter, then approach this essay by selecting one type of schema (person, role, event) and consider how this schema type affected your ideas and beliefs about the Duke case.

2. Read the excerpt below by a journalist who covered the Duke lacrosse case for *Newsweek*. She is writing about Crystal Mangum, the woman who accused the players of rape. The column is from 2010, four years after the case occurred. The column was occasioned by new charges against Mangum that included attempted murder, arson and child abuse.

    > I ended up spending eight weeks in Durham over a year of reporting on the lacrosse case, devoting a good deal of time to trying to figure out who Crystal Mangum was, following her trail into the worst parts of town. Though I never met her, I came to know a troubled woman and her hometown, a city still raw with racial bitterness.
    >
    > At the time of the rape accusations, Mangum was a mother of two, working as an escort, and taking classes at North Carolina Central University. NCCU was the first publicly supported black liberal-arts college in the country, but it has struggled over the years to get adequate funding. The distance between the campuses of Duke and NCCU was a few miles and a lot of resentment. Students I spoke with at NCCU's campus soon after the rape charges were filed had no doubt that the lacrosse players were guilty but would

beat the rap. One student told me, "This is a race issue. People at Duke have a lot of money on their side." Another student said, "It's the same old story. Duke up, Central down." He said he wanted to see the Duke students prosecuted whether they were guilty or not. "It would be justice for things that happened in the past," he said. For me, it was one of the more eye-opening moments of the whole case."[27]

   a. Finish this sentence: *"The NCCU students had no doubt the lacrosse players were guilty but would beat the rap"* because . . . . Because why?

   b. Why is there so much resentment between Duke and NCCU? What is the author leaving unstated here?

   c. Brainstorm at least one story idea that stems from the comments in this column excerpt. Pitch it to a small group for discussion.

3. Test the Rashomon effect by selecting a recent event in your community or on campus and discuss the event with at least four other people. Compare perceptions, memories and judgments toward the event. Try to figure out why differences exist within their conclusions.

4. Think of a story you've done in which the self-fulfilling prophecy may have played a role in the reporter-source dynamic. Or, if you haven't yet had a reporting experience, think about these questions in light of a different interaction, such as between you and a waiter or waitress, or between you and a new professor. The person who is the focus of your expectations is called a "target."

   a. In a brief paragraph, describe the situation. In a second paragraph, explore how you might have changed your attitude and acted more neutrally toward the target. Think about factors such as the words you used, your body language, your tone of voice, if you stood or sat, the volume of your voice or where you focused your eyes.

   b. Can you recall another time when your treatment of a target was negative and what his or her reactions were?

   c. Can you recall a time when your treatment of a target was especially kind and patient. What was the reaction then?

5. Categorize the following based on whether the situation is more likely to prompt you to engage in schema-driven processing or stimulus-driven thinking:

- Making a trip to the grocery store
- Attending a lecture
- Listening to a defendant testify
- Observing a fundraiser by a racist organization
- Meeting the new president of the organization, who is multiracial

FOR review

- Apply the person, event and role schemas to a current story unfolding in the news.
- Draw a diagram to illustrate the dynamics of the perseverance effect, in which your initial opinion persists even in light of contradictory information.
- Explain to a peer at least one technique to combat the perseverance effect.

notes

1. Duke University Office of News and Communications, "Looking Back at the Duke Lacrosse Case," Duke University, http://today.duke.edu/showcase/lacrosseincident/, retrieved June 5, 2010.

2. Scott Jaschik, "Anger and Consequences," *Inside Higher Ed,* March 29, 2006, http://www.insidehighered.com/news/2006/03/29/duke, retrieved June 10, 2010.

3. Elliot Aronson, Timothy D. Wilson, and Robin M. Akert, *Social Psychology* (5th ed.). (Upper Saddle River, N.J.: Prentice Hall, 2005).

4. Susan T. Fiske and Shelley E. Taylor, *Social Cognition* (New York: Random House, 1984), pp. 173–74.

5. Aronson, Wilson, and Akert, *Social Psychology.*

6. Fiske and Taylor, *Social Cognition.*

7. Aronson, Wilson, and Akert, *Social Psychology.*

8. Robert M. Entman and Kimberly A. Gross, "Race to Judgment: Stereotyping Media and Criminal Defendants," *Law and Contemporary Problems* 71 (2008), p. 116.

9. Shahin Hashtroudi, Sharon A. Mutter, Elizabeth A. Cole and Susan K. Green. "Schema-Consistent and Schema-Inconsistent Information: Processing De-

mands," *Personality and Social Psychology Bulletin 10,* no. 2 (1984); Chris S. O'Sullivan and Francis T. Durso, "Effect of Schema-Incongruent Information on Memory for Stereotypical Attributes," *Journal of Personality and Social Psychology 47,* no. 1 (1984); Reid Hastie and Purohit A. Kumar, "Person Memory: Personality Traits as Ongoing Principles in Memory Behaviors," *Journal of Personality and Social Psychology 37* (1979).

10. C. Neil Macrae and Galen V. Bodenhausen, "Social Cognition: Thinking Categorically About Others," *Annual Review of Psychology 51* (2000).

11. Ibid.

12. Rogers Brubaker, Mara Loveman, and Peter Stamatov, "Ethnicity as Cognition," *Theory and Society 33* (2004), p. 44.

13. Entman and Gross, "Race to Judgment: Stereotyping Media and Criminal Defendants," p. 109.

14. Stuart Taylor Jr., and K. C. Johnson, *Until Proven Innocent: Political Correctness and the Shameful Injustices of the Duke Lacrosse Rape Case* (New York: St. Martin's Press, 2007).

15. Kurt Andersen, "Rape, Justice, and the 'Times'," *New York Magazine,* October 8, 2006.

16. Ibid.

17. Heather Kleider et al., "Schema-Driven Source Misattribution Errors: Remembering the Expected from a Witnessed Event," *Applied Cognitive Psychology 22* (2008).

18. Craig A. Anderson, "Inoculation and Counter-Explanation: Debiasing Techniques in the Perseverance of Social Theories," *Social Cognition 1* (1982); Fiske and Taylor, *Social Cognition*; E. R. Hirt and K. D. Markman, "Multiple Explanation: A Consider-an-Alternative Strategy for Debiasing Judgments," *Journal of Personality and Social Psychology 69* (1995).

19. C. G. Lord, M. Lepper, and W. C. Thompson, "Inhibiting Biased Assimilation in the Consideration of New Evidence on Social Policy Issues" (paper presented at the American Psychological Association, Montreal, Canada, September, 1980); Fiske and Taylor, *Social Cognition.*

20. Fiske and Taylor, *Social Cognition*; Gordon W. Allport, *The Nature of Prejudice* (Cambridge, Mass: Addison-Wesley, 1954).

21. Patricia G. Devine and Lindsay B. Sharp, "Automaticity and Control in Stereotyping and Prejudice," in *Handbook of Prejudice, Stereotyping, and Discrimination,* ed. Todd D. Nelson (New York: Psychology Press, 2009).

22. Ibid.

23. Karl G. Heider, "The Rashomon Effect: When Ethnographers Disagree," *American Anthropologist 90,* no. 1 (1988).

24. Aly Colon, "Q & A: Avoiding Bias. Interview with Gelareh Asayesh," Poynter Institute, http://www.poynter.org/content/content_view.asp?id=5852.

25. Fiske and Taylor, *Social Cognition,* p. 150.

26. Anderson, "Inoculation and Counter-Explanation."

27. Susannah Meadows, "Crystal Mangum's Return to Court: A Sad Final Chapter to the Duke Lacrosse Scandal" *Newsweek,* Feb. 22, 2010, http://www.newsweek.com/2010/02/22/crystal-mangum-s-return-to-court.html.

4

Story Without Stereotype

*How stereotypes may influence reporting in stealthy ways—
and what to do about it*

LEARNING OBJECTIVES

- *To be able to define stereotypes and list four of their attributes.*
- *To understand the potential influence of stereotypes on news reporting, including how sources are influenced by stereotypes.*
- *To know how to apply techniques to control the use of stereotypes in journalism.*

LOOKING DEEPER

Excellent journalists allow themselves to be surprised, even proven wrong, in their initial assumptions. They look beyond the "story that writes itself" for the more complex one that lies below the stereotypes. Kerry Luft, a senior editor and former international correspondent at the *Chicago Tribune*, did just that when reporting a story with a colleague on child welfare across the globe.

OA

The question behind the assignment was simple: Why do people have children they cannot afford? The answer was more complex and lingers with me still.

At the time, I was a foreign correspondent based in Brazil. The assignment was part of a worldwide series and an overall effort by my paper to explain the plight of children.

The family we found seemed perfect for our purposes: Seven little girls whose father and mother made barely $40 a month and lived in one of Rio de Janeiro's most notorious slums. Another baby was on the way.

This was a place where police had massacred several civilians just a year before, where young kids sat on street corners dealing drugs and where teenagers openly carried assault rifles slung over their shoulders. In the night, heavy weapons rattled in the streets, forcing the family to huddle in one small windowless room in their tiny house.

Meals were rice and beans and maybe a piece of chicken; the father had illegally tapped an overhead utility line to give the family electricity. In one of the world's most famous beach cities, these little girls had never seen the ocean. Nor had any of them had a birthday cake. Writing a story that portrayed the bleakness of their lives would be easy.

Yet as we reported more deeply, I saw more things. I saw an 11-year-old girl confident enough to lead her illiterate mother through Rio's complicated public transit system and into a doctor's office, where she calmly read the paperwork and explained to her mother what she should do. I heard how that same girl, given her first grilled cheese sandwich, ate just a bit and asked to wrap up the rest to share with her sisters.

I saw a whole flock of little girls race toward their father and embrace him as he came home exhausted from his work as a day laborer, and I saw his face light up.

I saw love, and I saw happiness, and I wasn't sure that I could say that these children had a miserable life. Poor? Yes. Dangerous? Absolutely. But not miserable.

In the years since I have had to remind myself many times of that difference. Too often I see reporters applying their own standards and mores to people who live in another society—both here and abroad—and it pains me.

I don't mean to suggest that all things are relative. Certainly reporters will come across actions and incidents that are reprehensible and indefensible by any civilized standard. More often, the situation is more nuanced than that, and if we ignore those nuances, we ignore the truth. By all means report. But please, try not to judge.[1]

ON ASSIGNMENT

pause&consider What was Luft's initial stereotype? What did he find on the reporting scene that supported that stereotype? What did he find on the reporting scene that contradicted that stereotype? What did Luft do that allowed him to see past his initial stereotypes? Read the excerpt from Luft's story in Appendix A and discuss it with a peer.

THE NATURE OF STEREOTYPES

Stereotypical stories may be easy to write, but they are rarely as surprising or as vivid as real life. Also, they often damage the people who are being stereotyped. **Stereotyping** is the application of beliefs about the attributes of a group to judge an individual member of that group.[2]

In 1922, Walter Lippmann, a journalist and cofounder of *New Republic* magazine, first used the word *stereotype*, a printer's term for making a mold of composed type, as a social scientific concept. The first chapter of his book *Public Opinion* was titled "The World Outside and the Pictures in Our Heads." Lippmann wrote that people don't respond to reality (the world outside) but to mental pictures—those pictures in our heads that he called "fiction."[3]

Stereotypes Can Simplify

People create those mental pictures, or stereotypes, to simplify perception and thinking processes. Lippmann noted that a characteristic of a stereotype is that it's in one's head before a person can critically think about it. "We are told about the world before we see it," he wrote. "We imagine most things before we experience them. And those preconceptions, unless education has made us acutely aware, govern deeply the whole process of perception."[4]

Stereotypes may be seen as a kind of role schema, which was discussed in Chapter 3. Specifically, stereotypes can be thought of as a particular type of role schema "that organizes one's prior knowledge and expectations about other people who fall into certain socially defined categories."[5] Stereotypes mean that certain behaviors are expected of people based on their age, religion, education or other factors. Other types of schemas, such as event or person schemas, guide perception and memory and other thinking-based judgments. But role schemas influence emotions and behavior. "To put it another way, deciding that some people have adopted the role of gang members does more than help you to notice and remember that they wear black leather jackets and drive motorcycles. It helps you decide how you feel about them."[6]

Education is essential to building awareness about stereotypical preconceptions.

Stereotypes Satisfy the Need for Story

When it comes to journalistic narrative, stereotypes can influence how news people portray essential characters. News stories sometimes lead the broadcast or make the front page because they fit a formula of what the audience, and sometimes the journalist, expects the news to be. How often is a story so satisfying because it fits with popular notions of what *should* be? Or, how people in certain situations *should* behave?

Consider the work of journalists Jayson Blair, formerly of *The New York Times;* Jack Kelley, formerly of *USA Today;* Patricia Smith, formerly of the *Boston Globe;* and Stephen Glass, formerly of *The New Republic.* Some of their stories read like scripts. The details perfectly fit the angles of their stories. The main sources were like well-cast characters. The story settings were as predictable as a movie set. But reality isn't as neat as all that: Each of these journalists was caught fabricating information and/or plagiarizing material. That's why they are all former journalists.

Deceptive journalists' fabrications capitalize on the human tendency for stereotypes that mesh into prearranged scenarios and predictable outcomes, researchers have noted.[7] These journalists were not immediately caught in their deceptions in part because their stories hung together so solidly. They rang so true; too true to be real, as it turned out.

For instance, Jayson Blair wrote a story based on information he took from a story written eight days earlier by a reporter with the *San Antonio Express-News.* The story was about a South Texas mother whose son, an American soldier in Iraq, was still unaccounted for after an attack on his maintenance convoy. The *Express-News* reporter wrote about Blair's plagiarism:

> One of the last stories Jayson Blair wrote before being unmasked as a liar and plagiarist contained these words: "Juanita Anguiano points proudly to the pinstriped couches, the tennis bracelet in its red case and the Martha Stewart furniture out on the patio. She proudly points up to the ceiling fan."
>
> Eight days earlier, I had written similar words about Anguiano in an article for my newspaper: "So the single mother, a teacher's aide, points to the ceiling fan he installed in her small living room. She points to the pinstriped couches, the tennis bracelet still in its red velvet case and the Martha Stewart patio furniture, all gifts from her first born and only son."

When I read Blair's story on the morning of April 26, it seemed possible, barely, that Blair too had visited Anguiano, a south Texas mother whose son Edward was the last American soldier missing in action in Iraq. But there was a problem: The Martha Stewart patio furniture wasn't on the patio. It was still in its box, next to the kitchen table. I doubted that Anguiano had found the energy to haul it outside after we spoke. Also, when she had pointed to the furniture, there had been no hint of pride, only pain.[8]

Blair, who never visited Anguiano and plagiarized his story from the *Express-News,* had assumed the furniture sat on the patio. Indeed, "in a stereotypical world, patio furniture is on the patio. In the real world, things are not so simple," wrote two researchers who studied the case.[9] Writing to stereotypes, to what journalists think people and settings typically look like, can mean missing the truth. Of course, stereotypes pose problems in addition to plagiarism or fabrication, including the power to unfairly and inaccurately portray people simply because they belong to a certain group.

Stereotypes Are Necessary

Despite their bad reputation, stereotypes are integral to the way our minds process information. Some basic attributes of stereotypes are:

1. **Pervasiveness.** All of us hold stereotypes. No one is free from stereotyping others. Stereotyping is as much a part of us as touching or tasting.

2. **Predictability.** Stereotypes help people make sense of the world. They provide people with a way to quickly categorize others. "Stereotypes provide us with a handy, albeit imperfect, basis on which to predict the behavior of individuals in the absence of any information about those individuals other than their membership in some group."[10]

3. **Positives.** Stereotypes are not automatically negative. They can be positive, as in, "Midwesterners are so friendly!" Problems arise when, instead of generalizing about a group, people exaggerate or oversimplify. They fail to individualize the traits of the group. They do not customize information to the unique situation. Then they are at risk of indicting entire groups of people.

4. **Partly true.** Stereotypes do often hold an element of truth. Stereotypes evolve because they stem from behaviors or characteristics that *are* often shared by people in a group. They are generalizations that on average tend to be true, but not always. How stereotypes affect the behavior of people toward one another is what really matters. The danger of stereotypes lies in the application of a generalization to an individual case. "Stereotypes matter because they have consequences."[11]

Stereotypes Can Be Unconscious

Perhaps the most troublesome stereotypes are those we don't know we possess. An explosion of research in recent years explores both the explicit (conscious) and implicit (unconscious) associations at play when it comes to our attitudes about others. We are aware of explicit stereotypes; for example, an individual may recognize he has a bias against extremely overweight people, believing they are ignorant or lazy even though he has no knowledge of their work ethic or intellect. **Explicit stereotypes** are the biases that you know you have. Conversely, **implicit stereotypes** are sneakier. They affect our attitudes and behavior without our immediate realization.

Project Implicit is a research collaborative aimed at measuring thoughts and feelings that exist outside conscious awareness or control. Project Implicit experts define an implicit stereotype this way:

> A stereotype is a belief that members of a group generally possess some characteristic (for example, the belief that women are typically nurturing). An implicit stereotype is a stereotype that is powerful enough to operate without conscious control.[12]

For example, someone might say she is not prejudiced toward lesbians (an explicit attitude) but act in a manner that indicates she is (reflecting her implicit attitude). In one study, the higher people tested on having unconscious negative feelings toward lesbians, the more socially distant they acted when alone with a woman who was allegedly gay. They smiled less, made less eye contact, had more tense body posture, were less friendly overall and showed less interest in conversation with a lesbian than with a heterosexual in the same setting.[13]

pause&consider Take a Project Implicit test to gauge your implicit associations about characteristics such as disability, weight, skin color or religion. You can find the Project Implicit link at this book's website, www.hhpcommunities.com/overcomingbias. When you learn your results, note your emotional reaction. Were you surprised? Do you agree with the results?

JOURNALISTIC CONSEQUENCES OF STEREOTYPES

Some stereotypes justify systems of discrimination, such as systems based on racial, sexual, disability or age discrimination, note researchers John T. Jost and David L. Hamilton in their writing on stereotypes in our culture. "Stereotypes are used—implicitly and explicitly—to . . . imbue existing forms of social arrangements with meaning and legitimacy; they preserve and bolster the status quo."[14] The researchers summarize the impact of stereotypes on thinking; a partial list is included in the left column of Exhibit 4.1.[15] The effects are translated into journalistic practice in the right column.

Stereotypes are particularly tempting to grab hold of when we have little time. The more multitasking we are doing, the more our thinking relies on stereotypes.[16] The more so-called "cognitive load" or "processing load" a reporter is under—juggling phone calls to police and prosecutors, helping edit the video and recording voiceovers, talking with her editor to move the story higher in the broadcast—the more she will rely on those mental pictures as opposed to carefully considering anti-stereotypical information. In a

Visual images promote stereotypes

"The list is endless and always injurious: African Americans play sports. Latinos are gang members. Native Americans are alcoholics. Wheelchair-using individuals are helpless. Gays are effeminate. Lesbians wear their hair short. Older adults need constant care. Anglos are racists or rednecks. Homeless people are drug addicts. These and other stereotypes are perpetuated by visual messages presented in print, television, motion pictures, and computers—the media."

Paul Martin Lester,
"Images and Sterotypes"[17]

world in which journalists are increasingly called on to fill multiple roles or make do with shrinking resources, it is especially important to be wary of a reliance on stereotypes for mental shortcuts.

exhibit 4.1   HOW STEREOTYPES INFLUENCE REPORTING

Stereotypes tend to . . .	In journalistic terms, that means:
direct people's attention to certain information and exclude other information.	When reporting on a murder in a low-income neighborhood, the reporter focuses on the stereotypical run-down houses and graffiti; not the organic food in the witness's kitchen and the PBS DVDs on the bookshelf.
color the interpretation of the information.	When met with ambiguous information, the reporter interprets it in line with his stereotype. So the halting English of the witness, a new immigrant, is seen as a sign of low intelligence, not of fresh arrival to a new land and language.
play a role in eliciting from others the very behavior that confirms biased expectations.	He's so sure the witness is unintelligent that the reporter speaks to her slowly and loudly, asking simple, close-ended questions that could only elicit a "yes" or a "no." He is left with a notebook of single-word answers, confirming his biased expectation that the witness isn't all that bright or thoughtful.
influence the way that information is remembered.	Writing up his notes at his laptop, the reporter most easily remembers the information that *doesn't* fit his stereotypic portrayal. "What were those PBS DVDs doing there?" The props that were out of place in his mental picture required extra thinking that made the information lodge in his memory. This can work in a journalist's favor, helping the reporter more easily recall fresh or incongruent information—but *only* if the reporter has time to think about the discrepancy.[18] And time is something in short supply in newsrooms.
serve as hypotheses that are tested and disproportionately favored in the interpretation of new information.	The reporter's angle is about a poor neighborhood held hostage to yet another murder in a slew of gang killings. While writing his lead, the reporter gets the crime data he's been waiting for; the murder is the second in 18 months for the neighborhood—not good, but hardly a "slew," either. Unwilling to see the data as disproving his hypothesis, the reporter instead sticks with the bloodbath angle and attributes the 18-month "lull" in murders to a corresponding rise in burglaries and robberies.

Source: Items in column 1 are adapted from Jost and Hamilton, 2005.

STEREOTYPES: JOURNALISTS AND SOURCES

The way in which journalists portray news sources can contribute to the public's understanding and opinion about whole groups of people in our society. In turn, news sources, particularly officials and organized groups, also communicate to the public through the news media. Sources' messages, delivered through quotes and news events, from rallies and meetings to campaigns and conventions, can relay stereotypes to the public.

When Journalists Stereotype Sources

Examples abound of news media coverage that furthers societal stereotypes of groups of people in our society. For example, local television newscasts overrepresent African Americans as perpetrators and underrepresent Latino victims when the amount of news coverage is compared to actual crime statistics.[19]

Entertainment and news media have presented a distorted portrayal of mental illness as dangerous, unpredictable and leading to criminality. This portrayal results in stigma and discrimination toward people with mental illness.[20] Research has shown that news media representations of people living with AIDS also negatively influence audience perceptions.[21]

More than 50 percent of Westerners surveyed, including people in the U.S., surveyed think that Muslims are fanatical. But then,

Awareness of socioeconomic biases

Steve Gunn, a longtime journalist and Director of Strategic Products and Audience Development at *The Charlotte Observer,* notes that young journalists in particular need to be aware of their socio-economic stereotypes and biases:

> Class is a very interesting issue. I don't see a lot with racial stereotypes that much, but class discrimination or class stereotypes is a very interesting thing. Journalism used to be a blue-collar profession. We all get paid really well, and that's good news. But does that take you away from the heart of what journalism used to be, which is the underdog, the common man's thing? I see with a lot of young people . . . they feel like they are entitled and therefore they are not as sympathetic to people who maybe are not as high up the ladder as they are.[22]

exhibit 4.2 CHARACTERISTICS ASSOCIATED WITH MUSLIMS AND WESTERNERS

Characteristic	Muslim views of Westerners (%)*	Western views of Muslims (%)*
selfish	68	35
violent	66	50
greedy	64	20
immoral	61	23
arrogant	57	39
fanatical	53	58
respectful of women	44	22
honest	33	51
tolerant	31	30
generous	29	41

* Median % of Muslims across seven Muslim countries who say each of these traits describes people in Western countries and median % of non-Muslims across the U.S., Russia, and four Western European countries who say each of these traits describes Muslims.

Source: Pew Research Center's Global Attitudes Project, Spring 2011. Reprinted with permission.

more than 50 percent of Muslims think Westerners are fanatical (see Exhibit 4.2). These views are shaped in part by news portrayals.[23]

In another example, news media coverage of female corporate executives still carries with it negative stereotypes about women and their abilities. For example, when Carly Fiorina was named chief executive of global technology giant Hewlett-Packard, the coverage included sexist references that her male counterparts likely didn't suffer. According to one analysis of media coverage: *"U.S. News & World Report* referred to her as a 'former receptionist' and the 'consummate corporate cheerleader.' *Fortune* described her as 'affable and stylish, dressed in a brown Armani pantsuit,' commenting further that Fiorina 'seems as comfortable with power as any woman could be.'" The *Fortune* piece concluded with "Expect to see her on the covers of *Fortune, Business Week,* and *Forbes*—heck, maybe she'll even make *InStyle."*[24]

The stereotypes that journalists may have about a person or group can prevent them from tapping those individuals as sources. That's a missed opportunity, and it's neglecting part of the job, which is to tell the public about entire communities, not just selected parts of them.

When Sources Stereotype Other Groups

News sources are no different from journalists in their cognitive habit of stereotyping others. But news sources don't have professional training as journalists do. They may make no effort to avoid making intentionally biased comments, or they may make biased comments unintentionally. Journalists must understand and clarify the information from sources that hint (or perhaps reek) of unfair stereotyping.

When sources speak in stereotypes, reporters and editors have decisions to make. If the quoted comments are from a brief person-on-the-street interview, journalists are likely inclined to dismiss the comments outright as prejudicial and move on to other sources. Or, if the source is a politician, to scramble to immediately publish the offensive language.

Sometimes, a source's comments are laced with stereotypes and it's unclear whether the source is conscious about how ugly his or her generalizations are; in these instances, journalists should probe. Instead of accepting a source's general bashing of an entire category of people, ask follow-up questions that aim at the specific and personal. Seek to understand the context in which the source is framing the comments. Unpack the statements; push the source to clarify meaning. The quotes may still be highly prejudicial, but a journalist who has ferreted out the specific intent and, often, background of the source can then forcefully and clearly characterize the source and his or her comments without fear of misstating a position.

Stereotypes are heavily dependent on who is speaking, about whom they are speaking, the place in the world the source is from and the historical time frame being referenced.[25] For example, suppose a source, "Joe," declares that blacks are more violent than whites. Is the source himself a black man from the South or a white businessman? Are the comments set in contemporary society? David Schneider in *The Psychology of Stereotyping* writes:

> When Joe says that blacks are more violent than whites, he may mean, but not bother to say, that this stereotype applies only to unemployed

and undereducated black males, and even then only to a minority under certain circumstances (say, black males of this description who are
engaged in gang activity). In his own mind, he may be quite clear that
he does not mean to say that black lawyers and truck drivers are more
prone to violence than their white counterparts.[26]

Some probing questions for Joe: How does he characterize violence? Does he mean strictly physical assault against strangers or
aggression toward family members too? What are his criteria for
violence? What specific group of black men does he have in mind?
And what are his perceptions of that group?

Reporters should avoid assuming that they understand toward
whom the stereotype is aimed, which group of people, and the specific
context that the prototypical Joe Source has in mind. The reporter's
concept of the group referenced, the time frame or the setting being
referenced might be very different from that of a source. Assumptions
on the part of the reporter that he and his source were thinking of the
same context for a given comment can lead to calls and emails from
irate sources charging, "I was misquoted!"

When Sources Stereotype Journalists

The public possesses strong stereotypes about journalists that may
act as barriers to journalists when they are pursuing stories. For example, these stereotypes may frustrate journalists' efforts to land an
interview or gain access to citizens.

As Exhibit 4.3 indicates, news consumers have strong feelings
about journalists' accuracy and professionalism. None of these categories of criticism directly state that "journalists stereotype a lot."
But they do show a general wariness and negative view about how
journalists act, a set of characteristics applied to the news industry as
whole. For instance, the majority of respondents to a Pew Research
Center for People and the Press survey[27] didn't think that journalists got the facts straight and thought journalists tried to cover up
mistakes. An individual journalist may be professional, focused on accuracy and represent a respected news outlet, but he still is faced with
these stereotypical criticisms of the press that he must overcome.

Depending on the reporting situation, the expectations of journalists about how they will be perceived by sources can affect how

exhibit 4.3   INCREASING CRITICISM OF PRESS ACCURACY, OPENNESS

News organizations . . .	July 1985 %	Feb 1999 %	Sept 2001 %	Nov 2001 %	July 2002 %	July 2003 %	June 2005 %	July 2007 %	July 2009 %	85-09 Diff
Get the facts straight	55	37	35	46	35	36	36	39	29	−26
Stories often inaccurate	34	58	57	45	56	56	56	53	63	+29
Don't know	11	5	8	9	9	8	8	8	8	
Willing to admit mistakes	34	26	24	35	23	27	28	28	21	−13
Try to cover up mistakes	55	66	67	52	67	62	62	63	70	+15
Neither/don't know	11	8	9	13	10	11	10	8	9	
Highly professional	72	52	54	73	49	62	59	66	59	−13
Not professional	11	32	27	12	31	24	25	22	27	+16
Neither/don't know	17	16	19	15	20	14	16	12	14	

Source: Pew Research Center for People and the Press, 2009. Reprinted with permission.

journalists behave. Remember the self-fulfilling prophecy? Scholarship on communicating across cultures notes that if someone expects to be ignored or dismissed due to others' prejudices, the person may act in self-defeating ways.[28] Journalists report across cultures. Self-defeating behavior on the part of a journalist may cause him to fail to make a second attempt at interviewing a hostile source, or not press for an answer out of certainty that sources won't give a reporter who doesn't share the same race or ethnicity a straight answer anyway.

Teresa Puente, founder of *Latina Voices*, a website of stories by or about Latina women, has had to grapple with that sense that sources wouldn't talk to someone like her because of her ethnic background. When working at a small paper in California, Puente was assigned to cover an anti-immigration rally as a general assignment story to run the next day. Puente is not an immigrant, but a third-generation Mexican American. She tells about covering that event and feeling that sources assumed she was strongly pro-immigration:

My whole career, people look at me and make assumptions about me. I had to go into this crowd of people who were against immigration and in I walk—a brown woman with a reporter's badge. I am assuming they will assume what my beliefs are. They were looking at me probably with assumptions and I was looking at them with assumptions. I assumed they were racist.

That was a time I thought, OK, I have to put aside whatever my personal thoughts are and be a reporter. I had to put aside my assumptions and my worries about their assumptions. I had to do my best to ask the questions and interview them like I would any other sources. I did have to separate my personal feelings on the topic. That was very difficult to do. A daily story ran in the paper the next day. I didn't get any complaints, so I assume it was fair.[29]

pause&*consider* Think about a time when people made assumptions about you. What was the assumption? Was there a reaction or consequence because of the assumption? When working as a journalist, how can you use that feeling of frustration over being categorized to avoid doing the same to sources? Share your ideas with a peer.

MANAGING STEREOTYPES

With extra effort, it is possible to dismantle the stereotypes we hold about others. At a minimum, changing stereotypes requires time, attention and effort. But we don't have to settle for automatic stereotyping as a consequence of everyday thinking, or everyday reporting. Two initial steps to help combat one's natural tendency to stereotype are to:

1. **Individualize:** The act of seeking out information that is particular to an individual makes it easier to recognize the uniqueness of that person and to see the person as something more than a member of a particular group.[30]

2. **Self-Analyze:** The extent to which you readily accept negative stereotypes is linked to your personality. Knowing yourself will help you know how carefully you need to vet your work for

stereotypes. People who are highly cognitive (who like to think a lot) are less likely to stereotype.[31]

Another way to help assess and adjust your attitude toward others is to figure out your social dominance orientation.[32] The Social Dominance Orientation Scale in Appendix B describes a general attitude toward others, toward social groups and one's regard for various groups' implicit value. It measures the extent to which a person desires his or her own social ingroup to dominate and be superior to outgroups, or social groups to which one does not belong. It is a general attitudinal orientation toward relations between groups: Should they be equal or hierarchical? Should some groups be superior and others inferior?

This orientation also measures the extent to which an individual believes in policies and structures that support sexism, racism, nationalism, cultural elitism, liberalism and conservatism, among other ideologies. It's important to remember that this orientation, while remarking on an individual's personality, is designed to illustrate that in any given society, there are different kinds of people who have different roles and different effects on each other.[33] Also remember that this is simply one small measure of one's thinking. It is meant to use as a tool that invites you to think about how you view others and social hierarchies.

The journalist Walter Lippmann encouraged self-awareness to know the sources of our stereotypes. He urged easy modification of the ways in which we categorize others:

> If our philosophy tells us that each man is only a small part of the world, that his intelligence catches at best only phases and aspects in a coarse net of ideas, then, when we use our stereotypes, we tend to know that they are only stereotypes, to hold them lightly, to modify them gladly. We tend, also, to realize more and more clearly when our ideas started, where they started, how they came to us, why we accepted them.[34]

Replacing Our Stereotypes

Rewiring our stereotypes, especially the negative ones, and replacing them with more neutral responses is like breaking a bad habit. It requires awareness of the bias, motivation to correct it and control over the specific behavior.[35] The elimination of a bad habit requires essentially the same steps as the formation of a habit. Researchers outline these steps:[36]

1. **Decide to stop the old behavior.** In this case, negative stereotyping.

2. **Remember your resolution.** Type a note into your mobile phone. Program it into your virtual calendar for a reminder alarm every day at lunch. On your keychain, put an orange key that undoes nothing but your stereotypical thinking.

3. **Engage a rival response.** Each time you realize you are thinking of a negative stereotype, think about your personal beliefs toward negative stereotyping. You are essentially trying to train your mind so that when the automatic negative stereotype arises, you engage a rival response that is more neutral.

So if perhaps you hold a stereotype that all Latinos are undocumented immigrants, think instead about Latinos in terms of subsets; seasonal immigrants who have work visas, legal residents and native-born U.S. citizens. As your rival response, it may also help to have in mind an outstanding person who is from the group about which you hold a negative bias.

4. **Don't give up.** You won't be free of nasty stereotypes overnight, and you'll also fail on occasion in your efforts. Try and decide repeatedly to substitute neutral categories for negative ones. The more success you have at asserting your new attitude, the more natural it will become. We've all quit something; smoking, caffeine, being chronically late, a loser boyfriend or girlfriend. It takes daily recommitment.

Education Elicits Empathy

Diversity education has been shown to reduce prejudices and stereotypes in those who are interested in social and political equality for all people.[37] Diversity education is based in part on a piece of advice you've probably often heard: "Put yourself in the other person's shoes."

It's called empathy.

Consider how you would feel in your source's position. Spend time in her world to understand the challenges and joys. It will help you better see the wisdom or stupidity of a source's decisions and what motivates her choices. Taking the perspective of someone unlike yourself, and looking at the world through her eyes, can significantly reduce bias and negative stereotyping that stems from placing people into categories and groups.[38] Some reporters even choose to live for a time in the neighborhood of their beat to better understand the community, notes Rick Hirsch, managing editor at the *Miami Herald*:

> One of the things we struggle with as a news organization is that so often, we bring people from outside to cover communities they don't know. So everything is new and news to them. But . . . [if] you live in a neighborhood, [then] you understand things in a different way than if you just parachute in. The most successful community reporters are ones that really know their neighborhoods well.
>
> Just because it's boring to you doesn't mean it's not important to people in the neighborhood. Something that is new or changing in a neighborhood can mean a lot to that neighborhood. It's common for people to think, "What are they getting so upset about?" And if you don't know the answer to that question, then there's probably more reporting to do, because people care a lot about home. People protect home. And things that they think threaten [home] are really, really newsworthy in the local, local sense. You may not care about it on the other side of town, but in your neighborhood, it matters.
>
> Walking in someone else's shoes is a cliché, but some of the best reporters I've worked with have done just that.[39]

exploration EXERCISES

1. In the next month, actively seek out a news story to report that involves a group about which you hold negative stereotypes.

   a. Before reporting, write two paragraphs about your beliefs and attitude toward that group. Then, input those paragraphs into a free online tool such as Wordle that creates a visual depiction of your text (www.wordle.net). The software generates a "word cloud" that gives greater prominence to words that appear more frequently in the source text. What words are most prominent?

   b. Implement the four steps outlined in the Replacing Our Stereotypes section of this chapter to try to change or set aside your negative stereotype.

   c. After completing your news story, write two more paragraphs of personal reflection about the group and input that text into Wordle. What words are more prominent?

    d. Compare your visual "word clouds" and note any changes in prominent words.

2. Complete one of the exercises at UnderstandingPrejudice.org (www.understandingprejudice.org/demos). The exercises include a questionnaire to assess how mixed one's beliefs are regarding women and equality (the ambivalent sexism inventory), a quiz to test IQ about Native Americans, and an interactive presentation to illustrate how segregation occurs.

    a. After completing one of the exercises, blog about your results and your reaction to them.

    b. In your blog, consider how your attitude on the given topic might affect your journalism. Consider ways to combat any negative effects of that attitude on your work.

3. The excerpt below is from Susan Sontag's "The Double Standard of Aging," which ran in the Sept. 23, 1972, *Saturday Review*. The article explores the stereotypes of beauty in U.S. culture, and how aging affects perceptions about women's beauty:

> To be a woman is to be an actress. Being feminine is a kind of theater, with its appropriate costumes, décor, lighting and stylized gestures. From early childhood on, girls are trained to care in a pathologically exaggerated way about their appearance.... And a woman who spends literally most of her time caring for, and making purchases to flatter, her physical appearance is not regarded in this society as what she is: a kind of moral idiot. She is thought to be quite normal and is envied by other women whose time is mostly used up at jobs or caring for large families.... Women are more vain than men because of the relentless pressure on women to maintain their appearance to a certain high standard.[40]

    a. Using Sontag's comments as inspiration, shoot a video or compile a slideshow of stereotypical expressions of beauty in America as well as images that challenge those stereotypical expressions.

    b. Since Sontag wrote this article decades ago, consider whether her comments on vanity and standards of appearance now apply to men in the U.S. as well.

    c. You might consider which, if any, particular socioeconomic groups are being referenced in the excerpt and how her comments are specific to aging in America. Let your conclusions be evident in your video or slideshow.

   d. Post your multimedia package online and invite user comments.

4. Read the following excerpt from Paul Martin Lester's article about stereotyping and the media, including the news media:

> Most media experts come up with several reasons why the media stereotype: advertisers that demand quickly interpreted shortcut pictures, lazy or highly pressured reporters who do not take or have the time to explore issues within their multifaceted and complex contexts, limited diversity in news organizations, journalists' presumptions that readers and viewers only accept images of diverse members within a limited range of content categories, and—regrettably and often denied—culturism. *Culturism* is a term that describes the belief that one cultural group—whether based on ethnicity, economics, education, etc.—is somehow better or worse than some other cultural group. Culturism may explain why mainstream media are slow to cover human catastrophes in remote sections of the world such as Rwanda, Somalia, and South-Central Los Angeles.[41]

Identify an example of news coverage that stereotypes a group of people and briefly respond to the following:

   a. Define the stereotype.

   b. Explain how the coverage perpetuates the stereotype.

   c. Consider whether culturism may be at work in the text or image: Does the coverage depict a specific cultural group as better or worse than others in the U.S.? How so? What groups are being compared?

   d. Propose a different way to cover the same news event or subject without stereotyping.

FOR review

- List at least four ways in which stereotyping can influence journalistic practice.
- Formulate a rival response to a stereotype you hold.
- Role-play how a journalist might respond when a source negatively stereotypes others during an interview.

notes

1. Kerry Luft, Interview with author, 2010.

2. M. R. Banaji and A. G. Greenwald, "Implicit Stereotyping and Prejudice," in *The Psychology of Prejudice: The Ontario Symposium,* Vol. 7, ed. M. P. Zanna and J. M. Olson (Mahwah, N.J.: Erlbaum, 1994), p. 58.

3. Walter Lippmann, *Public Opinion* (New York: Macmillan, 1922), p. 12.

4. Ibid., p. 90.

5. Susan T. Fiske and Shelley E. Taylor, *Social Cognition* (New York: Random House, 1984), p. 160.

6. Ibid., p. 160.

7. Dominic Lasorsa and Jia Dai, "When News Reporters Deceive: The Production of Stereotypes," *Journalism and Mass Communication Quarterly 84,* no. 2 (2007).

8. Macarena Hernandez, "What Jayson Blair Stole from Me, and Why I Couldn't Ignore It," *Washington Post,* June 1, 2003, p. B05.

9. Lasorsa and Dai, "When News Reporters Deceive," p. 292.

10. Mark Schaller and Lucian G. Conway III, "From Cognition to Culture: The Origins of Stereotypes that Really Matter," in *Cognitive Social Psychology: The Princeton Symposium on the Legacy and Future of Social Cognition,* ed. Gordon B. Moskowitz (Mahwah, N.J.: Erlbaum, 2001). p. 165.

11. Ibid., p. 163.

12. Project Implicit, "Frequently Asked Questions," https://ImplicitHarvard.edu (IAT Corp., 2007).

13. Nilanjana Dasgupta, "Implicit Ingroup Favoritism, Outgroup Favoritism, and Their Behavioral Manifestations," *Social Justice Research 17,* no. 2 (2004).

14. John T. Jost and David L. Hamilton, "Stereotypes in Our Culture," in *On the Nature of Prejudice: Fifty Years after Allport,* ed. John F. Dovidio, P. Glick, and L. A. Rudman (Malden, Mass.: Blackwell, 2005), p. 220.

15. Ibid., p. 210.

16. Daniel H. J. Wigboldus et al., "Capacity and Comprehension: Spontaneous Stereotyping under Cognitive Load," *Social Cognition 22,* no. 3 (2004).

17. Paul Martin Lester, "Images and Stereotypes," in *Journalism Ethics: A Reference Handbook,* eds. Elliot D. Cohen and Deni Elliot (Santa Barbara, Calif.: ABC-CLIO, 1997), p. 69.

18. Fiske and Taylor, *Social Cognition.*

19. Robert M. Entman and Andrew Rojecki, *The Black Image in the White Mind: Media and Race in America* (Chicago: University of Chicago Press, 2001); Travis L. Dixon and Daniel Linz, "Race and the Misrepresentation of Victimization on Local Television News," *Communication Research 27,* no. 5 (2000).

20. Heather Stuart, "Media Portrayal of Mental Illness and Its Treatments: What Effect Does It Have on People with Mental Illness?," *CNS Drugs: Drug Therapy in Neurology and Psychiatry 20,* no. 2 (2006).

21. Dorothy Nelkin, "AIDS and the News Media," *The Milbank Quarterly 69,* no. 2 (1991).

22. Steve Gunn, Interview with author, August, 2010.

23. Pew Research Center, "Muslim-Western Tensions Persist," in *Pew Global Attitudes Project* (Washington, D.C.: Pew Research Center, 2011).

24. Catherine Daily and Dan R. Dalton, "Coverage of Women at the Top: The Press Has a Long Way to Go," *Columbia Journalism Review 39,* no. 2 (2000), p. 58.

25. David J. Schneider, *The Psychology of Stereotyping* (New York: Guilford Press, 2004).

26. Ibid., p. 331.

27. Pew Research Center for the People & the Press, "Press Accuracy Rating Hits Two Decade Low" (Washington, D.C.: Pew Research Center for the People & the Press, Sept. 13, 2009).

28. Jeffrey W. Breslin, "Breaking Away from Subtle Biases," in *Negotiation Theory and Practice,* 2nd ed., ed. J. W. Breslin and J. Z. Rubin (Cambridge, Mass.: The Program on Negotiation at Harvard Law School, 1993).

29. Teresa Puente, Interview with author, August, 2010.

30. Charles Stangor, "The Study of Stereotyping, Prejudice, and Discrimination Within Social Psychology," in *Handbook of Prejudice, Stereotyping, and Discrimination,* ed. Todd D. Nelson (New York: Psychology Press, 2009).

31. P. R. D'Agostino and R. Fincher-Kiefer, "Need for Cognition and the Correspondence Bias," *Social Cognition 10,* no. 2 (1992).

32. Felicia Pratto et al., "Social Dominance Orientation: A Personality Variable Predicting Social and Political Attitudes," *Journal of Personality and Social Psychology 67,* no. 4 (1994).

33. Ibid.

34. Lippmann, *Public Opinion,* pp. 90–91.

35. Dasgupta, "Implicit Ingroup Favoritism, Outgroup Favoritism, and Their Behavioral Manifestations."

36. D. L. Ronis, J. F. Yates, and J. P. Kirscht, "Attitudes, Decisions, and Habits as Determinants of Repeated Behavior," in *Attitude Structure and Function,* ed. A. R. Pratkanis, S. J. Breckler, and A. G. Greenwald (Hillsdale, N.J.: Erlbaum, 1989); Patricia G. Devine, "Stereotypes and Prejudice: Their Automatic and Controlled Components," *Journal of Personality and Social Psychology 56,* no. 1 (1989); Fiske and Taylor, *Social Cognition.*

37. Laurie A. Rudman, Richard D. Ashmore, and Melvin L. Gary, "'Unlearning' Automatic Biases: The Malleability of Implicit Prejudice and Stereotypes," *Journal of Personality and Social Psychology 81,* no. 5 (2001).

38. Adam D. Galinsky and Gordon B. Moskowitz, "Perspective-Taking: Decreasing Stereotype Expression, Stereotype Accessibility, and In-Group Favoritism," *Journal of Personality and Social Psychology 78,* no. 4 (2000).

39. Rick Hirsch, Interview with author, August, 2010.

40. Susan Sontag, "The Double Standard of Aging," *Saturday Review,* Sept. 23, 1972, p. 22.

41. Lester, "Images and Stereotypes," pp. 70–71.

5

Understanding Culture, Understanding Sources

How social groups serve as lenses for looking at the world

CHANGING PERCEPTIONS

When he worked at a mid-size paper in California, M. E. Sprengelmeyer reported about a group of Mexican residents in the ironworks trade. They traveled back and forth from the California community of Oxnard and their homes in Ocotlán, Mexico. Sprengelmeyer, now a reporter and publisher at the paper he bought in Santa Rosa, New Mexico, tells about his experience reporting across cultures and borders, wryly highlighting the clichés that littered his path:

ON ASSIGNMENT

The perception was that one family gets a foothold in America and they bring someone else and they bring someone else, and pretty soon Ocotlán is taking over our pretty little California community! So that was going to be the story. It was going to be a story about how their lives are down there; how terrible their lives in Ocotlán are, and how one comes to pull himself up by the bootstraps so they can all get to California.

We thought that was the story—these guys from Ocotlán bringing each other up to the good country where all the streets are paved with gold and all that. (At the time, I was living in a 500-square-foot apartment with rats and cockroaches.)

Outside their home there was no yard. It was built right up to the street. It had an imposing wooden gate. There was crumbling plaster on the outside. And right there, I am thinking, "Ah ha! Squalor!" I was like, "Yeah, here we go."

Then they open up the gate and we go inside: It was immaculate and it went on and on and on. It was a house that was U-shaped, with a courtyard and fountains. It was the nicest house I had ever been in in my life.

Over the course of a week, they taught me what was really going on; people were developing a nice business in Mexico, figuring out the market is a lot bigger in the United States, living in the United States, loving the United States, but having no intention of settling in the United States, or becoming Americans. They are like swallows, going seasonally. The family had two existences, one up here and one down there. They had developed a cross-border life back and forth, but in their hearts, they considered Ocotlán their home.

The story was written the way it turned out, not the way it was conceived.

You've got to do the reporting and follow it where it goes. It became kind of an emotional story about their hearts being rooted in Mexico instead of a cliché of "We want to live in America."[1]

pause&consider Read an excerpt from Sprengelmeyer's story in Appendix A.[2] If possible, access the entire series through a newspaper database or the URL provided at the top of his excerpt in the appendix. Do you think the story turned out as he described it in the last paragraph of his reflection? Identify specific details that show the family's "hearts being rooted in Mexico." Discuss this with a peer.

UNDERSTANDING CULTURE

Culture is a learned set of shared interpretations about the world. Culture describes socially transmitted behavior patterns in a fairly large group of people. People learn about culture through interactions with family, friends, teachers and others in their community.[3]

Culture isn't just about a race or ethnicity. Groups of people organized around important and constant commonalities create cultures, too. Culture can be about income, as in a culture of poverty or middle-class culture. It can be about sexual orientation, as in a lesbian, gay, bisexual or transgendered (LGBT) culture. It can be organized around religion, as in a Mormon or Amish culture. Culture has lasting effects and is a serious, often stable presence in someone's life as opposed to a transient affiliation for a brief period, such as a teen into Goth aesthetics and music.

A culture provides its members with knowledge about how to communicate with others and how to interpret their behaviors. Having said that, not every member of a culture shares the same beliefs and values with the same intensity. For example, a son might not be as patriotic as his father even though they may both be military veterans.

Beliefs, values and norms form the basis for culture. *Beliefs* concern what the world is like and what is true or false. *Values* involve judgment of good and bad and what is important. *Norms* have to do with appropriate behavior and expectations. Let's take a closer look at norms because they are the outward manifestation of beliefs and values.[4] Norms are what journalists are most likely to observe when interviewing sources.

"One should think twice before applying the norms of one person, group or society to another. Information about the nature of the cultural differences between societies, their roots, and their consequences should precede judgment and action."

INTERCULTURAL SCHOLAR GEERT HOFSTEDE[5]

Cultural norms, or simply **norms,** offer directions for correct and moral behavior. Cultural norms are strongly engrained in our lives, but we aren't always aware of norms' impact on thinking and behavior until we come up against other cultures' values and beliefs. For example, one of the norms in the culture of poverty is that any extra money is shared. While middle-class culture emphasizes self-sufficiency, people in poverty often have an outlook that advancement is impossible, so one might as well share or spend any extra money immediately. That a person in poverty would not save an extra $50 she lucked into but instead throw a party with the cash or immediately lend it to a friend may seem incomprehensible to a middle-class person. To a person in poverty it may seem cruel to hoard extra money when family or friends could benefit from it.[6]

Cultural norms influence the way many Americans dress (shirts are expected for men and women in public places); eat (with silverware); greet one another (look in the eye, smile); and communicate (people use different word choices and tone when addressing their boss than when addressing their buddies.) The story about the Ocotlán family migrating back and forth from Mexico to the United States shows a particular cultural value of cherishing one's homeland and a cultural norm of bringing any financial success to one's native land and to support family living there.[7]

pause&*consider* Identify the cultural norms that guide your daily behaviors and decision-making. Think about your norms in regard to how you respond to authority, how you define independence, and what success looks like to you. Compare your thoughts with those of a peer.

REPORTING IN A MULTICULTURAL SOCIETY

When a journalist so understands a culture that she selects salient and meaningful facts about that culture for a news story, she is demonstrating **accuracy of perception**. Accuracy of perception has two components: The first is truth. The second is an understanding of the people being covered, meaning a grasp of the beliefs, values and norms that influence a social group's behaviors and decisions.

The first of the Project for Excellence in Journalism's core principles states that "journalism's first obligation is to the truth." The second is that journalism's "first loyalty is to citizens" and to serving the public interest. This principle means representing all groups in a society. "Ignoring certain citizens has the effect of disenfranchising them," according to the PEJ principles. Audiences should be able to expect representation in their news accounts.[8]

"Responsible journalists are sensitive to the difference between religion and culture, and the fact that they often overlap. Many traditions or beliefs considered religious are actually cultural, limited to a certain region or group."

REUTERS' *HANDBOOK OF JOURNALISM*[9]

Accuracy of perception requires understanding a culture well enough to understand its complexities. Certainly cultures share important commonalities, but they also contain subgroups and differences. Within any broad culture is variety. For example, the demographic of Latino or Hispanic encompasses a wide spectrum of ancestries. Latinos who live in the United States come from and are descended from many different countries, including Mexico, Puerto Rico, Cuba, El Salvador, the Dominican Republic, Guatemala, Colombia, Honduras, Ecuador and Peru.[10] Jessica Durkin, who served on the board of the National Association of Hispanic Journalists and who helps grow online, independent news publishers, says, "You cannot address the Hispanic community as a whole. News reporters should be sensitive to the context of the community and who is in it. You should specify if it's predominately Puerto Rican, for example, and try to convey some of the nuance and specifics of the community."[11] Consider applying the Fault Lines framework explained in Chapter 1 *within* cultures, to better see the distinctions between cultural subgroups.[12]

COVERING CULTURES: EDUCATION, CONTEXT, PERSPECTIVE

In order for audiences to understand and *want* to read, watch or listen to news stories about cultures different than their own, news coverage needs to include three components:

1. **Education:** The facts and history behind issues, events or actions.
2. **Context:** The circumstances and conditions within which events, ideas or statements occur or exist.
3. **Perspective:** The diverse viewpoints of people involved, particularly views that are relevant and credible.

The Robert C. Maynard Institute for Journalism Education puts it this way: "We cannot make assumptions about what our audiences know and do not know and about their frames of reference."[13] Frames of reference are the ideas, assumptions and conditions that dictate how consumers will approach and understand the news. Frames of reference are the context in which audiences receive and process information. It is critical that audiences understand the significance of a news event. Consumers won't stick with stories that confuse them; they will stick with stories that enlighten, explain, encourage and even enrage them.

To apply these three guidelines, let's look at how news outlets depicted Muslim Americans' plans to build what was depicted as a mosque near the former site of the World Trade Center. Some news commentators didn't do much to educate their audiences, instead mischaracterizing where the building would go and just what it was, as in this *New York Post* column:

> A mosque rises over Ground Zero. And fed-up New Yorkers are crying, "No!"
>
> A chorus of critics—from neighbors to those who lost loved ones on 9/11 to me—feel as if they've received a swift kick in the teeth.
>
> Plans are under way for a Muslim house of worship, topped by a 13-story cultural center with a swimming pool, in a building damaged by the fuselage of a jet flown by extremists into the World Trade Center.[14]

However, to truly *educate* readers, many journalists were specific about the proposed location, which was two blocks away from the World Trade Center site. A *USA Today* article even put it right in the lead: "The wife of the imam of a proposed Islamic community center two blocks from Ground Zero in New York City on Sunday did not rule out building it at a different site."[15] Other coverage was also careful to specify that the proposed building being planned was a not a dedicated house of worship for Muslims, but a cultural center with a prayer room, sports facilities and auditorium.[16]

Context is important in covering this issue, as the reason for controversy over the plans for the proposed community center is solely because of its proximity to the twin towers of the World Trade Center, which collapsed in the Sept. 11, 2001, attack by members of al-Qaeda, the militant Islamic group. This proposal wouldn't be a news story without those conditions.

The many *perspectives* on the proposal for the center, originally called Cordoba House, were listed in a posting by *Huffington Post* blogger Skye Jethani:

> An expert in constitutional law might see the Cordoba House controversy as a First Amendment issue and demand that the Muslim-Americans organizing the project be allowed to proceed without impediment. A politico might see the matter as an opportunity to score easy points with constituents (right or left) by supporting or denouncing the "Ground Zero mosque." And a member of the media might see the issue as a powder keg guaranteed to draw an audience and therefore pursue

whatever means to keep the controversy alive. But I'm not a lawyer, a politician, or a journalist. I'm a pastor. And when I look at the matter it isn't the legal or political arguments that get my attention—it's the fear. . . . Many within my evangelical community are responding from the most un-Christian of motives: fear.[17]

Not every story can hit the mark on all three components—education, context and perspective. Sometimes, one component is far more essential than the others in accurately conveying what's happening. A local school board decision banning headgear of any kind in public schools isn't a story until a journalist brings the education component to coverage of the decision: Board members didn't consider the boys from Jewish families in the district, some of whom who wear a kippah, or skullcap, to school.

Race vs. ethnicity

Ethnicity is about social grouping. It refers to common social, cultural, religious, ancestral, linguistic or other affiliations. Some definitions of ethnicity include race, but race cannot include ethnicity. *Race* refers to biological characteristics.

Conveying Cultural Identity

A news story that isn't clear is a news story that will be ignored. News stories about ethnic cultures often do a good job of conveying the identities of sources with titles and positions, but a poor job of conveying the identities of everyday citizens, particularly if the citizens are of an ethnicity other than the reporter's. Wash away muddy characterizations with these lines of questioning:

1. **Self-identification.** How does the source describe herself—by country of origin? As an American? The response helps illuminate how a source might perceive herself within the surrounding society. Explore contradictions and benefits of being a global citizen.

2. **Language.** Is there encouragement to speak the native language often in the home, or do parents encourage youth to speak only English? How bilingual are the family members? These distinctions often convey the number of generations a family has lived in America, how much the

family emphasizes pride of country of origin and how the family has approached the adoption of American cultural norms of language.

3. **Family background.** Understand the extended family's history. For example, Asian Americans may be perceived as foreigners when in fact many families have been U.S. citizens for generations. What generation immigrated to America? Why did they come: Were they fleeing political, religious or sexual persecution? Were they seeking better economic opportunities? Or did they move because they found something else appealing about the United States? How many members now in the United States are foreign-born or native-born? How many generations interact in the home? What educational levels have been attained by each generation? What different or shared skill sets are represented?

4. **Ethnicity and religion.** Is the source's ethnicity often associated with a religion? Is it a valid association? What influence does faith have on his or her everyday life? For example, a common myth about people of Arab descent is that they are *all* Muslim. But only about 20 percent of the world's Muslims are from the Middle East or North Africa[18] and many Arab Americans are Christian.

Journalistic Standpoint

Like everyone else, journalists have a standpoint on the world, as discussed in Chapter 1. Remember that a journalist's culture and history influences his standpoint. Standpoint can also influence the questions he asks and the answers he considers acceptable and reasonable.

A note on assimilation vs. acculturation

Be aware of the power of the word *assimilation*, as in the absorption and integration of an ethnic culture into the dominant culture. The term can suggest a negative outcome, as in something lost to a larger, more powerful force, the giving up of part of one's heritage to adjust to a new home country.

Depending on the story context, the term *acculturation* may be preferred. Acculturation describes an exchange that is two-way, as both cultural groups interact and change each other over time, through intermarriage or language, for example. Acculturation is the modification of a culture as a result of contact with a different culture. Use the word that best describes what is actually happening.

Suppose a journalist is looking into the problem of homelessness in his community. He's told by city officials that downtown retailers are suffering because of homeless people harassing shoppers on the streets. Many of the homeless people, the reporter discovers, are mentally ill. Some were removed from state mental health institutions, and efforts were made to assimilate them into society with the help of community mental health services. But those services were underfunded and the workloads too great for so few staff. So, many people aren't getting the treatment and oversight they need to stay well.

The reporter on this story at first sees it as a simple city policy story: Clean up the downtown streets for people who want to spend money. The city council is looking into ways to ban loitering, panhandling and other behaviors, thus targeting the homeless population. He isn't all that interested in the homeless people, in part because his efforts to interview them go nowhere. He thinks their responses to his questions are bizarre or irrational.

However, the reporter has good success with interviewing retailers, in part because the reporter's father was a jeweler. He grew up hearing lectures at the dinner table about the importance of a steady flow of foot traffic into a store. He heard many times how customers want easy parking and hassle-free shopping. His standpoint on this story is pro-retailer; he can't help it, it's in his genes.

A solution for the reporter is to interview advocates for and relatives of people who are mentally ill in the event he can't find primary sources who are able to communicate clearly. He also could include the background of the homeless problem, which emerged only after the institutions closed and local funding for services was cut. He could acknowledge to himself his bias against the homeless people and ask a caseworker to accompany him while interviewing, in hopes the caseworker can identify conversant sources. In short, the journalist needs to acknowledge that his pro-business stance is only one perspective in a story that goes beyond just hassle-free shopping.

In addition, journalists must think about the perspective inherent in their questions when interviewing sources from different cultures. Sometimes, journalists' own biases are embedded in the way they word questions, implying blame or criticism of sources' actions because they don't match journalists' own norms. To better understand the power of questions and perspective, consider how questions about sexual orientation or physical abilities can be framed.

For instance, "A Heterosexual Questionnaire" was written by a psychologist to highlight the cultural norm of heterosexuality by reversing the questions often asked of gay and lesbian people by heterosexual people. Among the questions: "What do you think caused your heterosexuality? When and how did you first decide you were a heterosexual? Is it possible your heterosexuality is a phase you may grow out of?"[19] Similarly, for people with disabilities, Exhibit 5.1 highlights the different perspectives inherent in the two questions.[20]

The first question is from the able-bodied point of view as dominant, functional and "adequate." The second question turns the tables on that perspective. (The first question was taken from an actual survey administered by government personnel to people with disabilities in Britain in the 1980s.) The lesson here is not that journalists need to ask convoluted questions to ensure no offense to any source, but instead to think about the different perspectives from which a journalist as well as news sources may view issues and events.

Ingroups and Outgroups

Standpoint comes into play when considering a key aspect of social cognition, the concept of ingroups and outgroups. No, you are not back in high school, with cliques and popularity contests. But the principle isn't so different.

Outgroup members are outsiders, people not in your social group, and often seen as inferior. **Ingroup** members are those in your own social group, or people with whom you share similar interests and attitudes.

exhibit 5.1 QUESTIONS AND STANDPOINT

"Do you have a scar, blemish or deformity that limits your daily activities?"

"Do other people's reactions to any scar, blemish or deformity you may have limit your daily activities?"

Journalists need to understand ingroups and outgroups because group membership—their own and that of their sources—influences perceptions, perspectives and people's definitions of truth. Exhibit 5.2 frames basic findings about ingroup and outgroup membership in terms of journalistic decisions.

exhibit 5.2 INGROUPS AND OUTGROUPS: JOURNALISTIC DECISIONS

ASSUMPTION #1	People in outgroups are all the same.

Journalistic application: Reporter Kali interviews a Japanese American student who just won a public school math contest. She leads her story with: "Everybody knows that the Asians are good at math."

Research shows: People see those in outgroups as less variable and more homogenous than their own group. They are "all alike." Therefore, people are willing to make inferences about outgroup members with little knowledge about them. Based on meeting one person in the group, they make generalizations about the entire group. This sort of categorization relates to both schemas and stereotyping.[21]

ASSUMPTION #2	People in outgroups are less complex.

Journalistic application: Twenty-four-year old Kali doesn't believe that old people do all that much, so how could they be interesting? She mistakes sedentary lives for sedentary minds. Her profile on residents in the town's new assisted living complex paints them simplistically, with an existence limited to knitting classes on Tuesdays and Sunday dinners with visiting family. She doesn't take time to look for the depth and personality in individual residents: The woman in Room 203 who plays Delta blues on the harmonica. The man in Room 321 who on Thursdays offers Latin classes for his fellow residents.

Research shows: The conceptions people hold about outgroup members are less complex than those they have about ingroup members. For instance, young people view old people along fewer dimensions than they do other young people.[22]

ASSUMPTION #3	People slant their perception of the behavior of those in outgroups.

Journalistic application: In her cover story on a local youth center, Kali investigates a tip that a group of Mexican American teens are instigating fights there. She spends a couple of nights observing at the center. She perceives the loud, boisterous behavior of the Mexican American youths as violent and incendiary, but the loud, boisterous behavior of the hometown teens she perceives as goofing around. Her story reflects her bias.

Research shows: How people categorize others—as being in an ingroup or an outgroup—influences how they interpret their behaviors. For instance, a child taking an eraser from another child may be seen as aggressive if he is black but simply assertive if he is white.[23]

When covering outgroups, journalists are wise to listen closely when sources make unsubstantiated allegations that rely on in-group acceptance of cultural norms. For example, a study of 356 stories about gay men and lesbian women published by *Time* and *Newsweek* over a 50-year span from 1947 to 1997 showed that while the presence of prejudicial allegations certainly declined in the news coverage over that time, the allegations from sources continued to appear without evidence to support them and without journalistic skepticism to balance them. A common allegation by sources was that men who were gay were sexually predatory and that gays and lesbians were a threat to children—or, more specifically, that they would "recruit," "seduce" and "molest" children. The lesson from these findings, noted the study author, is to seek evidence and challenge assertions rather than accepting characterizations at face value.[24]

pause & consider Conduct a brief online search of news feature stories about people who are gay or lesbian. Select a story or broadcast transcript to read. Assess whether negative depictions of gays and lesbians by sources are included in the story without adequate evidence to support them. Compare your findings with those of the study mentioned above. Has coverage containing prejudicial allegations diminished? Has the type of prejudice changed?

Unfairly judging others is not the exclusive domain of ingroup members. People in outgroups hold biases about others too. For example, nearly 80 percent of LGBT people of Asian and Pacific Islander backgrounds said they experienced racism within the primarily white LGBT community, according to one survey.[25]

Journalists of color are often assigned to the minority affairs beat.[26] Covering one's own culture—one's own "ingroup"—can pose its own challenges. In one of my classes that conducted an in-depth reporting project on our community's African American neighborhood, two black student journalists found it more difficult to interview local residents than did their white peers. Why? Said one student at the end of the project:

> Sources kept saying to me, "Well, you know how it is. You know what I'm talking about." They assumed I'd know how they'd finish their

thoughts because I was black too. I had to keep saying, "No, I don't know what you're talking about. Explain it to me." Because I really didn't know. I couldn't assume.

STRATEGIES FOR REPORTING ACROSS CULTURES

Journalists reporting across cultural boundaries can take steps to improve the accuracy of their perceptions. To promote accuracy and correct context when reporting about cultures, a journalist should:

- **Know his or her individual standpoint and outlook on the world.**
- **Make people the *subjects* of news coverage, not the *objects*.**[27] Instead of writing a news story observing that overweight women are wearing miniskirts and other clothing often thought of for the size-4 set, write a fashion story about new styles for plus sizes. The first approach objectifies a community of people. The second approach contributes to that community.
- **Create new categories to define a source or situation.** Instead of seeing a source, a woman in a wheelchair, as a disabled person, see her as her occupation defines her; as a scientist or artist or swim coach, for example.
- **Focus on process, not outcome.** Focus on how an interview is conducted instead of just completing it. The process of communication involves all sorts of nuances and cues—word choice and body language, inflection and silences. When a journalist focuses on the process of communication he is more able to make an authentic connection to a source.
- **Approach sources as individuals, not as part of a monolithic group.** Avoid allowing one member of a culture to speak for or represent the entire culture.
- **Avoid single-topic coverage.** For example, go beyond crime coverage in a low-income neighborhood to depict the many people there living productive, interesting lives.

Identify Ethnic Cultural Patterns

Being aware of patterns within groups can help journalists better understand ethnic cultures in particular. Ethnic cultural patterns affect group members' thinking about their actions and behaviors. A reporter is more informed when she understands a particular culture's approach toward the major aspects of life—such as work, interpersonal relations or the concept of time. This information helps when reporting on members of that culture. Exhibit 5.3 demonstrates the wide range of approaches different cultural groups may take toward major aspects of life.

Journalists serve both themselves and their news audiences when they do background research into ethnic cultures' norms and values. For example, Vietnamese people honor courtesy, people who are older and those in authority. A Vietnamese daughter may not correct her father in an interview situation, even if he is providing incorrect information. The reporter may be wise to also interview the daughter separately. The daughter would not want her father to "lose face."

exhibit 5.3 CULTURAL CONTINUUMS[28]

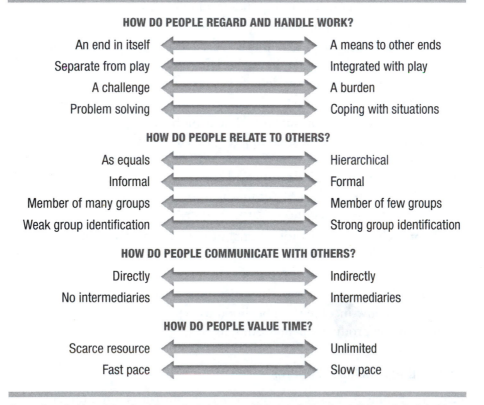

HOW DO PEOPLE REGARD AND HANDLE WORK?

An end in itself	⟷	A means to other ends
Separate from play	⟷	Integrated with play
A challenge	⟷	A burden
Problem solving	⟷	Coping with situations

HOW DO PEOPLE RELATE TO OTHERS?

As equals	⟷	Hierarchical
Informal	⟷	Formal
Member of many groups	⟷	Member of few groups
Weak group identification	⟷	Strong group identification

HOW DO PEOPLE COMMUNICATE WITH OTHERS?

| Directly | ⟷ | Indirectly |
| No intermediaries | ⟷ | Intermediaries |

HOW DO PEOPLE VALUE TIME?

| Scarce resource | ⟷ | Unlimited |
| Fast pace | ⟷ | Slow pace |

Source: Compiled from *Intercultural Competence: Interpersonal Communication Across Cultures,* 3rd ed., by Myron W. Lustig and Jolene Koester, Tables 4.3, 4.4, 4.7. Copyright © 1999 by Addison Wesley Longman.

Value Patience

Patience in reporting is a characteristic not often preached in journalism schools or championed in harried newsrooms. But an extra few hours, a second interview or another visit to the scene can mean a far richer story, the kind that people Tweet and re-tweet, remember and share with others. Whenever possible, journalists should try to return to a community after filing an initial breaking news story and have conversations with everyday people and non-officials who have experiences with the issue at hand. The journalist who takes time to circle back stands in contrast to other reporters and conveys to local residents a genuine interest in forming accurate conclusions.

Annie Shreffler had to be patient and gain the trust of one neighborhood's residents before they would explain its culture to her and her public radio listeners. In August, 2008, Shreffler was reporting a story for WNYC, a public radio station in New York City. A 9-year-old boy, Shamshawan Kelly, had been killed when he was inadvertently caught in the crossfire of a shooting in the Crown Heights neighborhood of Brooklyn. Some three days after the shooting, Shreffler was sent to do a piece on the event. She details how she handled entering the Crown Heights subculture:

OA Going into Crown Heights to cover a shooting was not an original story. It's a neighborhood famous for its riots and violence. I knew I needed to go there and not be the 25th reporter to ask the same questions. I sat down on a stoop with a guy who wouldn't talk unless I put away my microphone.

We talked forever. He told me I couldn't handle "the real news." That's how he put it. He talked about how a corrupt system full of players in Manhattan is what brings guns into his neighborhood. He hinted that if the city really wanted to crack down on violence, it could, but it was full of people who didn't care about his neighborhood.

He introduced me to passersby because he enjoyed the sport of watching me try to get an interview. He dared me to speak to one woman coming down the street, and she told me off. "You can't handle what I could tell you," she declared.

Finally one of his friends agreed to an interview. He gave us great, honest clips to play for the evening broadcast. By the time I had talked with him, I had a much better sense of the place and the people. That never would have happened if I had just hustled the guy for a sound bite and taken off.

This story took me way out of my comfort zone by sending me into what felt like hostile territory. I was white in a black neighborhood with its share of poverty and violence, and I was holding a microphone. I looked like I didn't belong and that I wanted something for nothing.

What the people there didn't know was that I lived in the Bronx; I didn't feel like I was in unfamiliar surroundings. What I felt uncomfortable about was being such an obvious outsider, and so unwelcomed! That made me tense. But I dealt with it by asserting my right to be there and convincing someone that I was interested in the story from that street. It took time, so I decided not to give in to pressure or do anything desperate. I decided to plant myself and figure it out.[29]

Shreffler's patience paid off in good quotes for a daily broadcast. Sometimes, the patience needs to last more than a day. It might take months to develop trust with sources wary of news reporters who parachute in, demand information and leave until the next crisis occurs.

Practice "Big Umbrella" Journalism

Inclusive journalism begins with taking people and events from the narrow categories in our minds and placing them in broader contexts. We have to revise our mental placement of groups, from ingroups and outgroups, to an inclusive **"Big Umbrella"** that encompasses all groups. Shifting someone's membership from a confining outgroup to a common ingroup changes our perceptions of them. The idea is that since people are programmed to best like the group they are in, why not defuse stigmas by putting outgroup members under the same ingroup umbrella?[30] The concept behind this model of thinking is not that people still don't categorize, but that their categorization is broader and more inclusive.

Interestingly, this model doesn't mean that devotion to a smaller, more elite group disappears, but the two coexist; this is a **concentric loyalty.** Two distinct groups can exist within a larger group—like parents and children in one family. This model recognizes that people rightly desire to retain membership and allegiance to their ethnic culture, for example, but that they can also retain that ethnic identity while seeing themselves as members of their surrounding culture as well.

Journalists can apply the Big Umbrella concept to their own thinking as well as to their reporting and writing. A journalist interviewing a local woman who follows Islam might show the woman as a devout Muslim but also determine whether or not the woman perceives herself as belonging to the local secular community as well, and how those two roles set the stage for cultural exchange, intersection or conflict. This type of reporting seeks to go beyond a one-dimensional depiction of the woman.

Some stories are so good *because* the reporter has captured the duality of a situation. For example, imagine a story prompted by the news that a teenager who is overweight has founded Big Is Beautiful, a fat acceptance campaign at her public high school. The story may be occasioned by the founding of the group but also detail the many ways the teen is similar to, and seeks acceptance from, the very peers who have teased her. The story works well because it captures the tension of a teen shuttling between her vocal activism and her efforts at belonging.

When journalists apply the Big Umbrella approach to sources, they recognize the source's unique culture and its influences while also placing individuals and issues in a broader societal context. This dual-minded strategy allows for relevant differences among groups of people to be highlighted while avoiding an "us vs. them" depiction of the world.

exploration EXERCISES

1. As Latinos began relocating to the coast of South Carolina, *Carolina Morning News* wanted to recognize the demographic shift. The Hilton Head–based paper decided to create a regular section of the newspaper devoted to the growing Latino community in town. Then-editor Kyle Poplin changed his mind about the section after he spoke with a leader in the Latino community.

   "He said, 'Why would you do that? We don't want to be seen as separate. We want to be part of the community.' It had felt really good when we had first thought of the idea, but he was absolutely right."[31]

   a. Why might a special section be a negative instead of a positive development in coverage?

   b. Assume you are the editor at a news outlet based in your community. Select a cultural group in your community that you think is underrepresented in current news coverage.

   c. Map out an editorial strategy that will frequently include that cultural group in daily coverage without separating them into an outgroup. Some ideas to consider include: Designing a mobile application that posts citizen reviews of ethnic restaurants in town; compiling a source list of people who represent various cultural viewpoints or expertise; mandating a specific number of sources per news account; or providing regular Q and A interviews with members of that group. Try to think of at least three unique techniques. Share your strategic plan in a PowerPoint presentation or do a mock pitch to an editor.

2. Class and financial standing are not always as evident as cultural borders in the same way that race, ethnicity or gender are. But economics are a significant part of people's lives. Class is more than what you can afford to buy. It also involves power. People of different classes often relate to one another in different ways. People may judge affluent people as "snobby" or "selfish" just as they judge people on public assistance as "lazy" or as "scammers." Select one of the following exercises to explore your economic history and perspective:

   a. Use a free online software tool such as Timeglider to make a timeline of your economic life. Start with the economic circumstances into which you were born. As you compose your timeline, include the highs and lows in your economic life. What was your first job, its pay and how formal was it? Consider the difference between a job and a career; which did your parents have? Note the spaces and places in which you grew up. Consider adding photographs to your timeline to illustrate your economic circumstances. Upload the timeline for others to see. Think about how your class standing influences your perspective on the world.

   b. Make a list of statements that explain the norms of your economic class[32] and share them with peers. To get you started: What do you value as "possessions"—people, things or one-of-a-kind objects? Is money to be used, to be managed or to be invested? When it comes to food, is it most important to have enough, to have it be tasty or to have it well presented? Is clothing chosen as an expression of individual style or based on the label and quality? Think of other norms to include in your list of statements. Compare your norms with others' norms.

    c. Write a brief essay about how popular culture has framed your perceptions of consumerism and affluence. What television shows influenced your ideas about wealth and how people should live? Which performers or celebrities do you follow and why? What cues do you take from them about the trappings of success? Share and compare with peers.

3. Select a current controversy involving a distinct cultural group that is playing out in the news media. Ideally, choose a local issue.

    a. Remembering that audiences need three components in coverage that involves multicultural reporting, assess the coverage on the basis of those three elements: *Education* about issues, events or actions; the *context* of issues, events and actions; and inclusion of all relevant, credible *perspectives*.

    b. Summarize your assessment in a brief memo and include a story pitch suggesting one new approach to covering the issue.

4. Commonly held stereotypes portray overweight workers as more emotionally unstable and harder to get along with than their "normal-weight" colleagues. But in a study of the relationship between body weight and personality traits involving 3,500 adults, researchers found that adults who were overweight and obese were not significantly less conscientious, less agreeable, less extroverted or less emotionally stable.[33]

    a. Talk with a peer about the challenges posed by doing a story about the very real problem of a lack of fitness in the American public today while still respecting people's natural body size and shape and without furthering stereotypes.

    b. Interview a health expert in your community to understand the issues involved in America's escalating problem with obesity.

    c. File the highlights of your interview as a tip sheet for your classroom or newsroom.

FOR review

- List at least six cultural norms that you follow.
- Explain to a peer the three components necessary for covering cultures.

- Apply one strategy for reporting across cultures to a story you are currently reporting or one in the news.

- Identify a news story in which a more inclusive "Big Umbrella" approach could be applied instead of a narrow take on the issue. Explain the more inclusive angle on the story.

notes

1. M. E. Sprengelmeyer, Interview with author, August, 2010.

2. M. E. Sprengelmeyer, "Bringing It Home: U.S. Earnings Mean Better Life for Melgozas in Mexico," *Ventura County Star,* April 6, 1997.

3. Myron W. Lustig and Jolene Koester, *Intercultural Competence: Interpersonal Communication across Cultures,* 3rd ed. (New York: Longman, 1999).

4. Ibid.

5. Geert Hofstede, *Cultures and Organizations: Software of the Mind* (New York: McGraw-Hill, 1991), p. 7.

6. Ruby K. Payne, *A Framework for Understanding Poverty* (Highlands, Tex.: aha! Process, 2005).

7. Pew Hispanic Center, "Country of Origin Profiles" (Washington, D.C.: Pew Hispanic Center, April 22, 2010).

8. Project for Excellence in Journalism, "Principles of Journalism," Pew Research Center, www.journalism.org/resources/principles, retrieved May 16, 2011.

9. Reuters staff, "Reporting About People," in *Handbook of Journalism* (New York: Thomson Reuters, 2008), http://handbook.reuters.com/index.php/Main_Page, retrieved Sept. 1, 2010.

10. Pew Hispanic Center, "Country of Origin Profiles," http://pewhispanic.org/data/origins, retrieved Aug. 17, 2010.

11. J. Durkin, Interview with author, August, 2010.

12. Maynard Institute, "Fault Lines: Cultural Diversity Training in the Workplace" (2011), http://www.maynardije.org/faultlines.

13. The Maynard Institute, "Fault Lines, Chapter VII: Perspective Exercises" (2011), http://www.maynardije.org/fault-lines-chapters-ix-and-x, retrieved Aug. 10, 2011.

14. Andrea Peyser, "Mosque Madness at Ground Zero," *New York Post,* May 13, 2010.

15. Rick Hampson, "Imam's Wife Says, 'We Understand'," *USA Today,* August 23, 2010.

16. Matt Sledge, "Just How Far Is the 'Ground Zero Mosque' from Ground Zero?," *The Huffington Post* (July 28, 2010), http://www.huffingtonpost.com/matt-sledge/just-how-far-is-the-groun_b_660585.html, retrieved on Sept. 15, 2010.

17. Skye Jethani, "An Evangelical Response to the 'Ground Zero Mosque'" (July 30, 2010), http://www.huffingtonpost.com/skye-jethani/an-evangelical-response-t_b_664580.html, retrieved on Sept. 15, 2010.

18. Pew Forum on Religion and Public Life, "The Future of the Global Muslim Population" (Washington, D.C.: Pew Research Center, Jan. 27, 2011).

19. Martin Rochlin, "The Heterosexual Questionnaire," in *The Meaning of Difference: American Constructions of Race, Sex and Gender, Social Class, Sexual Orientation, and Disability,* ed. Karen E. Rosenblum and Toni-Michelle C. Travis (Boston: McGraw-Hill, 2008), p. 175.

20. Michael Oliver, "Disability Definitions: The Politics of Meaning," in *The Meaning of Difference: American Constructions of Race, Sex and Gender, Social Class, Sexual Orientation, and Disability,* ed. Karen E. Rosenbaum and Toni-Michelle C. Travis (Boston: McGraw Hill, 2008), pp. 177–78.

21. Susan T. Fiske and Shelley E. Taylor, *Social Cognition* (New York: Random House, 1984); Samuel L. Gaertner and John F. Dovidio, "Categorization, Recategorization, and Intergroup Bias," in John F. Dovidio, Peter Glick, and Laurie A. Rudman, eds., *On the Nature of Prejudice: Fifty Years after Allport* (Malden, Mass.: Blackwell, 2005); Susan T. Fiske, "Social Cognition and the Normality of Prejudgment," in *On the Nature of Prejudice: Fifty Years after Allport,* ed. John F. Dovidio, Peter Glick, and Laurie A. Rudman (Malden, Mass.: Blackwell, 2005).

22. Fiske and Taylor, *Social Cognition;* Fiske, "Social Cognition and the Normality of Prejudgment."

23. Ibid.

24. Lisa Bennett, "Fifty Years of Prejudice in the Media," *The Gay & Lesbian Review Worldwide* 7, no. 2 (2000).

25. Alain Dang and Cabrini Vianney, "Living in the Margins: A National Survey of Lesbian, Gay, Bisexual, and Transgender Asian and Pacific Islander Americans" (New York: National Gay and Lesbian Task Force Policy Institute, 2007).

26. R. Shafer, "What Minority Journalists Identify as Constraints to Full Newsroom Equality," *Howard Journal of Communications 4,* no. 3 (1993).

27. David Tuller, *The Reporting Diversity Manual* (London: Media Diversity Institute, 2004), http://www.media-diversity.org, retrieved July 17, 2011.

28. Lustig and Koester, *Intercultural Competence: Interpersonal Communication Across Cultures,* Ch. 4.

29. Annie Shreffler, Interview with author, June, 2010.

30. Samuel L. Gaertner and John F. Dovidio, "Categorization, Recategorization, and Intergroup Bias."

31. Kyle Poplin, Interview with author, 2010.

32. Payne, *A Framework for Understanding Poverty.*

33. Mark V. Roehling, Patricia V. Roehling, and L. Maureen Odland, "Investigating the Validity of Stereotypes About Overweight Employees: The Relationship Between Body Weight and Normal Personality Traits," *Group and Organization Management 33* (2008).

Training the Reporter's Eye

*What gets journalists' attention can influence
how they portray events and explain behaviors*

ON THE LOOKOUT FOR AUTHENTICITY

Reporter Ellen Warren kept her attention focused on the "real people" at the Washington, D.C., funeral of a member of the president's Cabinet who died while in office. At the time, Warren was a Washington-based national correspondent for Knight-Ridder newspapers. She looked beyond the elite members of the audience from Congress, the Cabinet, the national political scene and diplomatic corps to find the people who had known U.S. Secretary of Commerce Malcolm Baldrige for decades. In them, Warren found the down-home, informal eulogies that other outlets missed. Here's how her story began:

In the driveway of the National Cathedral, long after the bigwigs had left, Commerce Secretary Mac Baldrige's cowboy buddies stood around stiffly and talked about President Reagan's eulogy of their friend.

They couldn't have said it better, they said. Then, they did.

Junior, Smokey, Rags, Ken, Ron and the others, rodeo friends from 20 years back and more, lingered after the Washington-style memorial service Wednesday, sharing memories that had nothing to do with trade policy and the value of the dollar and the matters of commerce that were Malcolm Baldrige's life in the capital.

"Mac never got enough roping. He'd call in the middle of the day and ask me if we could rope a pen. He'd show up in his suit, take off his tie and his coat, rope five or six [calves], get his head clear and go back and face Congress," remembered Ken Schiffer, who keeps Baldrige's quarter horse on his Virginia ranch outside Washington.

"My oldest boy roped with Mac two weeks ago, and they placed second," said Paul Crotta, who like the other rodeo friends is a businessman in his cowboy off-hours. "My wife just sent him his winnings check."[1]

How did Warren find those cowboys? As she tries to do with every story, Warren, now a senior correspondent for the *Chicago Tribune,* got to the reporting scene early and stayed late, after the formal event was over. That's when the interesting things often happen, when most of the news media have left.

Warren pays attention to the opportunities for exclusive information no one else has, and also for behind-the-scenes players who often are the closest to the issue in question. She explains:

OA

I hung around the National Cathedral in D.C. after the funeral. That's when I saw a group of fellas jawing on the steps who absolutely could not be Washington bureaucrats. With their corrugated skin, their slouchy looks, for sure they were cowboys and old pals of Baldrige, who was well known to have had a real cowpoke life. I knew if they were who I thought they were, then they'd have more colorful stories than the bureaucrats and the stuff I'd heard from the speaker's list of Washington elite at the funeral.

When reporting, I watch what the other news outlets are paying attention to, but I also try and look beyond the staging and the surface. I watch people's body language, the pictures on the wall, the small details. Often, they're the things that bring a story to life; and those details can open up new avenues for questions that a source might not be sharing. I scan a reporting scene for the basics—the 5ws and the H—but also for the unexpected and the authentic. I try to catch people being themselves, and when I do, I try to stand back and observe carefully. I try not to put any conditions on what I take in.[2]

As Warren's story illustrates, what journalists pay attention to and what they ignore shapes news coverage. (Go to www.hhpcommunities.com/overcomingbias for more on Warren's reporting.) A journalist can sometimes uncover a more authentic version of a story by foregoing yet another interview with elite sources such as a government official, a spokesperson or others highly skilled at imposing their perspective of an event on the news media.[3] Sometimes, seeking out interview subjects who are less media savvy and who are not paid to have a particular point of view is crucial to achieve comprehensive coverage of an event or issue. In short: Go for the cowboys with bona fide sunburns over the bureaucrats in cowboy hats.

WHAT PEOPLE NOTICE

Our senses and minds gravitate to certain kinds of people and events because of how our brain works. What journalists pay attention to matters to their reporting because our attention can influence what we remember, how we evaluate people and the extent to which we stereotype people. To start, let's look at what generally grabs people's attention:[4,5]

- **Novelty in one's immediate surroundings,** such as the person over 60 in a classroom full of 20-year-olds, or a person with only one arm who is checking out groceries for customers.

- **Objects and people that are bright, moving or complex.** For example, a woman in a red dress (bright), someone rocking in a chair (moving), or someone in a Hawaiian shirt amid gray uniforms (complex pattern).

- **Behaviors that don't fit one's preconceptions or prior knowledge of the person.** If you expect your source to be friendly and helpful, as he always has been, and on this day he is not, you pay increased attention to his behavior.

- **Behavior that is unusual given someone's social category.** For example, a white-collar professional coming to work in overalls.

- **Unusual behavior in general, especially the negative or extreme.** For instance, a loud, obnoxious audience member at a city council meeting.

- **The person in your immediate visual field,** such as the person seated right across from you at a long table.
- **People who have influence over us in some way,** such as a boss.
- **Things that are threatening,** such as civil unrest or a tornado.
- **Immediate, proximate happenings,** such as a hotel fire in the local community.

A pattern emerges that suggests the mind pays attention to the different, unusual or threatening. These qualities that the mind naturally notices are in many ways assets for journalists: The unusual and the extreme draw our attention, and such characteristics often drive news coverage. So why, exactly, do we notice what we notice? And what does that mean for the news?

What Gets Attention Is Newsworthy

What people naturally pay attention to has a striking similarity to what journalists pay attention to when working. These priorities are reinforced through the values of the U.S. news industry. Frequently mentioned news values include conflict, proximity, prominence, novelty, timeliness and human interest. Instead of thinking about news values as the guidelines for determining newsworthiness, journalists can think about them as the criteria for judging the characteristics of the information that *naturally* attracts people's attention.[6]

pause&*consider* Quickly scan the home page of your city's daily news outlet and write down the news values represented in the top stories. Then, compare those news items with the list of categories of information that get people's attention. How similar are the two lists?

Biological Influences on Attention

The news industry is not the only factor influencing journalists' attention. It goes back much, much further than that. For ages, humans have had an innate drive to gather and disseminate news as a survival tool. Surveying for nearby threats is biologically influenced; people are programmed that way.[7] Which brings us to cavemen. Or rather, early humans.

Human thinking can be seen as the interaction of both biology and culture. The majority of this book is focused on the influence of culture and society on how journalists think—social cognition. However, it's worth noting that biology influences thinking as well. It's called evolutionary psychology. Our ancestors' version of breaking news might have been something like: "Grunt! Tiger outside the cave! Beware!"

People are innately interested in news about deviant (as in abnormal or unusual) or threatening events or ideas because the brain is hardwired to scan the environment this way.[8] Plus, news that involves the abnormal, exceptional or threatening is usually bad: disasters, murders, coups, scandals. People pay attention to bad news because it's in their best interests, both biologically (for survival from predators and danger) and culturally (society encourages surveillance of what is right and wrong, what threatens the status quo). Our nose for news doesn't sniff out commonplace events; it follows the scent of unusually good things and the odor of unusually bad things.

The human instinct to watch for the threatening and deviant can help journalists pay attention to things that genuinely matter to the public. Biology is actually on the side of journalism. Examples of such coverage include stories about whether or not efforts to combat wildfires across the western United States are effective, or how the poor enforcement of safety regulations might contribute to a high death rate among construction workers in fast-growing areas such as the Las Vegas strip. Reporting on both of those topics won Pulitzer Prizes in 2009. These two examples (read both at www.pulitzer.org) focus on threats—in these cases, fires and dangerous work conditions. The stories may have been triggered initially by the reporters' instinct to look for problems or troubles, but they succeed by going beyond that. The "bad news" element may be what inspired those story topics, but vigorous research and reporting made them award winners.

Humans' brains are biologically and culturally wired to acknowledge the threatening or unusual, which explains why so much news is negative.

Cultural Influences on Attention

Throughout the ages humans have also been *taught* to be on the lookout for threats to safety or security, from looking both ways when crossing the street to guarding against a radical idea that might upset the status quo. Culture teaches people about what to pay attention to and why. Humans have an inclination toward surveying their environment and shaping information in order to emphasize what is divergent from the norm and what is socially significant.[9]

Note, however, that norms change over time. A marriage between a black woman and a white man made headlines and went to the U.S. Supreme Court in 1967 for violating Virginia's ban on interracial marriages. Today such marriages are commonplace and not news. In another example, rapes were typically not covered in the news media in the 1950s *because* of their sexual nature. Now, rapes are typically covered, particularly when the incident involves sensational details or someone prominent.[10]

What constitutes news, what our minds pay attention to as notable, is determined by both a genetic predisposition for surveillance and cultural determinates about what is the norm and what isn't. The cultural explanation for what humans pay attention to involves whatever deviates from the norm or the usual: What's different, extreme, prominent, controversial, sensational?[11] A locally born resident—white, English-speaking, middle-class—running for mayor in a small Montana town isn't unusual or particularly noteworthy, but a Nigerian-born Muslim running for mayor of a small Montana town is. News is not apart from culture, but fueled by cultural history and traditional practice.[12]

As society changes so does the news. Cultural norms change and evolve, and cultural norms in part dictate what is news. Journalists working in today's multicultural society cannot fail to notice what comes easily and automatically to their minds. But news people can pause to reflect and note what is being depicted as being *outside* a culture's norm by advocacy groups or political causes, for instance. Wise journalists who pause from the daily digital competition will see the quiet changes going on around them and can help news audiences see them, too.

One thing that strikes me, as a reporter in the Middle East, is that it's very easy to hear what you want to hear. Sometimes it's a little harder to let people say what they want to say.

ANTHONY SHADID, *WASHINGTON POST* REPORTER[13]

THE CONSEQUENCES OF OUR ATTENTION

Hey!

Look right here!

Don't you want to know why attention matters?

After all, what people find prominent or noticeable has consequences. Attention affects our perceptions of someone's influence over events, and also how we evaluate other people and events. So, a person who stands out in a group is seen as more influential. Simply because she stands out, she's credited with characteristics she may not possess.[14]

For instance, in a workplace setting attention is drawn to the serious man, with graying hair and dressed in a suit and tie, sitting in a conference room among mostly women and a few men in casual shirts and comfortable shoes. An outside observer sees him as the boss. He hardly speaks, so he's obviously smart, the observer figures. A man of few words. And he's powerful, because everyone seems to be deferring to him.

Turns out he's the janitor. He's at a retirement reception in his honor, so he dressed up. He's never been a big talker.

The lesson for journalists, especially when entering breaking events with little background or orienting information, is to avoid assigning characteristics to a source without evidence. Watch, listen and use that extra sense called common sense to figure out new situations.

Giving someone our attention also has the effect of exaggerating our existing judgments about the person.[15] If a person views a defendant in a criminal proceeding negatively, the increased attention from news coverage will likely cause the person to view the defendant even more negatively. Of course, reporters will have private judgments, so professional training and awareness of our attention becomes essential. A reporter covering the court trial must keep her attention on the empirical evidence, so that conclusions made in the resulting news account are based in fact.

Attraction to Vividness

The brain loves a treat: It is wired to pay attention to things that are **vivid**. Information that is vivid is emotionally interesting, concrete, and close to us, either in terms of our senses (first-hand information), in real time (the event happened just yesterday), or in actual space (the event happened in our own community).[16] Vivid information produces strong mental images. This is important because vividly presented information engenders memory. We tend to recall information presented vividly far more readily than information presented in a dull way.[17] Like the way you remember the experience of eating a triple chocolate cupcake better than a sugar-free bran muffin. People remember a car crash they passed on the way to work far more easily than the day's decline in the stock market.

Journalists in the 21st century are well acquainted with the power of vividness. Their news organizations encourage them to seek approaches to stories that will make a clear impression on news consumers. The livelier the lead and images accompanying the story, the more online hits it is likely to receive. This is why personal anecdotes often lead stories about abstract topics, such as the mortgage crisis or contaminants in drinking water. Triple chocolate, not bran.

Vivid information is also concrete and imagery-producing. Compare "Jack sustained fatal injuries in a car accident," with "Jack was killed by a semitrailer that rolled over on his car and crushed his skull."[18] Journalists use the power of vividness often in conveying the news. It is a useful tool that captures audiences' attention. Knowledgeable journalists know how to take the basic bran recipe (explaining federal health care changes for low-income children) and add enough tasty ingredients (personal anecdotes, an interactive graphic) to make consumers want to take a bite.

News Frames and Audience Attention

The conclusions that journalists make about an event shape the news story. Within each news account, certain elements get more attention than others and some elements are left out completely. This selection and emphasis of information is called framing. **Framing** is the magnifying or shrinking of elements to make them more or less *salient,* which means information that is noticeable, meaningful or memorable to an audience. In journalism, frames define problems, diagnose causes, make judgments and offer remedies.[19] The focus of journalists' attention affects news frames and in turn news frames direct the news audiences' attention.

News frames are extremely helpful to journalists, especially as journalists are under constant deadline pressure due to the nature of digital media. News frames allow journalists to quickly process lots of material and convey it to a general audience, putting it in some logical order and focus for their audience. A news frame guides a journalist in sorting through which details of a story to include, which to emphasize and which to exclude.

Frames and fairness

Journalists need to be aware of the power of framing on accuracy and fairness. The way that journalists frame a happening often reflects broader cultural themes and priorities. The words, phrases and images with which journalists choose to portray a news event may result in significantly different portrayals of the same event and different audience reactions. The presentation of public issues and events affects how news consumers understand them.[20]

Consider news coverage of a Ku Klux Klan rally in a small Ohio city. In an experiment, one group of participants watched a local television news segment that "emphasized the right of KKK members to speak to the public and, especially, the right of their supporters and the curious to hear what the Klan had to say."[21] The second group of participants watched a segment on the same event that instead "highlighted the disturbances that erupted during the rally and included images of police officers in riot gear."[22] The participants who saw a news story framing the rally as a matter of free speech expressed greater tolerance for the Klan than those who saw the story as one of potential violence.

Framing signals to news consumers what to care about and how to interpret events and people.[23] One framing analysis showed how the downing by the United States of an Iranian plane was called "a technical problem," but the Soviets shooting down a Korean jet was "portrayed as a moral outrage."[24] How one interprets the event depends on the news frame. In another example, how people assigned responsibility for the causes of poverty was dependent on news frames. Research participants either blamed society at large or the actual individuals in poverty, depending on whether the news media presented poverty as a general outcome or presented poverty in specific, individual cases.[25]

Just because the news media cover a story doesn't mean that news consumers pay attention. Sometimes the news coverage does not mirror the interests of news consumers. For instance, the coverage of Osama bin Laden's death by U.S. forces dominated 69 percent of the news stories in one week in May 2011, a near-record amount of news coverage; but only 42 percent of people polled said they followed the news of the Al Qaeda leader's killing more closely than other news that week. One in five consumers were interested in news about tornadoes and floods in the South and Midwest, but news organizations devoted only 5 percent of coverage that week to those stories.[26]

Visuals and framing

Framing can also be accomplished effectively through visuals. Visual framing includes the practice of selecting one image instead of another, cropping out certain details or otherwise editing the image. For example, showing many images of cheering people at a parade can give the impression of far more public support for a candidate or cause than may actually be the case. Have you ever been to an event and then watched coverage of it on television and thought, "That's not what I experienced at all"? Your reaction could be due to news media's framing of the event. Think about the impact on public opinion regarding an underdog presidential candidate when audiences are shown images of wildly cheering crowds versus sullen faces at the very same political rally. "A picture must stand for a thousand words, but also must replace a thousand other pictures."[27]

pause&consider Search online for two different images from the same news event and compare their content. Describe the frames being used to depict the event.

In news stories, visual framing can convey meanings that might be controversial or meet audience resistance if spelled out in text. One area of news coverage in which this occurs is the portrayal of African

Americans in negative news accounts. Here, images provide subtle stereotyping through implication and suggestion.

For example, a story about AIDS on a Dallas television station didn't verbally state that race and ethnicity were involved, but by repeatedly using images of African Americans dancing in nightclubs, stereotypes of black sexuality were reinforced.[28] In another instance, an NBC evening news story about people moving from welfare to work in

Images can often convey controversial meaning in more subtle ways than text does.

the 1990s showed a preponderance of images of African Americans. The first 14 shots were of black people, giving the sense that most people on welfare were black, though the voice-over did not explicitly state so.[29]

JOURNALISM AND THE ETHICS OF ATTENTION

If the unusual and abnormal attract our attention, then emphasizing what is *different* from the norm serves to emphasize the norm. But whose norm is being emphasized? Is there an overarching mainstream, traditional, American Cultural Norm? If so, is that the norm news organizations should use as their guidepost in determining whether events, people and ideas deviate from it? What do journalists do in a global society in which the news audience represents a multitude of cultures, and when perhaps even the immediate community is highly diverse? These questions probe how news shapes values and society, and journalists' responsibility to reflect *all* members of a society.

pause&consider Take a moment and free write or talk informally with a colleague about the questions raised in the paragraph above.

One way the news media tells consumers what is normal is by showing them what is deviant.[30] The news media can marginalize a group by portraying its members in a way that diminishes their validity or by simply by ignoring them. Social change, for instance, can be seen as innovative and enriching the current society, or it can be seen as a threat that upsets the status quo, a breakdown of normal operations that may lead to violence.[31]

News media legitimize the traditional and entrenched systems of power and privilege in America when reporters pay attention exclusively to official sources and spokespeople. A focus on prominent and powerful people also contributes to this legitimization. So does negative coverage of events and ideas that run counter to the status quo. Through this sort of coverage, the news media can bolster the current social structure.

Upholding Journalistic Standards

Excellent journalists keep their attention focused on *journalism's* status quo principles instead of a *society's* status quo values. As the world changes and diversifies, the tenets that journalists hold as sure and true become all the more important. Standards relating to attention and news coverage remind journalists to broaden the scope of their attention. The Project for Excellence in Journalism's principles urge journalists to:

- Place society's varied viewpoints and interests in context, instead of presenting only extremes and conflicts.
- Give attention in terms of news coverage that is proportional to the event. "Inflating events for sensation, neglecting others, stereotyping or being disproportionately negative all make a less reliable map" by which citizens can navigate society.
- Serve as an independent monitor of power. Journalists should be watchdogs of those in authority in a society. [32]

Filling the Gaps in Attention

Journalists can apply professional training and engage in reflective practice (as discussed in Chapter 2), to consider where their attention is focused even mid-story. Journalists cannot help what the mind is naturally programmed to notice. The schoolgirl wearing a hijab amid a classroom of bare heads will pop out visually. Fires and mayhem will and should always get coverage. Yet reflection, however brief, should reveal gaps in attention. It might include questions such as: What do I know and still need to know?[33] Did I cover all perspectives of this event? Who might have a stake in this issue or event that I haven't checked in with yet? Did one source in particular get special attention in the news account, perhaps too much? Why did I notice that? How do I know that? The journalist needs to know she can justify her thinking and decisions to colleagues, stakeholders in the issue at hand and the greater public.

Minding Attentional Blind Spots

Additional ways in which journalists can focus their attention on relevant news events and topics that broaden the scope of quality coverage include:

Look for the invisible. Because people naturally turn their attention to the novel and extreme, journalists need to train themselves to look where others don't naturally look. One of the most important things about attention is to note what *isn't* being noticed. Plenty of significant news is not vivid, dramatic or immediately threatening, such as the quiet rise in the number of children living in families where no parent had full-time, year-round employment, up to 23.1 million in 2009. While roughly one out of every four Asian and non-Hispanic white children lived without securely employed parents, nearly one in two American Indian and African American children did.[34]

The results of parental unemployment for children are an increased risk of poor health and poor performance at school, not to mention the reduction of benefits that come from stable economic conditions at home (the opportunity to enroll in music lessons or a baseball league, to have friends over for a birthday party, to have new shoes). Kids are easily ignored by society at large. They don't protest; they don't vote; they don't pay taxes. But their welfare has far-reaching implications for the greater public, including the strength of the future workforce.

Don't follow the pack. Just because a majority of the U.S. news media anoint an event, person or idea as newsworthy doesn't mean it is significant or meaningful to most of the population. What is newsworthy is a cognitive concept; it is a mental judgment.[35] Often, the most newsworthy angle is the one that best reflects the perspectives and reality of everyday citizens. This is why solid beat reporting is so valuable. Talk to everyday sources about *their* everyday concerns. Follow Twitter trends. Notice what people talk about on their

Facebook and Google+ accounts. Then do the reporting that provides critical, informed coverage about the public's concern.

Christi Parsons, who covered the Obama presidential campaign in 2008 for the *Los Angeles Times* and *Chicago Tribune,* says she enjoyed diving into campaign crowds to talk with people who made the effort to attend public events. Going beyond campaign speeches and press handlers, Parsons sought a context beyond the pack journalism of the campaign bus. She explains:

OA

ON ASSIGNMENT

When you're on the campaign bus, it's easy to narrow your focus to the news happening within the campaign "bubble." The frame of reference is very limited; it's just that bus, and the staffers and the candidate on it. Of course, in order to develop sources, break news and develop a deep understanding of the candidate and campaign, you simply can't do without the bus experience.

It's beneficial to have reporters rotate off the bus and to take turns being "ground support" for one another. The job of the ground support team is to pull back the lens, to see more and report more. Those reporters are working the telephones, meeting with sources in person, flying around the country and jumping into other campaign bubbles to develop the fuller picture.

Within the context of the campaign operation, reporters are getting similar information. And they are analyzing it in a similar way because their contextual information is so similar. The people who are free to pull back the lens and look at trends and patterns and evaluate things with a broader view are fewer and farther between.

There is less immediate reward for news outlets and news writers to think about things that way. Sometimes the thinking is, "Quick, what's the next thing we can put on the website?" It's not the long view. It's very short-sighted. We have to be disciplined and determined in order to rise above that.[36]

pause&consider Parsons notes that there is "less immediate reward" for news writers who try to evaluate things with a broader view. Why do you think that is?

Make the dull shine. Strive to make the significant interesting and relevant. Unfortunately for lazy storytellers, vivid information is not necessarily the most important information for news consumers.[37] Overreliance on vivid information can lead to errors of perception and judgment, such as the striking personal anecdote that only tenuously relates to the rest of the news story. Select what is truly informative over what is merely vivid.

The rising cost of food might not sound like a gripping news story, but the weekly struggle to feed a family on only food stamps can be the most important story of the day for a news outlet. The incremental, complex business decisions that compounded into the national financial meltdown and banking crisis that began in 2008 were not vivid, but their impact is still felt today throughout the world.

Challenge the status quo. Challenge it in your newsroom and in society. Question formulaic news coverage decisions in a newsroom or editorial meeting, inviting colleagues to reframe issues and consider them from different angles. This requires you to follow your own moral compass; journalists should have a personal conscience, a sense of ethics and responsibility that guides their work.[38] Journalists obviously need not embrace all ideas and all types of people as equally newsworthy, but they should strive to notice as much of the world as humanly possible, avoiding selective attention to an elite few in authority.

exploration EXERCISES

1. Watch where your attention takes you:
   a. Pair up with a colleague, preferably one who is different from you in a specific way, such as in regional background, political ideology, sexual orientation or physical ability.
   b. Attend an event neither of you have been to before. Ideally, select an event that focuses on some aspect of your or your colleague's culture that isn't shared by the other: a food tasting, a political rally, a gay rights parade, the local Special Olympics, and so on. During the event, take notes on what grabs your attention.
   c. If you do not have time to attend an event together, select a television show or movie that features the difference and watch the same episode, taking notes on what seems significant to you about the script, set and characters and what got your attention.

    d. Compare your findings to those of your colleague: What did you notice that your colleague didn't? What did you ignore or miss that your colleague didn't? What might be reasons for the differences or similarities in what caught your attention?

    e. Compare and contrast your separate perceptions in a brief presentation to a training group or class.

2. Review the top three stories over three to five days in your local news outlet. Select the stories from the student newspaper, a community radio station or an online site, and evaluate its coverage of current institutions, leadership, laws and policies. Decide whether or not the coverage furthers the status quo of your community. Consider how critical the coverage is. Are reporters asking sources: "How do you know? Why should people trust that? Who says so?"

    a. To do this review, record at least two of the following elements: The types of sources used (official or unofficial) and how often they are used; the types of story topics selected and their relative placement in the broadcast or online layout; which stories get visuals and the nature of the visuals used; the emphasis of the lead; the word choice—in particular note the verbs used to describe sources' positions on issues.

    b. Summarize your findings in a brief memo and state whether or not the coverage challenges current norms or provides a broader perspective on the community. Give specific examples to support your conclusion.

3. Award-winning journalist Marshall Allen of the *Las Vegas Sun* says that journalists need to "earn readers' attention"[39] by writing from the readers' point of view. See an example of how Allen and his colleague Alex Richards did this in their series on the thousands of cases of injuries, infections and deaths associated with stays in Las Vegas hospitals. The story is told in a variety of ways, including through primary documents, text, photos, videos and interactive maps. The series, called "Do No Harm: Hospital Care in Las Vegas," is online and also accessible through your library's newspaper database.

a. After reviewing the series, discuss in a small group how Allen and Richards earned your attention.

b. Identify the form of storytelling that was most engaging for you and explain why and *how* it got and kept your attention.

4. Keep an attention journal for two days.

a. On the first day, log entries at least three times a day (breakfast, lunch and dinner works well) about what was most noticeable about your routine environment in the last few hours.

b. On the second day, with the entries of the day before in mind, notice different aspects of your daily regimen. Also log entries three times a day. As you travel to work or school, note the people you normally see (or don't see), the language you overhear, the visual details around you.

c. Note any new information in your entries on the second day. Think about how you might employ this same devotion to noticing new things in your next assignment.

FOR review

- Summarize basic qualities that attract humans' attention and link as many of them as possible with a corresponding news value. (You'll likely repeat the same news value more than once.)
- Analyze how a news outlet has framed a text or visual news account.
- Identify a news story that you think indicates that the journalist "looked for the invisible" or didn't "follow the pack."

notes

1. Ellen Warren, "President, Friends Praise Baldrige's Cowboy Spirit," *The Miami Herald,* July 30, 1987.
2. Ellen Warren, Interview with author, November, 2010.
3. Robert M. Entman, "Framing: Toward Clarification of a Fractured Paradigm," *Journal of Communication 43,* no. 4 (1993).
4. Susan T. Fiske and Shelley E. Taylor, *Social Cognition: From Brains to Culture* (Boston: McGraw-Hill, 2008).

5. Pamela J. Shoemaker, "Hardwired for News: Using Biological and Cultural Evolution to Explain the Surveillance Function," *Journal of Communication 46,* no. 3 (1996).

6. J. David Kennamer, "News Values and the Vividness of Information," *Written Communication 5,* no. 1 (1988).

7. Shoemaker, "Hardwired for News."

8. Ibid.

9. Ibid.

10. Pamela J. Shoemaker and Stephen D. Reese, *Mediating the Message: Theories of Influences on Mass Media Content,* 2nd ed. (White Plains, N.Y.: Longman, 1996).

11. Pamela J. Shoemaker, L. H. Danielian, and N. Brendlinger, "Deviant Acts, Risky Business and U.S. Interests: The Newsworthiness of World Events," *Journalism Quarterly 68,* no. 4 (1991).

12. T. Koch, *The News as Myth: Fact and Context in Journalism* (Westport, Conn.: Greenwood Press, 1990); Shoemaker, "Hardwired for News".

13. Anthony Shadid, "The Iraq Experience Poses Critical Questions for Journalists," *Nieman Reports* (2004), http://www.nieman.harvard.edu/reports/article/100828/The-Iraq-Experience-Poses-Critical-Questions-For-Journalists.aspx, retrieved August 8, 2011.

14. Fiske and Taylor, *Social Cognition: From Brains to Culture.*

15. Ibid.

16. Richard Nisbett and Lee Ross, *Human Inference: Strategies and Shortcomings of Social Judgment,* ed. James J. Jenkins, Walter Mischel, and Willard W. Hartup, Century Psychology Series (Englewood Cliffs, N.J.: Prentice-Hall, 1980).

17. Richard Nisbett and Lee Ross, *Human Inference: Strategies and Shortcomings of Social Judgment,* p. 47.

18. Ibid.

19. Robert M. Entman, "Framing U.S. Coverage of International News: Contrasts in Narratives of the KAL and Iran Air Incidents," *Journal of Communication 41,* no. 4 (1991).

20. Vincent Price, David Tewksbury, and Elizabeth Powers, "Switching Trains of Thought: The Impact of News Frames on Readers' Cognitive Responses," *Communication Research 24,* no. 5 (1997).

21. Thomas E. Nelson, Rosalee A. Clawson, and Zoe M. Oxley, "Media Framing of a Civil Liberties Conflict and Its Effect on Tolerance," *American Political Science Review 91,* no. 3 (1997), p. 571.

22. Ibid.

23. Ibid.

24. Entman, "Framing U.S. Coverage of International News," p. 6.

25. Shanto Iyengar, "Framing Responsibility for Political Issues: The Case of Poverty," *Political Behavior 12*, no. 1 (1990).

26. Pew Research Center for the People and the Press, "Death of Bin Laden: More Coverage Than Interest" (Washington D.C.: Pew Research Center for the People and the Press, May 11, 2011).

27. David Perlmutter and Gretchen L. Wagner, "The Anatomy of a Photojournalistic Icon: Marginalization of Dissent in the Selection and Framing of a 'Death in Genoa'," *Visual Communication 3,* no. 1 (2004).

28. Paul Messaris and Linus Abraham, "The Role of Images in Framing News Stories," in *Framing Public Life: Perspectives on Media and Our Understanding of the Social World,* ed. Stephen D. Reese, Oscar H. Gandy, Jr., and August E. Grant (Mahwah, N.J.: Lawrence Erlbaum, 2003).

29. Ibid.

30. Shoemaker and Reese, *Mediating the Message.*

31. Shoemaker, Danielian, and Brendlinger, "Deviant Acts, Risky Business and U.S. Interests."

32. Project for Excellence in Journalism, "Principles of Journalism" (Washington, D.C.: Pew Research Center, 1997), www.journalism.org/resources/principles, retrieved July 18, 2011.

33. Bob Steele, "Ask These 10 Questions to Make Good Ethical Decisions," Poynter.org (2002), www.poynter.org/latest-news/everyday-ethics/talk-about-ethics/1750/ask-these-10-questions-to-make-good-ethical-decisions/.

34. Annie E. Casey Foundation, *Kids Count Data Book*, summary of findings (Baltimore, Md.: Annie E. Casey Foundation, 2011).

35. Shoemaker, "News and Newsworthiness: A Commentary," *Communications 31* (2006).

36. Christi Parsons, Interview with author, 2008.

37. Kennamer, "News Values and the Vividness of Information."

38. Project for Excellence in Journalism, "Principles of Journalism."

39. Bill Kirtz, "How Award-Winning Investigative Reporters Earn Readers' Attention, Impress Advertisers," Poynter.org (2011), http://www.poynter.org/how-tos/newsgathering-storytelling/122403/how-award-winning-investigative-reporters-earn-readers-attention-impress-advertisers-work-around-editors/, retrieved August 4, 2011.

7

Critical Decisions Before Deadline

Why even experienced journalists neglect certain facts and what to do about it

LEARNING OBJECTIVES

- *To define and identify confirmation bias.*
- *To understand how confirmation bias and deadline pressure affect the information-gathering process.*
- *To be aware of biases in judgments that can affect thinking.*
- *To recognize how accountability may improve accuracy.*

A DISTORTED VISION

Disbelief. That was the tone taken by three Milwaukee television stations as they reported the findings of a scientific study on whether a reformulated gasoline that contained the additive MTBE was causing health problems.

Said Channel 6: "*Not* [emphasis in original] a health problem? Thousands of people have complained about the reformulated gasoline, saying it makes them sick."[1]

Channel 4's report asked: "Is reformulated gas dangerous to your health? A new report says no, but not everyone is convinced."[2]

Following the 1995 introduction of the new gasoline in Wisconsin, Milwaukee news reports provided researchers the opportunity to explore the impact of cognitive bias on news content.[3] The gasoline was part of a federal mandate intended to reduce smog in certain areas of the United States. But the requirement prompted controversy over detrimental health effects from airborne fumes and leakage into groundwater. Eventually, 3,500 health complaints from citizens were registered with either the state or Environmental Protection Agency (EPA). Wisconsin's Division of Health conducted a four-part study that was reviewed by scientists nationwide. The study and its reviewers found the additive had no link to the health complaints in Milwaukee.

Despite the fact that the review was conducted by scientists from 11 other state agencies, four universities, the U.S. Centers for Disease Control and Prevention and the EPA, the framework of the news coverage stuck to a conspiratorial tone. While skepticism is a wonderful trait in journalists, this time it was at the expense of balanced and informed coverage.

For example, Channel 4 found the sole member of the panel's 17 peer reviewers who didn't agree with the study's conclusion. The other 16 reviewers who supported the conclusion were not included in the coverage. Compounding that, the lone dissenter's complaint was never explained on air and his quotes were edited mid-sentence. Noted the researchers: The reporter interviewing the dissenter says to him, "The study is flawed, is what you're saying, the study *is* flawed." (Emphasis in original.) The dissenter replies, "Well the study, yea, the study's got a lot of problems, too." (Cut off midsentence.)

What is important in this example is not whether you think the gasoline additive is safe or not, but whether the television reporters gave news consumers enough fair and balanced information to make their own judgments. The television news coverage of the report suggested the journalists were biased toward reporting a particular point of view: The additive is dangerous to health. Their devotion to this story line permeated all aspects of their coverage, from selection of sources, interviewing style, the questions asked and inferences made.

pause&consider What other sources might the journalists have interviewed? What questions should they have asked to cover other angles of the story?

THE CONFIRMATION BIAS

The additive story demonstrated confirmation bias in action. **Confirmation bias** is the tendency people have to seek, interpret and remember information that reinforces their preconceptions. A confirmation bias happens when people give more weight to evidence that confirms their hypothesis and undervalue evidence that could disprove it. It often takes more mental energy to reconsider a hypothesis than to find ways to fit information into an existing framework or decision.

Journalists demonstrate a confirmation bias when they search for, interpret or remember information in such a way that support for their hypothesis, or story angle, becomes likely—*whether or not the hypothesis is actually true.* The best way to test a hypothesis is to try to disprove it. But too often, people try to confirm their hypotheses instead.[4]

> Confirmation bias is the tendency for people to search for, interpret or remember information to support a preconception and ignore contradictory information.

When deadline pressures are imposed on a story, information processing is simplified. People tend to go with information that confirms their working hypothesis even when inconsistent information is clearly present. For journalists, that may mean that they seek out information that confirms their story angle to the exclusion of other perspectives, especially if incorporating conflicting information means missing their deadline.

Recognizing Confirmation Bias

The gasoline additive story is useful in illustrating the effects of the confirmation bias. It shows how the actions resulting from confirmation bias can lead a reporter to unfairly portray a person or group of people in the news. Researchers have explored many aspects of confirmation bias and many of their findings can be applied to journalism. For instance, a reporter succumbing to confirmation bias might:[5]

- Remember information that confirms the hypothesis or story angle better than information that disconfirms it.

- Seek out only sources that she thinks will support her hypothesis.
- Treat sources critical of the hypothesis in an aggressive or argumentative way.
- Interpret unanswered questions in a way that infers hypothesis confirmation.
- Give the comments of sources supporting the hypothesis more emphasis, space or more prominence in a story.
- Evaluate sources and information confirming the hypothesis less critically.
- Regard disconfirming information as unusual, superficial or of poor quality.

The Story Process and Confirmation Bias

At several stages in the story process, confirmation bias can play a role. Let's go back to the gas additive story for an example of the cognitive processes involved in reporting a story.[6]

Categorizing information

First, a journalist takes new information, such as the report on the additive and health problems, and places it in a mental category (or schema; see Chapter 3) based on his past experience and knowledge. The category will influence how the reporter interprets and weighs any subsequent information he discovers. Reporters covering the additive story categorized it as a consumer piece as opposed to a government story or a health story, for instance.

Once a news event is slotted into a category in a journalist's mind, ideas take shape about story angles and story focus. The consumer framework that was used for the additive story sets up a different hypothesis than a health framework. Compare the different approaches of: "Drivers having to buy gas that may make them sick" vs. "What is the medical proof that it does make them sick?"

Also, the consumer point of view led to interviews with drivers at the pump, who were portrayed as sources equal to, if not more significant than, scientists. In fact, each television station broadcast its report from a gas station, and each TV station's coverage featured person-at-the-pump interviews.

Forming a story angle

Angles naturally stem from the category into which the story is placed in a journalist's mind. If the consumer angle is understood as describing how people buy and use things, then regulations that dictate how people must consume things often encourage skepticism: *How* do they know the additive is safe? *Who* says it is? *Why* does this need to be regulated? All three stations expressed some level of doubt about the study findings. The consumer complaint angle was further strengthened when one station noted the "thousands" of people reporting health problems to state and federal hotlines. The actual number of complaints was in question, but was estimated at 1,500 to 3,500. The stations' reporters didn't sort through those numbers to figure out how many people were actually sickened by the gas or to acknowledge that no one knows the actual number of complaints.

Reporting the story

The story angle is then tested through reporting, which gets at the questions asked, how they are asked and to whom. If a confirmation bias is in full force, the journalist can select sources sympathetic to his story angle and ask them leading questions to elicit responses that support his story hypothesis. He can aggressively question sources contradicting his hypothesis and interpret ambiguous answers in favor of his angle. The abrupt editing of the interview with the dissenter by Channel 4, quoted earlier, illustrates how directive questioning can seem to prove or disprove a hypothesis. In addition, the sources selected by the stations for reaction to the study's findings each in one way or another indicated that the state's report was not to be trusted. Four individuals critical of the health report (a politician, a bureaucrat and two scientists, one an outspoken opponent of the additive) are given the same play as the 20 scientists who support the report. Finally, once a journalist confirms his hypothesis, he often stops reporting.

Finishing the Story

All journalists, regardless of mindset, have to decide when to stop reporting and conclude that the story is ready for online, broadcast or print. Confirmation bias comes into play when this decision is premature and made because an easy or an anticipated answer is reached. The brain is "frozen," or closed, to new information. The coverage on the additive report ended once the story angle was confirmed.

The decision to stop reporting is often compounded by deadline pressure. Journalists are under the dual pressures of having to report accurately *and* quickly. One study found that the most frequent reason for ending the reporting and research process was deadline pressure.[7] Exhibit 7.1 summarizes the tensions at play for journalists as they decide whether or not to stop reporting. The decision depends both on the time allowed to research a decision *and* the need to avoid errors. These competing tensions are explored in the next section.

Knowing when to keep going

New York Times staff writer Andrew Martin was assigned the banking beat at the tail end of the financial crisis that shook the country in the late 2000s. One story he reported involved whether people were being unfairly kicked out of their homes because of paper-

exhibit 7.1 FREEZING OUT INFORMATION

A journalistic tension exists between beating the competition by uploading or broadcasting first and reporting a story fully so it is accurate. Research[8] shows that:

FREEZING — *The Digital Compromise* — **UNFREEZING**

If people are under increased time pressure, such as a story deadline, their minds quit gathering information and stop considering alternate hypotheses more quickly than if time pressures didn't exist.

With online news sites, journalists can publish incomplete but accurate information and keep reporting, filling in gaps in knowledge with online updates. This way, journalists don't completely "freeze" the information-gathering part of the story process but can also get news to consumers quickly.

If people know their judgments will be evaluated (such as by news audiences) and accuracy is important, they delay "freezing" their search and allow their minds to be open to new information and possibilities.

work problems or because they couldn't pay their mortgages. The latter scenario might indicate a fairly straightforward story involving class—people with low incomes extending beyond their means to buy a home. But in the excerpt below, Martin describes the information-gathering and evaluation process that he and his colleague followed to report this problem that touched homeowners of *all* incomes throughout the United States. Martin had to actively suspend any allegiance to a specific story angle to be open to all kinds of information and differing perspectives in the reporting.

OA Some of the nation's largest banks temporarily stopped foreclosing on homes because of revelations that fraudulent documents were being used to justify the foreclosures in court. In short, the banks were handling so many foreclosures that they had low-paid clerks rubber-stamping affidavits—documents swearing that the facts in the case are true—without actually verifying the contents.

So anyway, as this story unfolded, two very different versions of events emerged. While acknowledging mistakes, the banks said that these were mere clerical errors that could be fixed easily. And many argued that these homeowners were "deadbeats" who weren't paying their mortgage bills and who deserved to be evicted once the paperwork problems were resolved.

The flip side of this, from consumer attorneys and advocacy groups, was that this was yet another example of the banks screwing consumers. Some argued that submitting fraudulent affidavits on the court was an affront to the justice system that would take years to unravel. And the lawyers for the homeowners argued that their clients deserved some compensation, if not their homes.

How do you report a story that one side says is a non-story and the other says is one of the biggest stories of the decade? The answer is simply to talk to everyone—the banks, the consumer types and the homeowners themselves—and report what you find out.[9]

ON ASSIGNMENT

Knowing when to stop

Martin says he knows when he is finished reporting in part because he feels comfortable writing a definitive sentence. Martin reported the mortgage story over the span of a couple weeks while also juggling other stories. When time pressure is an issue, Martin acknowledges to readers what he is still uncertain about. The key, he says, is to be honest and don't fake what you don't know. Some questions, Martin adds, can't be answered no matter how much reporting is done:

OA

ON ASSIGNMENT

So for instance, in this story on the homeowners, we stated upfront that it may be impossible to know how many homeowners have legitimate claims against the banks. And then we laid out three different stories from homeowners who say they were victims in some way, attributing like hell what they were telling us.

As for confirmation bias, the only way to avoid that is to make sure that you get—and understand—the other sides' viewpoints and give them a chance to express those viewpoints in your story. It's okay to have a working hypothesis, as long as you seek out and listen to the other sides and accurately reflect their viewpoints in your story.

If you can't get the other sides' views, the best thing is to not run the story. If that's not possible, or the other sides don't want to comment, then you need to show that you made a sincere effort to get their perspectives.

Giving Both Sides

Once Martin and his colleague stopped gathering information and crafted the final story for publication, they found that both sides were right, to a degree. The banks had a credible argument that most of the people affected were indeed delinquent on their mortgage payments and would ultimately lose their homes anyway. The critics were right that the legal issues involved were far more complicated than the banks were letting on.

Was the nationwide foreclosure story about class as well? Were the people delinquent on their mortgages mostly lower class? The foreclosure stories started out focusing on people of lower incomes, says Martin, but as the economic recession continued, the foreclosures spread to middle- and even upper-class homeowners. The stories became focused on geography, as the foreclosures became concentrated in a handful of states. Martin concluded that the perception among some people ("primarily those with stable jobs and a comfortable living") that those in foreclosure were all low-income deadbeats was too narrow a view. The result just wasn't that simple.

pause&consider Read the beginning of the story by Martin and his colleague in Appendix A. Decide whether the lead anecdotes support the main point of the story.

OTHER JUDGMENT BIASES AND HEURISTICS

Confirmation bias is one of the more prevalent biases in human judgment. But several others are also common and equally challenging to the journalistic credo of accuracy. For journalists, decisions are inherent in the job; they pepper the reporting process from story selection to final editing, and typically they are private— an individual journalist is often on his or her own in making these split-second determinations. Each journalist has to be on the lookout for personal biases as well as those of sources.

Journalists can address mistakes in judgment by:

- understanding how good judgments are made
- understanding common errors in reasoning
- asking probing questions
- avoiding leading questions
- seeking evidence
- relying on probability over intuition

Hardest of all is having the courage to recognize when the facts don't fully support the version of the story that will put it at the top of the broadcast. As a reporter sorting through facts, anecdotes, observations and quotes, remember that a story is only as good as it is right.

pause & *consider* Identify a news story from recent months in which a news organization published too early, without complete facts or with erroneous information. An example is the breaking news coverage of the shooting of U.S. Rep. Gabrielle Giffords in January, 2011, which initially reported that she had died.[10] Discuss with peers how to put safeguards in place to catch mistakes before they go public.

Fortunately, many of the ways in which the brain works are highly efficient and good enough for everyday living. Heuristics are mental shortcuts or "rules of thumb" that allow people to make judgments quickly and avoid constant thought about every action they take. In general, these shortcuts are highly useful, though sometimes they lead to serious errors.[11] A very brief tour of five heuristics and biases gives one a sense of why trusting our own or our sources' hunches, intuition, memory or gut is a bad idea if we're aiming for journalistic accuracy and fairness—particularly when covering people unlike ourselves.

Representative Heuristic

This mental shortcut has to do with the way people tend to judge probabilities on the basis of similarity. Problems arise from such generalization.[12] Just because someone is judged as similar to a parent population—a man who seems gay because his mannerisms and dress are similar to the stereotype of a gay man, for instance—doesn't mean he belongs in that group. Reporters need to be especially wary of such subjective judgments by sources and avoid rewarding them with publication.

Availability Heuristic

People judge the probability of an event by the ease in which previous instances of it can be brought to mind. The more readily we can think of instances of something happening, the more likely we think it will be to happen again.[13] This is called the **availability heuristic.** Such as, "This source is trying to get me to investigate racial discrimination in hiring practices by the city. Hmmm. I can think of two African Americans and a Native American who got hired or promoted by the city in the past few years. I just don't see a story here." With this bias, story leads go uninvestigated simply because of our faulty logic that if we can remember something easily, it must be happening a lot.

The Conjunction Fallacy

A third judgment flaw is the **conjunction fallacy,** which happens when two events that can occur separately are seen as more likely to occur together rather than separately. As in: "She is physically disabled, so she must also be mentally disabled." The probability is much higher that the woman is physically disabled *or* mentally disabled as opposed to both. This bias can mean that a journalist is too willing to find connections that aren't valid. The key is to test assumptions: Just because a woman is against abortion doesn't mean she is a Republican. Just because someone is over 70 doesn't mean he is unproductive. Just because someone is from a low-income area doesn't mean she didn't go to (and finish) college.

Anchoring Heuristic

A fourth bias is the **anchoring heuristic.** This is when people base estimates and decisions on "anchors" or familiar positions and then adjust for a final answer. However, people are typically biased toward their initial position and don't make sufficient adjustments. They change their answer slightly relative to the anchor position without thinking more critically about it.

For journalists, the anchoring bias can be wrongfully used, especially when conducting reader polls or in questioning sources, for example. A journalist can lodge a number favoring that story angle into the heads of sources, and most people will unknowingly base their reactions on that number. As in: "Other metropolitan areas are raising residential taxes by about $250 a year per homeowner to help pay for housing for people who are homeless. Should our city council adjust taxes more or less than that?" In reality, what other cities are doing has little or nothing to do with the city in question. Due to current housing, the number of homeless people and current tax levels, the city may need to raise taxes by $500 a year to address the problem. The $250 figure is irrelevant. But it will now be stuck in people's minds as they formulate an answer.

Hindsight Bias

Anyone who watches TV news and certainly any reporter will find **hindsight bias** instantly familiar. The hindsight bias describes how people view something that has happened as being relatively inevitable before it happened.

"People believe that others should have been able to anticipate events much better than was actually the case. They even misremember their own predictions so as to exaggerate in hindsight what they knew in foresight."[14] How many times have reporters interviewed a neighbor after the kid next door committed a crime and the neighbor said confidently: "I always knew that kid was a bad apple. I told everyone who'd listen that he was trouble, and no one paid attention to me"?

pause & consider Select one of the judgment biases in the previous section and identify a time at which you fell victim to it. Share your recollection with a small group.

TOWARD BETTER DECISION-MAKING

Both the desire to be accurate as well as the expectation of accountability can improve decision-making and keep reporters from falling into the bias traps discussed in the previous section. For reporters, this should be welcome news! After all, the journalism profession expects both accuracy and accountability, as highlighted in the Society of Professional Journalists' ethics code:[15]

- **Seek truth and report it.** Journalists should be honest, fair and courageous in gathering, reporting and interpreting information. Journalists should test the accuracy of information from all sources and exercise care to avoid inadvertent error. Deliberate distortion is never permissible.

- **Minimize harm.** Ethical journalists treat sources, subjects and colleagues as human beings deserving of respect.

- **Act independently.** Journalists should be free of obligation to any interest other than the public's right to know.

- **Be accountable.** Journalists are accountable to their readers, listeners, viewers and each other. Journalists should clarify and explain news coverage and invite dialogue with the public over journalistic conduct; encourage the public to voice grievances against the news media; admit mistakes and correct them promptly; expose unethical practices of journalists and the news media; abide by the same high standards to which they hold others.

Accuracy

A devotion to accuracy helps correct judgment biases. When people are motivated by accuracy in their decision making, they expend more effort on reasoning through issues. They pay more attention to relevant information. They process it more deeply and more carefully when they desire to be accurate.[16] So many good things come from a desire to be accurate.

With that said, however, research shows that people are more likely to arrive at conclusions they *want* to arrive at and not necessarily the most accurate one. They just have to be able to justify their conclusions.[17]

What does all of this mean for journalists? It means the professional commitment to getting the story right should stand above getting it first. A drive to be first can lead to expediently confirming a preconceived story angle. The discipline-wide emphasis on accuracy helps support a journalist's own motivation for accuracy as an end to itself and over any motivation to arrive at a particular conclusion. Editors help by championing a search for truth above the confirmation of any neat hypothesis that pleases a publisher or shareholders.

Accountability

Accountability helps to counter some judgment biases. **Accountability** is the implied or clearly expressed expectation that one will be called upon to justify one's beliefs, feelings or actions to others.[18] For journalists, this happens automatically when work is published or broadcast. Accountability involves the expectation that journalists will have to explain their news reporting decisions to others, including their colleagues, editors, sources and news audience. Simply put: Can you defend your story as factual and fair?

In general, people who are accountable to an audience, as journalists are, think about arguments from more than one side. They tend to take more things into account. People think at a more complex level and with more open minds when they know they will be accountable to an audience.

Self-critical thought, meaning a person is on the lookout for bias and is expending a lot of mental effort in making decisions, is most likely activated when decision makers know from the start that they will be accountable to an audience. It's also strongest when the audience (a) has views that are unknown; (b) is interested in accuracy; (c) is reasonably well informed; and (d) has a legitimate reason for inquiring into the reasons behind a judgment.[19]

Sounds a lot like a news audience, doesn't it?

Journalists know they have a lot of people to answer to when making judgments in reporting and writing a story. That knowledge encourages journalists to regularly monitor what influences their judgment; in addition, it can help them anticipate counter-arguments, weigh their merits impartially and factor those most relevant into their overall opinion or assessment of a news situation.[20] If a person knows *before* she makes a decision that she will have to justify it, she will explore options more impartially and more thoroughly and try to make the best decision possible. If our hypothetical decision-maker isn't held responsible for a decision until *after* it is made, she rationalizes her decision and looks for reasons to bolster it.[21] For example, just look to the fumbling efforts at justification by journalists caught fabricating and plagiarizing.

Accountability implies that positive or negative consequences hinge on one's decision. Positive consequences include having one's story get the most daily reads, lead the broadcast or receive recognition by the editor-in-chief. Negative consequences include receiving online complaints about the story, having to air a correction or being put on probationary status. In particular, audience feedback via online comments can be swift and mighty, especially in the case of an obvious slant or inaccuracy.

A notable downside to accountability is that if a reporter knows the audience prefers a specific outcome, she may be inclined to distort the decision process to justify that outcome.[22] News organizations may slant coverage in an attempt to match their audience's preferences, researchers assert.[23] An example of "giving the people what they want" is evidenced in newspaper coverage of immigration. For instance, due to pressure to please audiences, news organizations close to the U.S.–Mexico border were found to be more likely to provide negative news coverage of immigration.[24] Continual exposure to negative news coverage reinforces negative public attitudes about immigrants and immigration, and a cycle ensues.

Sometimes, accountability causes decision-makers to overthink and give irrelevant information too much significance. A journalist's overthinking of information can be offset by editors who provide essential distance and perspective on news coverage. In one amusing example, study participants trying to predict a hypothetical student's grade point average were so concerned that they would be held accountable for their prediction that they considered such irrelevant information as the fact that the student had failed to date the same person for more than two months. They would have fared much better if they'd focused on the single valid predictor of success, which was, shockingly, the number of hours the student studied per week.[25]

Accountability to Yourself

Part of a journalist's job is reactive: Find out what is happening, how, to whom or what, when and why. This part of the job is physical: Get the information.

Another part of a journalist's job is proactive: How will I select, interpret and present this information? This part of the job is cognitive. It involves choices and decisions.

A journalist's decisions are often made quickly in the heat of battle. So make this decision now: Find time to reflect on how your mind makes decisions and what errors you have repeatedly made in your past judgments. Seek training to improve decision making. Look for patterns. ("I always seem to cut off my reporting too soon because I want more time to write"; "I trust my memory too much and don't dig up my past notes to check information"; "I tend to pay attention to silly data"; "I am too eager to focus on sources who agree with my story angle.") Be accountable to yourself and decide to address one shortcoming in the next breaking news battle you're in. The battle will come soon enough. There's always another chance to be even better.

exploration EXERCISES

1. Try your hand at being purposefully biased in your reporting.

   a. Select a newsworthy local event or issue.

   b. Decide what bias you are going to adopt on this event or issue. What will be your predetermined slant on the story? (e.g., Cost-cutting is leading to a lower-quality education for students at a given university.)

   c. To show your understanding of how confirmation bias can influence all stages of the story process, write a paragraph on each of the following areas: story categorization or type and its effect on story focus; reporting and interviewing choices; selection of information and when to freeze out new information. Show how you would apply bias each step of the process to arrive at your predetermined conclusion.

   d. Finally, read through your strategy for producing a biased story. Write a closing paragraph about how you feel after reviewing your choices. Comment on what version of the truth remains—if any.

2. Read the string of online reader comments on a major news story in your community.

    a. Note the sorts of issues that the news audience raises in reaction to the coverage.

    b. In what ways do the comments hold the journalist(s) on the story accountable? Are the comments focused on accuracy? Do they offer a different perspective not considered in the account? Question the story focus? Mention missing information or offer other angles to pursue?

    c. Discuss and compare your findings with those of your colleagues.

3. Think of a time when you tried so hard to be right and accountable for a decision that you overthought to the point of making a wrong one. (This may happen when you overthink what an editor or professor wants in a news story.) Write a one-minute monologue of what went on in your head.

4. Some journalists covered the forecasted pandemic of the H1N1 virus, commonly called the Swine Flu, in 2009 with reports about a widespread panic over the virus. However, there wasn't much evidence of panic in the public. That didn't stop some reporters from insisting there was and showcasing their confirmation bias in action. Select one of the following exercises:

    a. Listen to an expert's take on how the news media can't resist a panic story. Download an interview with Eric Klinenberg, a professor of sociology who has researched panic coverage, from the news radio program *On the Media*. For the MP3 download, go to www.onthemedia.org/transcripts/2009/05/01/01.[26] React to the *OTM* piece in a small group discussion.

    b. Select a sample of news coverage of the 2009 H1N1 virus from your outlet of choice. Evaluate whether confirmation bias is at play in the story.

    c. The sociology of disasters tells us that in general, when there are crises, people *don't* panic. Can you think of other news coverage of crises that you think didn't warrant panic coverage? Find an example of such coverage and write a paragraph describing it.

FOR review

- Explain confirmation bias to a friend.

- List the five judgment biases or heuristics described in the chapter.

- Notice the point at which you freeze out new information when reporting your next news story.

- Name the two techniques that improve decision making.

notes

1. Craig W. Trumbo, Sharon Dunwoody, and Robert J. Griffin, "Journalists, Cognition, and the Presentation of an Epidemiologic Study," *Science Communication 19* (1998), p. 257.

2. Ibid., pp. 258–59.

3. Ibid.

4. Margit E. Oswald and Stefan Grosjean, "Confirmation Bias," in *Cognitive Illusions: A Handbook in Fallacies and Biases in Thinking, Judgement and Memory,* ed. Rüdiger F. Pohl (New York: Psychology Press, 2004).

5. Charles G. Lord, Lee Ross, and Mark R. Lepper, "Biased Assimilation and Attitude Polarization: The Effects of Prior Theories on Subsequently Considered Evidence," *Journal of Personality and Social Psychology 37,* no. 11 (1979); Trumbo, Dunwoody, and Griffin, "Journalists, Cognition, and the Presentation of an Epidemiologic Study"; Oswald and Grosjean, "Confirmation Bias"; Raymond S. Nickerson, "Confirmation Bias: A Ubiquitous Phenomenon in Many Guises," *Review of General Psychology 2,* no. 2 (1998).

6. S. Holly Stocking and Paget H. Gross, *How Do Journalists Think? A Proposal for the Study of Cognitive Bias in Newsmaking* (Bloomington, Ind.: ERIC Clearinghouse on Reading and Communication Skills, 1989).

7. E. K. Parsigian, "News Reporting: Method in the Midst of Chaos," *Journalism Quarterly 64,* no. 4 (1987).

8. Tallie Freund, Arie W. Kruglanski, and Avivit Shpitzajzen, "The Freezing and Unfreezing of Impressional Primacy: Effects of the Need for Structure and the Fear of Invalidity," *Personality and Social Psychology Bulletin 11,* no. 4 (1985); Arie W. Kruglanski and Tallie Freund, "The Freezing and Unfreezing of Lay-Interferences: Effects on Impressional Primacy, Ethnic Stereotyping, and Numerical Anchoring," *Journal of Experimental Social Psychology 19,* no. 5 (1983).

9. Andrew Martin, Interview with author, November, 2010.

10. For a useful recap, see Mallary Jean Tenore's January 10, 2011, column at www.poynter.org titled "Conflicting Reports of Giffords' Death Were Understandable, but Not Excusable."

11. Amos Tversky and Daniel Kahneman, "Judgment Under Uncertainty: Heuristics and Biases," in *Judgment under Uncertainty: Heuristics and Biases* (1998 ed.), eds. Daniel Kahneman, Paul Slovic, and Amos Tversky (Cambridge: Cambridge University Press, 1982).

12. Louise Almond, Laurence Alison, Marie Eyre, Jonathan Crego, and Alasdair Goodwill, "Heuristics and Biases in Decision-Making," in *Policing Critical Incidents: Leadership and Critical Incident Management,* eds. Laurence Alison and Jonathan Crego (Portland, Ore.: Willan, 2008), p. 154.

13. Ibid.

14. Baruch Fischhoff, "For Those Condemned to Study the Past: Heuristics and Biases in Hindsight," in *Judgment under Uncertainty: Heuristics and Biases,* ed. Daniel Kahneman, Paul Slovic, and Amos Tversky (Cambridge: Cambridge University Press, 1982), p. 341.

15. Society of Professional Journalists, "Code of Ethics" (1996), http://www.spj.org/ethicscode.asp, retrieved July 15, 2010.

16. Ziven Kunda, "The Case for Motivated Reasoning," *Psychological Bulletin 108,* no. 3 (1990).

17. Ibid.

18. Jennifer S. Lerner and Philip E. Tetlock, "Accounting for the Effects of Accountability," *Psychological Bulletin 125,* no. 2 (1999).

19. Ibid.

20. Ibid.; Hal R. Arkes, "Costs and Benefits of Judgment Errors: Implications for Debiasing," *Psychological Bulletin 110,* no. 3 (1991).

21. Lerner and Tetlock, "Accounting for the Effects of Accountability."

22. Richard P. Larrick, "Debiasing," in *Blackwell Handbook of Judgment and Decision Making,* eds. Derek J. Koehler and Nigel Harvey (Malden, Mass.: Blackwell, 2004).

23. David P. Baron, "Persistent Media Bias," *Journal of Public Economics 90,* no. 1–2 (2006); James T. Hamilton, *All the News That's Fit to Sell: How the Market Transforms Information into News* (Princeton, N.J.: Princeton University Press, 2004); Regina P. Branton and Johanna Dunaway, "Slanted Newspaper Coverage of Immigration: The Importance of Economics and Geography," *Policy Studies Journal 37,* no. 2 (2009).

24. Branton and Dunaway, "Slanted Newspaper Coverage of Immigration."

25. Philip E. Tetlock and Richard Boettger, "Accountability: A Social Magnifier of the Dilution Effect," *Journal of Personality and Social Psychology 57,* no. 3 (1989).

26. *On the Media,* "Stop, Drop and Roll," National Public Radio, http://www.onthemedia.org/transcripts/2009/05/01/01, retrieved August 7, 2011.

The Power of
Words and Tone

When words can suggest unintended meanings

- *To understand the significance of speaker, audience and context on the meaning of words.*

- *To recognize four problematic areas of word choice: Otherness words, politicized words, judgment words and code words.*

- *To learn three tools to become more attuned to word choice and tone: The Blab Test, challenging sources and the Language Self-Check.*

WRITING FROM A POINT OF VIEW

A student in my class wrote a powerfully honest first-person narrative about the demographic changes that had transformed her formerly all-white childhood neighborhood into a mix of white, Latino and African American residents. Early in the story, the student described how her walk to school had changed over time:

"Walking down the block, I felt safe, wandering from street to street with my brother. Over time, things began to change. By the time I was starting school, the neighborhood was no longer the all-white neighborhood that it had originally been . . . walking down the street to my bus stop in the morning went from being perfectly safe to dangerous."

The ending of the student's story draft read this way:

"My family moved out of our house in the beginning of 2006. I drove by it earlier this year to see it for the first time since we moved. The front steps that we had lined with pots of flowers were now cluttered with children's plastic toys, and a barbeque grill was chained to the porch railing. The two front windows in which we'd hung white curtains now had large Mexican flags proudly displayed in each window. I looked over at my brother.

"'Wow,' I said, 'things really have changed.'"

Her facts were correct. It had a nice sense of closure, with driving by to check things out after years have passed. So what was the problem?

pause&consider How, if at all, would you edit the student's essay? Discuss your changes with a peer.

The writer unwittingly linked an all-white neighborhood with perfect safety while portraying a diverse neighborhood as dangerous. Written this way, the story becomes about the author's belief that the formerly all-white neighborhood was better on many levels than the diverse one it had become. While her feelings were real, there is no evidence that the danger was real.

In her ending, the comparisons that the student set up in her sentences were concerning. Each comparison suggested that her family's way was the right way for the house to look, and that this new Latino family had it all wrong. Without intending it, the student was imposing her ideas about what the outside of a home, particularly one occupied by a "decent" family, should look like.

pause&consider How might the author honestly report on the changes in her neighborhood without ethnic bias?

Here's what we did. We removed the phrases describing what *had* been there and rethought the choice of the word *cluttered*. After all, children's toys left on the front porch could signify fun and family time. The resulting edits conveyed a more neutral tone while still capturing what the house looked like years later:

> My family moved out of our house in the beginning of 2006. I drove by it earlier this year to see it for the first time since we moved. Various children's toys happily littered the front steps, and a barbeque grill was chained to the railing. A large Mexican flag was proudly displayed in each front window. I looked over at my brother.
> "Wow," I said, "things really have changed."

pause&*consider* Compare the word choice in both endings. Do you think the second version works? Is it neutral enough? In terms of the first paragraph of her essay, what changes could be made to address the writer's assumptions about safety and neighborhood demographics while still retaining her point of view?

LANGUAGE AND MEANING

Words are flexible. Their meanings change depending on influences such as politics, religion, economics, history, culture or geography. Keith Woods, now vice president for diversity in news and operations at National Public Radio, has identified how the meanings of words change depending on speaker, audience and context:[1] *Who* is speaking to *whom* and *in what circumstances.* The answers influence the meaning of the words used and how journalists determine the significance of statements.

exhibit 8.1 UNDERSTANDING CONTEXT

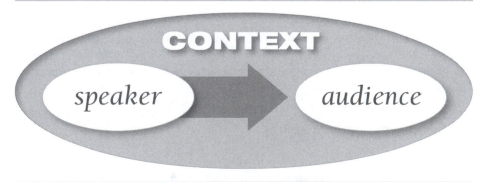

For example: "A man (speaker) asking a female colleague (listener) to get a cup of coffee during a meeting (context) does so at the risk of coming across as chauvinistic."[2] By contrast, a female boss (speaker) asking a male subordinate (listener) to get a cup of coffee during a meeting (context) comes off as asserting her authority in the organization. A female colleague asking another female colleague to get a cup of coffee during a meeting is likely seen as collegial. The same request for coffee is assigned different meaning based on who is doing the asking to whom.

Another example would be a teenage African American male (speaker) calling his black friend (listener) the "n-word" in irony and solidarity (context). The same word spoken by the teens' white football coach (speaker) to the same black friend (listener) during practice (context) has a different meaning charged with a history of hate and racism.

Think about the ingredients of speaker, audience and context as you read the following anecdote:

OA

ON ASSIGNMENT

A student in one of my classes was reporting a story on the level of lesbian, gay, bisexual and transgendered activism on our campus. He kept asking sources about "the queer culture on campus" and wasn't getting far. Finally, the head of the university's program on students who are LGBT told him that while being reclaimed by some in the gay community as an affirming term, the word *queer* is still seen as a label many felt was offensive, particularly when used by a heterosexual male.

The student learned a lesson about the importance of speaker, audience and context. People within the LGBT community could use the term *queer* in conversation to others in the LGBT community far more acceptably than could a straight reporter asking interview questions. Once the student reporter dropped the term from his intro pitch to sources, his interviewees were far more receptive.

Mobile technologies allow reporters to file early and often. Since digital news travels well beyond a news organization's coverage area, the context of cultural comments and images is critical. Context allows consumers of all backgrounds to better understand the significance of news events.

THE MEANINGS OF WORDS

Many words really have two meanings: (1) the literal definition, its **denotation,** and (2) the association the word carries, its **connotation.** Connotations suggest a meaning apart from the explicit word. For example, the denotation of the term *9/11* is simply a date on the calendar, the 11th day of the 9th month. But the political, social and physical realities of the attacks in New York, Virginia and Pennsylvania on September 11, 2001, make up its connotation. Because they have both a literal and a suggested meaning, certain words and phrases require extra thought before going into a news package. These words and phrases fall roughly into four categories: Otherness words, politicized words, judgment words and code words.

Otherness Words

Some words needlessly highlight someone's "otherness." Otherness is relative. You are not an "other" in your own social group. But you're an "other" to the social groups that you are not a part of. So whose social group gets to decide otherness? One example is that in the past, the U.S. news media mentioned a subject's race only to alert the audience that the person was not white.

Most reporting is a form of representing the "other."[3]

To avoid "otherness" words, journalists should think twice about the descriptors they use and ask themselves:

- How relevant is the term?
- Is it accurate?
- Is it helpful to understanding the news issue at hand?
- What does its use convey to the news audience?
- If it is used, is it as specific as possible?
- Why is it being used? Justify the inclusion of the descriptive language.

So in a story about a local public school's efforts to accommodate an influx of students who are Latino, a journalist could argue that it's important to note the students' common background, but it may not be relevant to include the students' immigration status. Similarly, in describing a teenager accused of a violent act, is it pertinent to the story to mention he was adopted?

Basic research is a defense against unfair generalizations. For instance, the Muslim population in the United States is not monolithic, but news accounts sometimes portray it as such. Muslims represent many different cultural and ethnic backgrounds. A journalist should not assume that an Arab American is Muslim, and vice versa. While news consumers may be accustomed to the word *extremist* used in conjunction with Islam, the religion, just like any other, has followers who are on the fringes. The majority are moderate followers who want for their neighbor what they want for themselves. However, this is not to say that all mentions of religious identity, ethnicity or other descriptors are bad. The more that Muslims and other "outgroups" are woven into the fabric of daily news reporting, the better the journalism gets. The voices are not singled out as exceptional or special but are one perspective amid many.

"Language reflects the culture from which we emerge," wrote author and activist bell hooks.[4] Carefully consider the implications before mentioning someone's race or ethnicity, religious affiliation, sexual orientation or other status in a news account. Ask yourself: Is the status relevant to the news or relevant because it seems so different from *your* life and background?

Descriptions of story subjects must meet the criteria of relevance, accuracy and specificity to make it into a news story.

If it *is* important to mention someone's status, then be specific. "A member of the Ojibwa people" is more descriptive and orienting than the term *Native American*. Describing someone as "a member of the LGBT community" seems to hide information; describing him as a man who is bisexual explains one important part of his identity.

Politicized Words

Some words have become highly politicized. The passage of time brings new issues and new labels that journalists must think deeply about before legitimizing them in a news story. Journalists should avoid word choices in news stories that obviously promote or comment upon a particular political agenda, such as *pro-life* and *pro-choice*. Better to use more straightforward terms such as *abortion rights supporter* and *anti-abortion advocate*.

Sometimes a word has the power to slant an audience's interpretation of a news story. Consider the use of the label *illegals* to refer to undocumented immigrants. The word *illegals* is shorthand for *illegal aliens.* The National Association of Hispanic Journalists describes both *illegals* and *illegal aliens* as negative terms to describe the millions of undocumented people living in the United States.[5] Calling someone an *illegal* is not only grammatically incorrect, but also implies the person is a criminal. The label *alien* used to describe a foreign-born person who is not a naturalized citizen is not only bureaucratic-speak, but also serves to cast someone as strange and from another world. The *Associated Press Stylebook* recommends *illegal immigrant* to describe someone who has entered or resides in the country illegally.

Whether a label is politically biased depends on one's perspective, notes teacher and scholar Martin Levinson:

> What's the difference between a "freedom fighter" and a "terrorist"? Were the victims at the Abu Ghraib prison in Iraq subjected to "abuse" or "torture"? Are organizations that comment on news reporting "media watchdog groups," or are they "pressure groups"? Don't look to the dictionary to answer these questions. Their answers depend on how people perceive things.[6]

Some labels highlight cultural divides in the U.S. and beyond its borders. For example, serious debates have ensued over the use of the word *terrorist.* The debates typically focus on the use of the word as describing an action (a violent, politically charged act) and on the nationality of the perpetrator (a foreigner or a U.S. citizen). In the wake of reporting on a software engineer who flew a plane into IRS offices in Austin, Texas, the editor of *Newsweek* launched an internal email thread on the definition of a terrorist and who should be labeled a terrorist. It's an important discussion. The editor then decided to publish the thread, which included this comment from a *Newsweek* reporter referring to the IRS attacker:

> This guy was a regular guy-next-door Joe Schmo. Terrorists have beards and live in caves. He was also an American, so targeting the IRS seems more a political statement—albeit a crazy one—whereas Abdulmutallab was an attack on our freedom. It's kind of the idea that an American can talk smack about America, but when it comes from someone foreign, we rally together.[7]

Given this definition of terrorists—people with beards who live in caves—what label should be given to an American citizen who employs terror as a political weapon? The reporter's frank statement about who is deemed a terrorist includes an "us vs. them" quality that embodies the "otherness" concept discussed earlier. The comment fails to consider the significant immigrant population in the U.S., and raises the question of who is an American in this scenario.

pause**&**consider If the news media in the U.S. only use the label *terrorist* for non-citizens, how does that affect the way in which audiences perceive those episodes of violence? Think about this for both U.S. and non-U.S. audiences.

Judgment Words

As journalists, we must evaluate language for judgment or assignation of blame. Judgment is implied in verb choices such as, "The man *admits* that he is gay." Or, "She *claims* that she isn't racist." These phrases imply negativity and doubt. Words such as *refuse* and *fail* imply rebuke.

News media polarize and play up opposites. It's no surprise that one news value is conflict. Judgment can seep into news accounts that cover conflict, simplifying positions to extremes that don't convey the full picture. Someone is a hero or a villain. Liberal or conservative. Winner or loser. Right or wrong.

Journalists are at their best when they can appreciate that most people live in the ambiguous, gray middle of society and not on the extreme fringes, where conflict often happens. The great gray middle is the origin of many valuable news stories, because those stories reflect the lives of average citizens. Writing that makes the everyday challenges people face as interesting and significant as they are to the people involved is truly artful and representative journalism.

In addition, avoid passing on judgment words through quotes without explanation. When a source, particularly one in a public position, whether a sports star or lawmaker, makes a knee-jerk judgment, do more than post it as fast as possible. "Gotchya" journalism doesn't enlighten or explain. Ask probing questions to figure out what the source has in his or her mind; what's behind the statement? Get experts to give context as to why the statements are insulting or insensitive or defamatory.[8] And try to report the comments in a way that launches public debate about the issue, as occurred with two photos discussed in the following paragraphs.

Words that assign blame shouldn't be used casually. When is someone *looting* and someone else *finding*? Is the most accurate word choice *taking* or *raiding* or *making off* when it comes to people removing goods from unattended grocery stores, as happened on a wide scale after Hurricane Katrina struck the Gulf Coast in 2005?

Two photographs of New Orleans residents surrounded by chest-high flood waters received different photo captions for what looked like the same thing. A controversy erupted online as the two photos were compared side-by-side. Photographers, journalists and others debated the use of the two verbs in the photo captions.

Aaron Kinney wrote on *Salon.com* that an image taken for the Associated Press shows "a young black man wading through chest-deep waters after 'looting' a grocery store, according to the caption. The young man appears to have a case of Pepsi under one arm and a full garbage bag in tow. In the other, similar shot, taken by (a) photographer . . . for AFP/Getty Images, a white man and a light-skinned woman are shown wading through chest-deep water after 'finding' goods including bread and soda, according to the caption, in a local grocery store."[9]

Chris Graythen, the photographer who took the photo of the man and woman, posted on SportsShooter.com the day before Kinney's article was posted: "I wrote the caption about the two people who 'found' the items. I believed in my opinion, that they did simply find them, and not 'looted' them in the definition of the word. The people were swimming in chest deep water, and there were other people in the water, both white and black. I looked for the best picture."[10]

The AP director of media relations was quoted as confirming that the photographer who took the image of the dark-skinned man did witness people looting a grocery store. "He saw the person go into the shop and take the goods and that's why he wrote 'looting' in the caption," said the director.[11]

The captions launched strings of posts debating the photojournalists' truthfulness and intent. Some posts argued about whether unconscious stereotyping of the black man occurred (similar to the discussion of implicit associations in Chapter 4). These cognitively based arguments suggested that involuntary negative associations with stealing and black people (and conversely, involuntary positive associations with *not* stealing and white people) influenced the word choice by the photojournalists.

The overarching lesson is the power of a single word: *looting* vs. *finding*. Just one word.

Code Words

Journalism that illuminates and educates uses concrete language. It avoids sweeping characterizations and relies instead on relevant detail. It shuns squishy labels that lump everyone together into the same basket: minorities, blue-collar workers, fundamentalists, activists. It avoids overgeneralizations in favor of individualizing actions and motivations. Quality journalism despises euphemisms. **Euphemisms** employ the use of a less direct word or phrase to avoid one that might seem offensive.

Euphemisms are intentionally vague so as to avoid bluntness. You might say a woman has "ample proportions" instead of asking the tough question to get this detail: She is 5 foot 2 inches tall and weighs 160 pounds. Journalists looking for a more polite or politically correct way to say something should consider more reporting. The urge to pad a story with squishy language may mean some difficult questions need to be asked to get at the real issues.

When interviewing a source for a story on public education, a PTO president in the school district might blame "those kids who can't speak English" for creating problems at particular schools. It's important to clarify about whom the PTO president is referring—locally born kids with bad grammar? Children from immigrant families? Bilingual students? Who? Give the actual number and percentage of the students in question compared to the district-wide population. Journalists need to follow up with sources who use the squishy language of euphemisms in order to seek clarity and specificity.

In addition, the words journalists *don't* use can deliver an unspoken message. What isn't said can be as important as what is. Reporters obviously cannot describe people in full. There's not the space or time or consumer attention to do that. But journalists should be aware of what they do omit when characterizing news subjects.

For instance, describing a woman throughout a story as "a mother," "a mom of three," and "a wife" emphasizes her familial role to the exclusion of other aspects of her identity. That might be appropriate if she is one of many sources in a parenting story, but not if the story is a personality profile. If the woman is also a partner in a local law firm and an accomplished marathoner, then describing her solely as a wife and mother portrays the woman in a discriminatory way.

LANGUAGE AND AUDIENCE

The words that journalists use influence their audiences. The subtle effect of words on audiences was shown in a study on racial prejudice in sports announcers' speech.[12] While sports announcers are not journalists, the study illustrates how words convey associations.

After reading transcripts from nationally televised NFL games, 180 undergraduate students (half white, half African American) had to guess whether the players were black or white based on the sports announcers' language. The names of the players and their teams and teammates were all disguised. The announcers were all white. The students correctly identified the race of the player 56 percent of the time—more often than expected by chance.

Noteworthy is the fact that the two transcripts in which students guessed incorrectly more often than correctly involved stereotypical racial descriptions. For example, an announcer said one player "lacked rhythm and all those things."[13] Students thought the player was black based on that statement, but he was white. The study shows that while the denotation of the words was correct, they carried a connotation that implied a player's race.

As the example above illustrates, words do more than simply inform; they often guide readers' and listeners' thinking. A student of quality Tweets will soon learn that an effective 140-character post quickly establishes an audience. A good Tweet uses words that are descriptive (*foul* does more than *unpleasant*), direct (say what you mean to say; "she's dying" instead of "she doesn't have long left"), simple (*get* instead of *procure*) and specific to its audience (a *gathering* for work clients vs. a *bash* for buddies). Which brings us to tone.

Setting a Tone

Tone is the style of writing and mood of a news piece, its personality. It might be conversational or intimate, business-like or sympathetic. Tone is determined by audience and subject matter and can influence the word choices a writer makes. Bloggers use casual and conversational language; slang and epithets are acceptable. You'll rarely find either slang or cursing in a straight news account, which is more formal.

Word choice can also set a tone. Note the word choices that convey an appropriately "insider" tone to a 2010 article that ran in *New Mobility: The Magazine for Active Wheelchair Users* about an emergency department director who became paralyzed in a car crash.[14] Its headline carries a shorthand for "quadriplegic" that you might not see in a mainstream news article: "Quad Doctors: In or Out?" Later in the text, there's more terminology, this time referencing the cervical vertebra injured: "How did this C6–7 quad convince the hospital and his malpractice carrier to grant him the seemingly impossible?"[15] Some readers might know that *quad* refers to *quadriplegic,* but the C6–7 reference describing the specific vertebrae injured in the lower neck is terminology unique to those patients and that medical community. Using those terms sets a tone of familiarity and expertise expected for the audience of that special interest magazine.

Sources and Tone

Journalists should be aware of adopting the tone of sources. Christina Samuels has been a staff writer for the *Washington Post* and the *Miami Herald*. She now covers local school districts for *Education Week*. Samuels' reporting on people with disabilities highlights the importance of tone when interviewing sources and selecting quotes. Samuels says she has to be on the lookout for sources using a tone that suggests that money is "wasted" on children in special-education classes.

Often this comes up in terms of school district budgets. There will be budget stories and the underlying question is, "Do we have to spend so much money to educate these special-needs kids?" With gifted kids, I don't think there would be the underlying tone of: "They don't really need it. Why are we spending so much money on kids who can't really do anything with it?"[16]

Samuels strives to detect the disparaging tone of sources and is careful not to allow that same attitude to seep into her word choices and her approach to stories.

pause&*consider* Read an excerpt in Appendix A from Samuels' story on the prom experience of a high school senior who is developmentally disabled. Note the tone of the story as you read the passage.

PRACTICING PRECISION

Every journalist has to use words to do his or her work, whether it is television and radio scripts, print or online news stories, blogs or photo captions. Crafting clear, accurate and informative sentences is fundamental to news writing. Strategies to avoid overly cautious or unintentionally insensitive language include:

Take the Blab Test

To examine your writing for euphemisms and overly broad language, take the Blab Test. For every abstract word or phrase, substitute a "blab."Stuart Chase called these ill-defined words "noises without meaning" in his book, *The Tyranny of Words*.[17] The Blab Test is a great way to highlight how much—or how little—you are actually communicating. Let's put the following sentence through the Blab Test:

The seeming explosion of welfare mothers is causing concern among many in this small town, as they see the abuse of food stamps and other government aid.

Translate that sentence into blab-speak: The *blab blab* of *blab blab* is causing concern among *blab* in this small town, as they *blab* the abuse of food stamps and other government aid.

Why did some words become blabs? Because they lacked specificity and precision. What is a "seeming explosion"? Either the number of parents on state assistance is increasing or it isn't. How can it be "seeming" to do so? And what constitutes an "explosion" of cases —10? 20? 100? What is a "welfare mother"? There are many types of government assistance, so be specific about which programs are experiencing an increase in caseload. How many is "many" and who

exhibit 8.2   REUTERS' GUIDELINES FOR WRITING ABOUT RELIGIOUS,
CULTURAL AND NATIONAL DIFFERENCES.[18]

1. "Seek precision with religious descriptions. 'Islamist' indicates an emphasis on Muslim principles. The adjective 'Islamic' refers primarily to the religion while 'Muslim' has both religious
   and cultural connotations. . . . Also be clear about distinctions within religions, indicating
   whether Muslims are Sunni or Shi'ite or noting which Christian denomination is involved."

2. "In cases where the line between nationalism, religion and culture is unclear . . . try to
   explain the historical and demographic background instead of glossing over the problem
   with oversimplified tags."

3. "When reporting on tragedies, we should be sensitive to the risk of implying that a Western
   life is worth more than an African or Asian casualty . . . [write] from a global perspective,
   while applying common sense and news judgment in cases where one group of victims
   deserves to be highlighted."

Source: Reuter's Handbook of Journalism, 2008.

are the "many"—citizens or local government officials or state workers? Be clear about why it matters that these people are concerned;
do they hold power to do more than be concerned? How do these
people "see" the abuse? Are they standing at the cash register when
the WIC stamps come out for ineligible items such as cigarettes?

Take the worn-out phrase, "He comes from the wrong side of the
tracks." What, exactly, does that mean? What's the right side of the
tracks? Who deems one side the wrong one? What are people really
saying when they use that phrase? That people in that neighborhood
are poor? Or not white? Or uneducated? Using specific words helps
avoid confusion and insult.

The multimedia news agency Thomson Reuters publishes *Reuters' Handbook of Journalism* written by and for its staff. Exhibit
8.2 includes three guidelines from the handbook regarding the use of
precision and common sense when writing about religious, cultural
and national groups.

Challenge Your Sources

Sources talk in euphemisms too. So ask and ask again to clarify
what people are saying. Jonathan Blakley, foreign desk producer at
National Public Radio, started out as a reporter in Detroit, where he
often heard sweeping generalizations about the city's violence:[19]

O.A. "People are dying in Detroit every day." You see that quote all the time. I grew up in Detroit. I was born and raised in Detroit. I've never been shot at nor have I ever shot anyone. And I didn't grow up in the richest part of Detroit. I grew up in a regular neighborhood.

I think: Really? People are getting shot every day? What do you mean? "Well, a guy got shot here a couple months ago." Well, that's different. Or, they say: "I don't feel safe." Now, we're getting somewhere; that is probably what that person meant.

"People are getting shot every day." That is a great quote. But is it true? I'd rather have the quote that may not sell as many newspapers or may not make the stock prices of some cable networks go higher. I'd rather have the quote of, "I don't really feel safe these days because . . ." rather than "People gettin' shot every day." You can easily get that quote.

You need to know more about a city before you just let someone say that. You also need to interview more than one person. This is a city built for 2 million people. Which part of the city are we talking about?

A news truck used to be a rarity. But in today's environment, you're videotaping yourself, so it's no big deal to have a microphone and camera in front of you. So a lot of times you have to be careful and looking out for someone telling you what **they** think you want to hear—be it in Baghdad or Detroit. As a reporter, you can't just walk away. You need to challenge folks. You need to ask: "What do you mean?"

When he was dean of the Poynter Institute, which provides training for journalists, Keith Woods provided advice on how to cover eruptions over word choices involving race and ethnicity. In the wake of controversial comments, journalists need to focus on gathering information before handing out judgment. Audiences need insight, not inflammatory coverage. Journalists need to understand sources' personal backgrounds and intentions before publishing. Woods suggests that journalists ask these questions to help audiences gain information after a news subject makes controversial comments:

1. **What did they say?** Don't get seduced by the sexy sound bite and leave out important facts. Be precise and avoid paraphrasing. That enhances fairness and sharpens accuracy.

2. **Why does it matter?** If someone has uttered a racial or ethnic insult, remember that not everyone knows the history or context of the words and, therefore, might not understand why anyone would be upset. That context also helps your audience put the remarks in

perspective and judge for themselves the severity (or lack thereof) of the words.

3. **What did they mean?** Beware of assumptions here. [They] might not mean what you think. Even if the words rank among the most profane or bigoted terms in the language, ask the neutral question: "What do you mean?" Another question that gets to the heart of the story: "Do you know why those words would anger some people?" Another: "What would you most want people to know about you right now?"

4. **Who are your sources?** Remember that opinions vary among and between people. If the insult is aimed at Arabs, don't just seek reaction from Arabs. Ask Latinos, Native Americans, white people, etc. That includes and expands perspective.[20]

Self-Check Your Language

If a story involves racial or other identifiers, and if it focuses on disenfranchised groups, before sending your story to an editor, quickly review this "Language Self-Check" to ensure your coverage is straightforward and balanced:

• **Use only relevant description** (e.g., is sexual orientation pertinent to the business story you are writing?).

• **Use labels with caution.** Labels encourage audiences to shoehorn all aspects of a person's behavior into a neat category. For example, one study showed that labeling a child as "poor" prompted people to label the child as less intelligent as well, even though no evidence was presented regarding intellect.[21] Instead, follow the next tip.

• **Use accurate, specific language.**

• **Vet quotes for negative stereotypes.** This doesn't mean you shouldn't run such quotes, but clarify what sources mean to say, and include context as to why the quote is offensive to some groups of people.

• **Use neutral language.** Avoid politicized terms or language that mirrors the viewpoint of influential sources.

Appreciating the power of words and tone to influence audience's understanding and perception of news events is critical for excellent journalism. A journalist has the opportunity to educate and inform, instead of to inflame or confuse. As journalists, many of us entered the profession because we love to write. Writing inclusively and with many perspectives in mind is challenging, but doing so means that journalists can attract a far broader and more diverse audience.

exploration EXERCISES

1. Read the August 11, 2009, piece by Cintra Wilson, style columnist for the *New York Times,* called "Playing to the Middle." It's about the JCPenney department store and is available online at http://www.nytimes.com/2009/08/13/fashion/13CRITIC.html. The column concludes with:

   > No matter how many Grand Slam breakfasts you've knocked out of the park, Penney's has a size for you. Ladies will find kicky little numbers that fit no matter how bountiful the good Lord made them; in the men's Big & Tall section, even Voltron could find office casuals.[22]

   a. Characterize the tone of the column. Is it helpful? Critical? Sarcastic? Informative?

   b. How was the tone established? Identify words or phrases that contribute to that tone.

   c. Do you agree or disagree with the *Times*' ombsbudman, who later wrote that he could feel "a virtual sneer"[23] coming through Wilson's tone?

   d. Explain your answers in a one-page blog posting, and reference the words or phrases you identified in answer (b) to support your conclusion. (Be aware that you are evaluating a column and not a straight news story, so more personality and viewpoint should be evident in the prose.)

   e. In a small group, brainstorm other ways that the author might have written about this topic that would be less offensive but still have voice and personality.

2. How should news outlets handle describing a news subject's race or ethnicity? Create a newsroom or classroom policy advising other reporters on the use of racial identifiers in news stories. Consider these questions when doing so:

a. In what circumstances might a racial or ethnic identifier be useful in a news story? How much does the identifier (such as "a Hispanic male") tell the audience about someone's looks? How different can people of the same race or ethnicity look? What is the effect on the news audience when a story notes someone's race and/or ethnicity?

b. Read "Racial IDs in Crime Stories: When Are They Fit to Print?" by Sally Lehrman, a senior fellow at the Institute for Justice and Journalism. It can be accessed through the institute's home page, www.justicejournalism.org. Also helpful is Mallary Jean Tenore's column at www.poynter.org from Aug. 17, 2011, about precise language and describing minorities. Make changes to your policy in light of either or both articles.

c. Publish your policy in an online discussion group or a journalism listserv for others to learn from and to offer feedback.

3. Select a news story you think illustrates one of the four problem areas of word choice: Otherness Words, Politicized Words, Judgment Words and Code Words. Circle the problematic word choice and explain in one or two sentences why it is problematic.

4. Put one of your recent stories through the Blab Test. Circle words that lack specificity and concrete meaning and replace them with blabs. Read your "blab-speak" story aloud. Then replace the blabs with words that add clearer meaning to your writing.

FOR review

- Select a word and give its denotation and connotation.
- Find an example from each of the four categories of problematic word choice.
- Put a recent story you reported, or one you recently read, through the Language Self-Check (p. 148) and note whether the story's words, phrases or tone needs to be changed.

notes

1. Keith Woods, "Diversity Tip Sheets: Is It Something I Said?," *Poynter.org* (2008), www2.poynter.org/column.asp?id=58&aid=137948, retrieved July 30, 2011.

2. Ibid.

3. Elfriede Fürsich, "How Can Global Journalists Represent 'Other'?," *Journalism 3,* no. 1 (2002), p. 80.

4. bell hooks, "Keeping Close to Home: Class and Education," in *Experiencing Race, Class, and Gender in the United States,* 5th ed., ed. Roberta Fiske-Rusciano (Boston: McGraw-Hill, 2009), p. 145.

5. National Association of Hispanic Journalists, "NAHJ Urges News Media to Stop Using the Term 'Illegals' When Covering Immigration," http://www.nahj.org/2009/09/nahj-urges-news-media-to-stop-using-the-term-illegals-when-covering-immigration/, retrieved July 30, 2011.

6. Martin H. Levinson, "General Semantics and Media Ethics," *ETC: A Review of General Semantics 64,* no. 3 (2007), pp. 257–58.

7. *Newsweek* staff, "Should Joseph Stack Be Called a Terrorist?," http://www.newsweek.com/2010/02/20/should-joseph-stack-be-called-a-terrorist.html.

8. David Tuller, "The Reporting Diversity Manual." (London: Media Diversity Institute, 2004), www.media-diversity.org; Tom Huang, "Beyond Political Correctness," *Poynter.org* (2011), http://www.poynter.org/how-tos/newsgathering-storytelling/diversity-at-work/23601/beyond-political-correctness/, retrieved August 4, 2011.

9. Aaron Kinney, "'Looting' or 'Finding'?," *Salon.com* (2005), http://dir.salon.com/story/news/feature/2005/09/01/photo_controversy/index.html, para. 2, retrieved August 6, 2011.

10. Chris Graythen, online post, member message board, *SportsShooter.com,* Aug. 31, 2005.

11. Kinney, "'Looting' or 'Finding'?"

12. Raymond E. Rainville, Al Roberts, and Andrew Sweet, "Recognition of Covert Racial Prejudice," *Journalism Quarterly 55,* no. 2 (1978).

13. Ibid., p. 259.

14. Aaron Broverman and Kent C. Loftsgard, "Quad Doctors: In or Out?," *New Mobility* (2010), http://www.newmobility.com/articleView.cfm?id=11728, retrieved June 6, 2011.

15. Ibid., para. 6.

16. Christina Samuels, Interview with author, 2010.

17. Stuart Chase, *The Tyranny of Words* (New York: Harcourt Brace, 1938), p. 21.

18. Reuters staff, "Reporting About People," in *Handbook of Journalism* (New York: Thomson Reuters, 2008).

19. Jonathan Blakley, personal communication, October 21, 2010.

20. Woods, "Diversity Tip Sheets: Is It Something I Said?"

21. J. M. Darley and P. H. Gross, "A Hypothesis-Confirming Bias in Labeling Effects," *Journal of Personality and Social Psychology 44,* no. 1 (1983).

22. Cintra Wilson, "Playing to the Middle," *New York Times,* August 11, 2009.

23. Clark Hoyt, "The Insult Was Extra Large," *New York Times,* August 22, 2009.

9

Attribution and Editing Without Bias

When to include data and how to determine cause

LEARNING OBJECTIVES

- *To learn to edit stories for relevant anecdotes and population-based data.*
- *To understand how to evaluate news accounts for incomplete explanations for causes of people's behavior.*
- *To self-assess two qualities of thinking style that may affect your journalism.*

QUESTIONING WHAT'S TRUE

The police department in Columbus, Ohio, launched a highly publicized campaign in the late 1980s to close crack houses, the homes from which dealers sold the pebble-sized form of cocaine. The Near East Side in Columbus was the area in which these homes were supposedly concentrated; it was a low-income neighborhood with mostly African American residents. Police raids with heavily armed SWAT teams became regular events on the homes there, with the mayor even bulldozing one supposed crack house. Television news stations broadcasted the near-weekly dramas, which often ended with police escorting a small band of handcuffed black men to jail.[1]

At the time, Michael J. Berens was a young reporter working at the *Columbus Dispatch*. He and a colleague began to wonder if the showy raids by police and politicians were really working. He describes the situation:

OA

ON ASSIGNMENT

The raids captivated the public. Politicians often tagged along with police to prove that the city was reclaiming its neighborhoods. At the height of the media circus, the mayor announced a plan to bulldoze documented crack houses. Indeed, the mayor drove a bulldozer into one home. Clinging to every side of the lumbering machine were city council members. The get-tough story and a large picture appeared in my newspaper. It was at this point in my career where I became tired of always accepting the "official word" about events. A colleague and I decided to examine the drug war.

We ventured into the Near East Side and went door to door in the crack neighborhoods. Some newspaper editors said that we were foolhardy at best. But the residents there wanted to talk. We talked to crack users and dealers. As word spread that we were open to hearing all sides, many people stepped forward.

We also used computers to quantify every arrest, every raid. In short, we found that the house the mayor had bulldozed was never a crack house. The whole event was a sham. We found that prosecutors dismissed 95 percent of the charges filed against the so-called crack dealers for lack of evidence. In most cases, police seized little more than a rock or two. These weren't dealers.

Most spectacularly, we found that narcotics cops had found a way to profit from the drug war. In short, the police chief resigned and dozens left the force or were reassigned. The story made national news. *ABC Primetime Live* profiled my partner and me.

This was my first investigative project. The stories spanned two years. I've never stopped. And I've never stopped questioning what everyone else believes is true.[2]

pause & consider Berens's crack house story refutes many stereotypes about drug dealing, poverty and black males. In what ways did the initial coverage play on those stereotypes?

Berens and his colleague, Roger Snell, used publicly recorded deeds, mortgages, maps, police documents and in-person interviews to put together an explosive account. Their stories showed the absence of bona fide crack houses in the neighborhood, exposed shoddy record keeping of cash and drugs seized in the raids, and revealed a pattern of questionable property ownership in the neighborhood by narcotics cops.

They didn't accept the explanations that officials and even other reporters gave to justify the raids. They didn't settle for the "good story" about taking back a neighborhood gone awry, and they looked beyond the accepted narrative about bad characters doing bad things. They made sure their explanation for the events was backed up by facts.

The reporting by Berens and Snell might have been based on numbers, but it was hardly dull. The *Columbus Dispatch* coverage led to an overhaul of the police department and the formation of an ethics panel to review officers named to certain assignments.[3]

ANECDOTE VS. DATA

People tend to favor anecdotes over data, and journalists are no exception. Too often, story trumps statistics in order to make deadline, enliven the account or cater to the audience. Nothing wrong with doing all three of those things. But journalists sometimes focus on the extreme example that makes for a lively tale but might not be truly representative of a neighborhood problem. To make a news account captivating, journalists seek out the dramatic elements of events sometimes to the exclusion of the larger perspective. And journalists know that distracted news audiences require attention-grabbing images, not a heap of numbers.

Numbers as Context

The preference for anecdotal instead of base-rate information can lead people to mischaracterize events. **Base-rate** information is data about the percentage of cases in a population, or the frequency with which an event occurs in a population. Base-rate information provides perspective. Such information might answer how many local grade-school children take free or reduced-price lunches, or the number of practicing Buddhists in a region, or the level of education attained by second-generation Guatemalans in a community.

Population-based data may not be scintillating, but it's more reliable than a string of specific individuals and their tales. It helps avoid language that hides a lack of concrete evidence; phrasing such as "seemingly" or "it appears that" or "some say." (This author has written all three phrases in her news writing career, she's certain.)

Knowing this, why do journalists sometimes overgeneralize based on a compelling anecdote instead of using more valid statistics to anchor a story?[4] The theories at work here are complex, but journalists should at least know that they, their sources and audiences tend to:

- Assume a sample from a particular population is highly representative of that population, and is similar to it in all essential characteristics.[5] *Example: One house from the Near East Side is essentially the same as any on the Near East Side: All are crack houses.*

- Concentrate on nonessential information instead of on relevant data when making a conclusion.[6] *Example: The number of houses in a neighborhood in which young black males reside is nonessential information when it comes to concluding whether they are crack houses.*

- Give undue consideration to descriptive information rather than statistical information and make unwarranted generalizations based on the vivid information.[7] *Example: A highly visual raid on a home led by a heavily armed SWAT team is inherently more captivating to the imagination than a collection of numbers on actual arrests made. News viewers may persist in believing that crack is a widespread problem in the neighborhood—even if the arrest numbers and police corruption cases indicate otherwise.*

Being aware of these basic tendencies will help journalists remember to seek out numbers to anchor a story.

pause&consider Read the excerpt in Appendix A from one of the *Columbus Dispatch* stories by Berens and Snell. Notice that the story leads with an anecdote and follows with data. How well do the two elements work together?

Editing With an Eye for Evidence

Editing is a process that occurs throughout the development of a story. In larger news organizations, photojournalists, reporters and the graphics team work together with editors to develop a story. In smaller operations, a single journalist might create text, photos and graphics singlehandedly. In either scenario, journalists producing the stories can and should serve as their own editors throughout the story process. Editing is about perspective. It invites the reporter to step back from his work and evaluate it from its initial premise: Is the foundational reporting there, or is the story built on information that hasn't been verified? Editing is the chance to check whether assumptions have overruled evidence. If so, revisions are the opportunity to correct your assumptions.

Journalists can build two questions into their self-editing routine, keeping both in mind *throughout the story process*, as they formulate a reporting plan, gather information and assemble their stories:

1. **Is there a use for base-rate data in the reporting?** Since base-rates describe how often something happens in a given population, they are useful in predictions. They also help determine the probability of events and offer information about general tendencies. They quickly give context and perspective. Cognitive biases are less apt to run wild when hemmed in by hard data. You can humanize the numbers with interviews and observation.

An example of base-rate data is the number of confirmed cases of cancer in children in a neighborhood near a nuclear power plant out of the total number of children living there. This sort of data helps prevent panic coverage and incorrect judgments about the randomness of events (which are more random than you think), particularly in small sample sizes.[8] While anec-dotal information is powerful and vivid, data is more reliable and valid. Stories about trends and patterns (such as crime and drug busts in a community) need data.

Remember that the plural of anec-dote is data.[9] In other words, look for personal stories that reflect genuine trends instead of squeez-ing a trend from a couple of good anecdotes.

2. **If an anecdote is used, is it relevant to the larger point of the story?** Journalists can't help how news consumers process information; people will always prefer a colorful story. But journalists can control how they themselves make judgments and ensure that the anecdotes they use are representative of the larger point of the news account. Anecdotes shouldn't be the extreme odd example, unless that example is clearly highlighted as the exception to a general pattern.

Let Numbers Keep You in Line

Reporters tend to go too easy on causes they support and with sources they like, notes Benjy Hamm, the editorial director at Landmark Community Newspapers, which owns more than 50 community papers in 15 states. Hamm used to be managing editor at the *Spartanburg Herald-Journal* in South Carolina, where he once edited a story about teen pregnancies. Hamm recalls that the reporter returned "all fired up" from his interview with a source at a local organization working to prevent unwanted pregnancies. But the reporter's pitch was weak. It had no numbers to back up sources' claims that there was a "crisis" of teen pregnancies in the area. Nationally, the number of teen pregnancies was down, so why not locally, too, Hamm wondered. He explains how the rest of the editing process proceeded:

We needed to ask, "What part of this is based on information versus assumptions?" So I said, "Go back to the source and ask what the teen pregnancy rate was 5, 10, 15 years ago." He came back and said, "They don't want to give me those numbers because that will take away from the story. The numbers aren't up here; it's just a crisis here."

The source's thinking was that if one teenager gets pregnant, that's a problem. We said we'll do a story about issues involved in teen pregnancy but we need the numbers. The assumption from the reporter was that this is terrible, this is bad; teen pregnancies are going up. [In the end we] were able to write about the difficulties of teen pregnancies along with an article about successful efforts to reduce the number of unwanted pregnancies.

Journalists often are criticized as being too cynical. I have not found that to be true for most of the people I've met in journalism. If anything, many journalists can be too trusting when it comes to causes they support, people they like and sources they trust. They can lower their guard and relax their standards when reporting on those topics and sources.

Who would oppose worthy efforts to reduce unplanned teen pregnancy? So, reporters—consciously or subconsciously—often see [the issue] as a cause to support through their news articles. That support can make them less likely to ask tough questions, to insist on documentation to verify claims, and to differentiate between fact and opinion. I see examples of this all the time when newspapers cover particular sources, government agencies and nonprofits. Editors need to challenge reporters to question conventional wisdom and ask tough questions of all their sources.

For example, if the police chief requests that the city council impose a curfew on people under age 17 because of late-night vandalism and violence, check out the numbers. A reporter did so when I was editor at a newspaper in Lancaster, South Carolina, and found no evidence of late-night crimes or mischief involving children under age 17. Upon questioning, the police chief admitted there were no problems. He said he was simply trying to avoid the potential for future problems.

So: Challenge your sources. Challenge the premise of your own story. Challenge the "facts." There are numerous examples of people telling reporters things that simply don't add up when you look at the numbers. You still may have a story; it's just a different, and better, story.[10]

pause&*consider* With a peer, make a list of a half dozen or so worthy causes that you support. Take one cause (such as a clean environment) and discuss hard questions you can ask sources to avoid a blindly positive news account on that topic.

The above sections describe the importance of editing to avoid basing stories on a single compelling anecdote or conventional wisdom and to determine when a story needs anchoring in data and statistics. Now, let's look at another way editing can eliminate assumptions that creep into stories. Revising your work as you report can help clarify cause and context and root out unintended bias in your writing.

EDITING FOR ACCURATE ATTRIBUTION

In journalism, *attribution* is the identification of the source of information in a news story. But in cognitive terms, the word **attribution** refers to how people explain the causes of behaviors and events.[11] People tend to attribute the cause of another person's behavior either to elements within that person (internal) or to environmental elements (external).[12]

Because reporters are in the business of trying to make sense of human behavior—to understand motivation and cause and explain it to the public—the concept of attribution has everyday utility for newsrooms. The mind can too quickly infer the personality traits of others. We assume that a person's behavior will be the same in very

ON ASSIGNMENT

different situations and circumstances.[13] These assumptions ignore the fact that behavior is often a function of the *situation* rather than a reflection of someone's personality, character or habits.[14]

For example, attribution errors can lead to the stereotype that successful women get to their position purely through long hours and hard work (external factors), not through their own intelligence (an internal factor). Attribution errors can perpetuate gender-based stereotypes by offering different explanations for the same behavior.[15] For instance, a sexist version of attribution would conclude that if a man succeeds at business, it's due to his innate abilities (internal). If a woman succeeds at business, it's due to luck, effort or affirmative action policies (external).

Attributions are inferences people generate to explain events, others' behavior and their own behavior. Attributions are a powerful force in all societies, as they seek to explain causes and, sometimes, to assign blame. How journalists assign cause to behaviors and events can have implications for how groups of people are viewed in the larger society, because news influences peoples' perceptions of events and others. Attribution has far-reaching effects. It is important for journalists to accurately label the causes of situations as much as access and time allow. For instance, a common tendency in a capitalistic society such as the U.S. is to attribute people's economic success to disposition: "He pulled himself up by his bootstraps." Or, "She worked her way out of poverty." By this rule, people deserve the economic fate they get.

Research indicates that how people explain the causes of mental illness or obesity affects how much citizens are willing to help people who are mentally ill or obese. If citizens believe people can control their conditions—that is, that the condition is due to internal, controllable factors, such as will power in the case of obesity—then they are less likely to help them.[16]

In a journalistic example, Wayne Drehs of ESPN.com found in Kurt Warner, who at that time was the Arizona Cardinals starting quarterback, an example of a man driven by his internal beliefs, not by his external circumstances. In 2009, Drehs spent time with Warner for a multimedia profile of the player. Drehs says he was careful to look for evidence that supported his explanation of the causes behind Warner's behavior:

ON ASSIGNMENT

Kurt Warner . . . could not be further from the stereotypes. The whole piece was about that. Here's this incredibly Christian man who had all these values yet goes to work everyday in a locker room full of men who cheat on their wives and go to strip clubs. Even with Kurt, I expected a certain type of Bible pusher, someone who would hammer at me with his religion and hammer at his teammates. His belief is, "I am going to live my life in the way of the Lord and my goal is that other people will see that and ask, 'How are you able to be that way?' And then I can tell them as opposed to standing on the bench in the locker room yelling."[17]

Drehs' piece makes conclusions about Warner's behavior and the causes for it. He sought to substantiate those conclusions with detailed writing and concrete specifics garnered from paying attention to a wide spectrum of information, not just Warner talking about Warner. In his writing, Drehs tried to show Warner in context. Here's the top of his story:

PHOENIX—It's a chilly, wet December afternoon in the alleged Valley of the Sun and a mud-covered Kurt Warner is lost. He's just finished helping build an elementary school playground and is driving home to stuff Christmas stockings for more than 100 foster kids when his cell phone rings.

It's Arizona Cardinals coach Ken Whisenhunt, congratulating the 37-year-old quarterback for making his third Pro Bowl, his first as a Cardinal. Warner asks which of his teammates made the team, then reacts to his own good fortune with the enthusiasm of someone who is yawning. . . .

And just like that, the conversation is over, the career renaissance complete. Eight years since Warner came out of an Iowa supermarket to lead the St. Louis Rams to a Super Bowl title, he is once again one of the top quarterbacks in the NFL. Despite his struggles the past two weeks, Warner's on-the-field success has shined an even stronger spotlight on his off-the-field deeds, which, depending on your perspective, are either saintly or too good to be true. . . .

On this day, at least Kurt Warner is lost. At least in the middle of all this selflessness, humility and utter lack of ego, the man is texting while driving, paying little attention to the road and can't remember if the path home follows I-10 East or I-10 West. Because otherwise, ugggh. Otherwise, this story might need to come with its very own barf bag. And Warner knows it.[18]

You can access Drehs' 2009 multimedia piece on Warner at http://sports.cspn.go.com/nfl/news/story?page=hotread17/kurtwarner.

Excellent reporters dig in and let evidence decide attribution: What fuels this subject? What drives his or her actions? How do we know?

Most people aren't great judges of their own behaviors. We're likely to interpret our worlds in order to maintain a strong self-image; successes are ours alone, failures are due to bad luck or other outside circumstances. That means we are actually not as cool/smart/great/cute as we think we are. So journalists should ask questions of not only news subjects but also a subject's friends and enemies in order to form more accurate attributions about a subject's behavior.

The Fundamental Attribution Error

One form of attribution is especially pertinent to journalists because it involves playing the role of observer, which is what news people do. Here's a quick multiple-choice quiz to better understand the concept behind the fundamental attribution error:

1. When you are speeding down the street late for work, you are violating the speed limit because:
   A. your alarm didn't go off
   B. your car wouldn't start
   C. you love to drive fast
   D. you couldn't find your keys/purse/wallet/cell phone

2. When a driver passes you on the right and is going 20 miles per hour faster than you, he's violating the speed limit because:
   A. his wife is in labor in the back seat
   B. he's irresponsible
   C. he has aggression issues
   D. he can't read speed limit signs

This brief quiz demonstrates how we often erroneously explain the causes of others' behavior: If you chose A, B or D for Question 1 and B, C or D for Question 2, then you have demonstrated the fundamental attribution error. The **fundamental attribution error** describes the tendency for an observer to *overestimate* the role of personal, internal factors in affecting behavior and to *underestimate* the influence of situational factors.

In the example above, *you* speed because of circumstances; it has nothing to do with you being incautious or disorganized. But *other* people speed because of their own idiocy; it has nothing to do with circumstances.

To put it in terms of the news profession, a reporter and editor may tend to explain behavior as due to a source's disposition—such as personality, habits or character ("that's just what he's like")—as opposed to the source's environment or circumstances. The fundamental attribution error is common in part because when people try to explain someone's behavior, their attention is usually on the individual and his or her appearance, language and outward attitude. Attention is focused less on the situational context or the relevant social roles, which can take longer to piece out when reporting.[19]

Imagine that a journalist observes a political candidate joking and laughing with people of her own ethnicity at a campaign stop at a local burger joint. Later that day, the journalist witnesses the candidate being reserved and serious with people of a different ethnicity at a fundraising session in a supporter's home.

pause & *consider* Make a quick mental list of possible reasons for the candidate's differing behavior at the two events.

The journalist would be committing the fundamental attribution error if he decided that the candidate's differing behavior was due to her inherent favoritism of people of her own ethnicity and a discomfort with people of other ethnicities. Actually, it is much more likely that the circumstances determined the candidate's behavior. The degree of formality of the venues dictated the style of the candidate's actions; the burger joint invited quips and banter, the fundraiser called for decorum.

The fundamental attribution error is also pertinent to journalists for a second reason: It can close the mind to alternate explanations for someone's actions. Studies in general suggest that the urge to explain a source's behavior in terms of her personality will cause a reporter to discount situational evidence *even* if the reporter knows that circumstances are influencing the source's behavior.[20]

Here's an example of this discounting in news work: A reporter on the court beat learns that a woman on trial for stealing money from her employer did so because she was broke and needed to buy food for her three kids. The reporter covers her hearing, at which the woman is bitter and sarcastic to the judge. "A thief's a thief," the reporter thinks, and his story focuses on how crafty and sinister she was about pilfering cash from the check-out drawer at the locally owned hardware store where she worked (and stole) for the past two years. He quotes the angry, betrayed owner extensively.

However, the reporter also learns the woman is a paycheck away from eviction. He chooses not to pursue this angle and concludes that basically she is lazy; after all, she hasn't used the food pantry available to her each week. Had he looked into bus routes to the pantry from her low-income housing complex, he'd have found the trip to and from the pantry (with three young children in tow) takes an hour each way. And, the pantry closes at 1 p.m. on Saturdays; she gets off work at noon on Saturdays. None of this is to say the woman isn't guilty or unpleasant or that she should have done what she did. But there's a more complete story here that goes beyond the rightfully angry employer.

Unseen situational forces such as poverty, racism and unemployment are "invisible social chains" that control people's behavior. So noted an influential social psychologist named Gustav Ichheiser in 1949, and his comments still have worth today. Ichheiser wrote that "the complete tragic blindness of the privileged concerning the life-situation of the underprivileged is the result of just this kind of not seeing the invisible factors in the situations of others."[21]

The next section discusses a way journalists can discover the invisible circumstances influencing sources' actions.

REPORTING AND EDITING FOR COMPLETE EXPLANATIONS

As a story takes shape, revising and editing to provide correct explanations for actions are among the most important tasks at hand. Audiences typically don't ask what other forces might have influenced the subject of a news story; they take the news accounts at face value. So a journalist must take the concept of cause seriously.

Seeking the Private Self in Sources

One way journalists can learn the motivations and causes behind sources' actions is to enter their private worlds. Doing so leads to a more accurate explanation for behaviors. It helps reveal the "invisible social chains" that direct some people's actions. This means interviewing a source in his apartment instead of meeting at a coffee shop. Watching him over a dinner with his family instead of at work. Going to his place of worship, or his weekly 7 a.m. pick-up basketball game. Journalists can make venue choices that assist their efforts to see beyond a person's outward appearance and public disposition.

Journalists' presence influences people's behavior. Reporters and photojournalists fortunate enough to get time to follow a story subject around for a length of time can melt into the background and no longer be seen as an audience. The journalistic observer needs to see how the source behaves when not on stage.

Journalists can fairly and fully explain their sources' behaviors by seeking circumstantial evidence for their actions. A full explanation is a fair explanation. As much as possible, journalists should consider a complete array of causes for sources' behavior. Interviews with a variety of sources can help determine cause. So might documents. Explore how forces of time, money, birthright, education and social network may explain a source's actions just as much as her character does.

A story's conclusions should be dictated by the most aggressive reporting that time allows. If a journalist doesn't have time to go beyond artifice and public statements, then a story should acknowledge that. It can be as straightforward as, "In public, at least, Source A seems confident and composed."

Know Yourself

A second way that a journalist can fully consider the motivations behind a source's actions is, ironically, to consider his or her own ways of thinking. It's helpful for editors to know journalists' individual styles as well. It's easier to address gaps and oversights in story coverage when working as a team. Interestingly, some people tend to attribute more readily than others. Two personality characteristics that affect the way people explain the behavior of others are category width and certainty orientation. Both have to do with one's thinking style.

Category width

Category width refers to how broadly a person categorizes things.[22] Is a woman selling cosmetics out of her home considered a businesswoman? A broad categorizer would say yes. A narrow categorizer would say no, because the professional trappings of a separate office, regular business hours, colleagues and office attire are missing. Broad categorizers allow for lots of discrepancy among members of the same category, while narrow categorizers generally do not.[23]

Broad categorizers tend to perform better than narrow categorizers on tests that require thinking about how things interrelate. Narrow categorizers tend to perform better on detailed, analytic processing. Broad categorizers are tolerant of conflicting information; they tend to search for the appropriate interpretation of a situation, such as evaluating the behavior of someone from another culture, rather than making an uninformed judgment. Narrow categorizers are unaccepting of conflicting information and tend to make strong judgments based on their own cultural viewpoint.[24]

Certainty orientation

Another personality trait that can influence a journalist's attributions about people is how certainty-oriented he is. People who are **uncertainty-oriented** have a need to understand others. They are open-minded and evaluate ideas on their own merit, integrating new and old ideas and changing belief systems accordingly.

Conversely, **certainty-oriented** people generally are not interested in finding out information about the world and others. They have a high degree of confidence in their explanations for strangers' behaviors. However, those explanations might not be correct.[26] While it is desirable to be authoritative in your reporting, this authority should not come from your own tendency to neatly explain behaviors but from fully reporting the circumstances.

Steve Gunn, Director of Strategic Products and Audience Development at *The Charlotte Observer,* noted how one story moved from narrow categorizing to broad categorizing:

> Life is unclear. Life is getting greyer and greyer and how you present a story should reflect that. We had a guy running for sheriff . . . and he basically outwitted the establishment and was not always following all the rules. So the first day story was very much, "This guy is like a crook." The second day story got more and more nuanced. It was more that "he'd worked his way up."[25]

Journalists who tend toward narrow categorization or who are certainty-oriented have to be aware of either tendency when assigning cause. Editors can ask reporters questions to prompt a review of interview questions and research to ensure the reporters didn't focus too soon and too specifically on certain elements of a story to the exclusion of other valid information. Together, editors and reporters can set goals for story coverage that includes an array of subjects.

Take the surveys on category width and certainty orientation in Appendix B to help you assess your own thinking style.

The professional tenets of journalism can help reporters develop good habits. It stands to reason that professional practices are especially helpful to journalists who tend to be narrow categorizers and certainty-oriented. Core tenets of journalism include fairness, accuracy and balance. Modern additions to that list include a commitment to represent all constituent groups in society, verification of information, providing a public forum for a variety of points of view and interests, and including news from all communities.[27] Striving to follow these principles on the job helps offset a disposition toward shunning new ideas, making strong judgments quickly or being closed-minded.

exploration EXERCISES

1. Now that you've identified your personality traits when it comes to category width and uncertainty-orientation using the questionnaires in Appendix B, take some time to reflect on the results. If possible, pair up with a peer to discuss your assessment.

   a. Can you think of instances in your life in which you demonstrated those tendencies?

   b. How might your tendencies affect your reporting accuracy?

   c. Identify three specific actions you can take to offset or strengthen your particular orientation.

2. During the 2010 Winter Olympic Games in Vancouver, British Columbia, Nodar Kumaritashvili, 21, a luger from the Republic of Georgia, fatally crashed in a training run on the notoriously high-speed track at the Whistler Sliding Centre. News reports subsequently grappled with the cause of the crash: Was it driver

error or the construction of the course that caused the athlete to lose control? Read the excerpts below from an editorial in *The Sunday Times* of London. The paper acknowledges that while the sport's professional association blamed the death on the athlete, concerns persisted about the dangers of the track.

> DEATH AT 90 MPH—Was Georgian Really the Only One to Blame for Crash That Killed Him at Winter Games?
>
> Having completed their investigation overnight, officials from the FIL concluded swiftly that the blame for the horrific accident lay not with the course but with the rider. Kumaritashvili, they said only a few hours after the seven-man Georgian team had marched into the opening ceremony for the 21st Winter Games wearing black armbands, a black streamer flying from the national flag, had made a fatal mistake, coming late out of turn 15 and losing control of his sled midway through the last of the 16 corners.
>
> Television viewers around the world saw the 21-year-old Georgian collide with both walls before being catapulted out of the shute headfirst into an unprotected trackside pillar.
>
> "Technical officials of FIL concluded that there was no indication that the accident was caused by deficiencies in the track," said the FIL. Officials denied Kumaritashvili had trouble on at least two of his six training runs on the track or that there were indications well before the accident that the track was dangerous. . . .
>
> But why, if the track was not to blame, did the officials lower the start, raise the height of the wall on the exit of curve 16 and alter the ice profile of the curve to reduce the risk of riders being hurled out of the track?[28]

a. Consider the different cultural or geographic viewpoints that might inform various news accounts' explanation of cause. To do this, conduct an online search for news coverage of the crash in U.S., Canadian and European outlets. Decide whether there is a pattern in the attribution of blame in this case. For example, do U.S. and Canadian news outlets emphasize Kumaritashvili's actions as a cause of the crash? Do European outlets dwell more on the course's speed and design?

b. How does attribution theory apply to this story? Write 2 to 3 paragraphs describing your findings and make conclusions about any differences in coverage.

3. Keeping in mind the points made by Benjy Hamm in the "On Assignment" on pages 158–159, look at teen pregnancy rates in your community.

a. Map out a plan to report a story using population-based data. Find the rates for your city or state and compare them with national figures.

b. Make a list of three places in your community in which you might find local sources to help humanize the numbers in a relevant way.

c. Identify the type of lead anecdote that would *not* be representative of your local situation. Then craft a hypothetical anecdote that *would* be representative.

FOR review

- Seek base-rate information for a news story on which you're working or for a story currently in the news.
- Explain the fundamental attribution error to a peer.
- Meet with an editor in your newsroom, invite one to class or conduct a Skype interview. Ask the editor to talk about his or her experiences with assigning cause to behaviors and events. Ask how cause or blame affects how cultural groups are viewed in the larger society.

notes

1. Michael J. Berens, Interview with author, 2010.

2. Ibid.

3. Roger Snell and Michael J. Berens, "Audit Clears Landlord-Police Officer," *Columbus Dispatch*, March 14, 1990.

4. Ruth Hamill, Timothy DeCamp Wilson, and Richard E. Nisbett, "Insensitivity to Sample Bias: Generalizing from Atypical Cases," *Journal of Personality and Social Psychology 39,* no. 4 (1980).

5. Amos Tversky and Daniel Kahneman, "Belief in the Law of Small Numbers," in *Judgment under Uncertainty: Heuristics and Biases,* eds. Daniel Kahneman, Paul Slovic, and Amos Tversky (Cambridge: Cambridge University Press, 1982).

6. Richard Nisbett and Lee Ross, *Human Inference: Strategies and Shortcomings of Social Judgment,* ed. James J. Jenkins, Walter Mischel, and Willard W. Hartup, Century Psychology Series (Englewood Cliffs, N.J.: Prentice-Hall, 1980).

7. Hamill, Wilson, and Nisbett, "Insensitivity to Sample Bias."

8. Tversky and Kahneman, "Belief in the Law of Small Numbers," p. 24.

9. Brad DeLong and Susan Rasky, "Twelve Things Economists Need to Remember to Be Helpful to Journalistic Sources," *Nieman Watchdog* (2006),

http://niemanwatchdog.org/index.cfm?fuseaction=background.view& backgroundid=0094, retrieved June 8, 2011.

10. Benjy Hamm, Interview with author, August, 2010.

11. B. Holton, "Attributional Biases," in *Magill's Encyclopedia of Social Psychology,* ed. N. Piotrowski (Pasadena, Calif.: Salem Press, 2003); Lee Ross and Craig A. Anderson, "Shortcomings in the Attribution Process: On the Origins and Maintenance of Erroneous Social Assessments," in *Judgment under Uncertainty: Heuristics and Biases,* ed. Daniel Kahneman, Paul Slovic, and Amos Tversky (Cambridge: Cambridge University Press, 1982).

12. Fritz Heider, *The Psychology of Interpersonal Relations* (New York: Wiley, 1958).

13. Ross and Anderson, "Shortcomings in the Attribution Process."

14. Susan T. Fiske and Shelley E. Taylor, *Social Cognition* (New York: Random House, 1984).

15. Ibid.

16. Patrick W. Corrigan, "Mental Health Stigma as Social Attribution: Implications for Research Methods and Attitude Change," *Clinical Psychology: Science and Practice 7,* no. 1 (2000).

17. Wayne Drehs, Interview with author, 2010.

18. Wayne Drehs, "Good Deeds Are Warner's Focus," *ESPN.com* (Jan. 29, 2009), http://sports.espn.go.com/nfl/news/story?page=hotread17/kurtwarner, retrieved October 6, 2010.

19. Fiske and Taylor, *Social Cognition.*

20. Ibid.

21. Gustav Ichheiser, "Misunderstandings in Human Relations: A Study in False Social Perception," *American Journal of Sociology 55,* no. 2 (1949), p. 47.

22. Thomas F. Pettigrew, "The Measurement and Correlates of Category Width as a Cognitive Variable," *Journal of Personality 26,* no. 4 (1958).

23. R. A. Detweiler, "Culture, Category Width, and Attributions," *Journal of Cross-Cultural Psychology 9,* no. 3 (1978).

24. R. A. Detweiler, "On Inferring the Intentions of a Person from Another Culture," *Journal of Personality 43,* no. 4 (1975).

25. Steve Gunn, Interview with author, August, 2010.

26. Richard M. Sorrentino and Judith-Ann C. Short, "Uncertainty Orientation, Motivation, and Cognition," in *Handbook of Motivation & Cognition: Foundations of Social Behavior,* ed. Richard M. Sorrentino and E. Tory Higgins (New York: Guilford Press, 1986); William B. Gudykunst, *Bridging Differences: Effective Intergroup Communication* (Thousand Oaks, Calif.: Sage, 1998).

27. Project for Excellence in Journalism, "Principles of Journalism," Pew Research Center (1997), www.journalism.org/resources/principles, retrieved May 15, 2011.

28. Andrew Longmore, "Death at 90 Mph—Was Georgian Really the Only One to Blame for Crash That Killed Him at Winter Games?," *The Sunday Times,* February 14, 2010.

10

Journalism and Reflective Practice

Cultivating an open mind

LEARNING OBJECTIVES

- *To understand what debiasing is.*
- *To know the three categories of debiasing.*
- *To know at least five strategies for debiasing.*

MAKING THE UNFAMILIAR, FAMILIAR

Thomas Curwen of the *Los Angeles Times* wrote about Ana Rodarte, a young woman with a disorder called neurofibromatosis that creates severe facial disfigurement. Ana looked very different from most people, and as Curwen wrote in his story, "The face is our calling card to the world. . . . It also elicits reactions from others that shape our lives. Every day we read faces and make assumptions about identity and character without any basis other than appearance."[1]

Curwen sought to go beyond surface definitions to explore Ana's inner life. In reporting the story, Curwen had questions about facial disfigurement, appearance and stigma. He describes how he used his emotions to guide his reporting:

OA

My reaction was complicated. I had seen a few photographs of Ana and was taken aback by the size of the tumors. These were clinical shots taken by the hospital (her face from three different angles), and I was surprised that the disorder had progressed as far as it had. I wasn't yet aware of her childhood surgeries.

When I met Ana, though, I immediately saw a young woman whose life had been defined by very difficult odds. She was shy, nervous and uncertain about her future. I couldn't help but feel empathy for her and admiration for her agreeing to go ahead with these surgeries and for letting the *L.A. Times* follow her.

All of these emotions—surprise, empathy, admiration—guided me throughout the reporting, and I wasn't particularly concerned about how they would distort the narrative because I knew that I wouldn't be alone in my reaction. All of our interactions with friends, family and strangers are constantly influenced and moderated by the judgments we make based on appearance—as determined by DNA or social pressure and fads—and I knew that readers would also have to sort through their own reactions to Ana. This is why I incorporated my impressions into the story (those first-person elements); they allowed me to be a foil for readers' own emotional reaction.

I framed the story with the idea that we're all different. Ana's differences are extreme, but by showing her daily life, her struggles and hopes, I hoped to focus on what she shares with everyone else.[2]

Curwen embarked on reporting Ana's story with labels leading the way—"neurofibromatosis," "disorder," "facial disfigurement." His story process echoes a lesson of inclusive reporting raised in Chapter 1 in my story about the migrant workers on the outskirts of metropolitan Chicago:

> This book is about how journalists acquire, filter and judge information, and how we must do our utmost to provide information as free from preconceptions and assumptions as possible. We must engage in label-free thinking.
>
> Part of the job of a journalist is to figure out which of the labels matter and *why*. We have to know the *why* in order to tell the right story, the truest story at that moment.

In writing about Ana, one could use the narrow label "disfigured" or the broader label "young woman with hopes for a future." The migrant workers in Chapter 1 could be labeled as "undocumented immigrants" or the more inclusive "fathers and husbands trying to make a living." Narrower labels are essential for accuracy and context. Broader, more inclusive labels are essential to make a connection with audiences; both are needed.

It took three years for Curwen to report the Rodarte story. He explains how stories that start at labels but then move toward inclusivity break down the barriers between "Us" and "Others" and are well worth the effort.

> I think that one of the greatest services that a newspaper can provide—along with its investigations and news reports—is a lesson in empathy. This is why I was drawn to Ana's story and why I believe it is newsworthy. I hope that in reading Ana's Story, readers will look beyond neurofibromatosis and think about the differences that define our lives (be it by DNA or culture) and understand that they are less important than we think.
>
> It's something of a cliché, I know, that we are more united by what we share than what we don't share, but I believe that Ana's story provided a fresh perspective. Of course, the terms were extreme (the tumors), but Ana was no different than anyone else her age: shy, cranky, hopeful, afraid.
>
> Journalists have been given a great gift by the nature of their jobs. They are allowed to get into the world and bring stories like these back to their readers. Without these stories, I believe our worlds could get very small and polarized and contentious. This is why I think stories like Ana's are important. They make the unfamiliar familiar.[3]

When journalists "tell the story of the diversity and magnitude of the human experience,"[4] they do so through common emotions and shared experience. For all the diversity in the world, there are things that connect us with others.

pause&consider What do you think Curwen means by the statement "without these stories, I believe our worlds could get very small and polarized and contentious"? Discuss this with a peer. Then, share a recent story in the news that helped make the world less "small and polarized and contentious" for you. Read an excerpt from Curwen's story about Ana Rodarte in Appendix A.

COMBATTING BIASED THINKING

Throughout this book are ideas to help journalists better understand how they think. As mentioned in Chapter 2, thinking about how you think is called *metacognition*. How the mind intakes, processes and categorizes information, how it reasons and how it focuses on certain pieces of information to the exclusion of others are all important factors in producing a news account.

Debiasing is the term used to describe techniques to reduce or eliminate distortions or errors in thinking and judgment, those habits of thought introduced in Chapter 2. These strategies for combatting cognitive errors and biases can be thought of as ways to cultivate a more open mind as a journalist.

Debiasing techniques in general shift the mental processing of people and events from automatic, rule-of-thumb thinking to conscious, controlled thinking.[5] A thoughtful journalist consciously considers information in an analytic way. The debiasing techniques break down into three general categories—cognitive, motivational and technological. We'll look at each later in the chapter.

Changing Thinking

We have given much consideration to understanding how and why people think the way they do. The good news is that it is possible to control and change some aspects of thinking. The evidence shows that automatic (as in instant and unintentional) stereotypes and prejudice are controllable.[6] Those who are *genuinely motivated* to be non-prejudiced with respect to race and ethnicity are more likely to succeed in achieving that goal.[7] Research also indicates that, in general, people motivated to be accurate can reduce judgmental biases.[8] That's great news for journalists, who strive to be neutral in their judgments and assessments of others; the profession demands it.

Other factors beyond motivation that may encourage journalists' unbiased thought and behavior include:

- Social norms, such as a newsroom culture that champions inclusive reporting and a diverse staff, or a news organization's decidedly ethical approach to doing journalism.
- Situational pressures, such as a critical and vocal source on the lookout for prejudicial coverage, may encourage more thoughtful assessments of news events.
- Social context, such as how a journalist wants to be seen by sources and the news audience—his or her reputation—may also limit a journalist's stereotyping or reporting bias.

Obstacles to correcting biased thought

Debiasing is hardly a guaranteed, one-size-fits-all fix. Correcting biased thought is difficult for many reasons, one of them being that prejudices are responses that stem from mental processing that is unconscious or uncontrollable. Simply put, people might not *mean* to be prejudiced, but cultural and social influences have clearly carved out patterns that dictate how their minds label and categorize others.

A person must actively reroute those categorizations and labels. And research tells us that a person *really* has to want to, because one's thinking is stingy when it comes to perceptions of others; the mind likes to economize its efforts.[9] Countering or correcting biases about others takes concerted, high-effort thinking.

As evidenced in this book, people's highly adaptive minds have many ways of thinking that fall far short of the journalistic standards of fair, balanced and critical. The result is that people may not know when their thinking is biased. That makes it hard to correct. And when a person does attempt to address what she thinks is a faulty assessment of someone, she may overcorrect or adjust in the wrong direction, making the assessment even more skewed.[10]

Preparing for debiasing

But enough with the bad news and disclaimers. Journalists have some built-in advantages when it comes to debiasing due to their profession. They aren't average citizens in this context.

In order to counter unintentional bias, a person first needs to be aware of it. The previous chapters in this book have focused on general areas where internal biases can appear. However, there are other ways to pick up on unintentional bias in your daily work. One way is through online comments. Audience feedback is timely and coverage-specific, and at the least, a journalist is exposed to the possibility that his work might be imbalanced. A person can become aware of his bias through introspection or by use of a corrective method.[11] A journalist might review a draft specifically for slanted word choice, or ask a source for feedback on the fairness of a published story's quotes.

A tool for journalists in seeking and responding to feedback is **crowdsourcing.** Crowdsourcing uses the collaborative information-gathering efforts of readers in reporting a news story. The journalist issues an open call for assistance, drawing on the knowledge of a wide range of people to find leads, information and sources. Crowd-sourcing allows journalists to gather ideas and represent perspectives that they otherwise might not have been able to find.

Jan Schaffer is the executive director of J-Lab: The Institute for Interactive Journalism, an incubator for news entrepreneurs at American University. Schaffer says that avoiding stereotypical treatment of a storyline or story angle, which she calls a "narrative," involves stepping back for context and seeking community input:

OA

Avoid the pack journalism mentality and the pack master narrative that so many journalists buy into without really questioning whether that narrative is the real narrative, or whether there is a narrative that is more compelling to readers. In terms of strategies, a lot of it is stepping back, and trying to figure what is going on: Is it true? Are there other avenues I can report? And then begin to really report it. You have to work at a place where an editor will trust your reporting. Look for more compelling stories so you can pitch a story and say, "Everyone is reporting this, but my reporting says this is happening."

If you look to the same old sources, you're probably going to get stuck in the same old master narrative everyone else is. Trying to cultivate different sources from different places from different points of view on a story is a no brainer but not enough people do it.

We go to people who have high titles but might not have high knowledge about the situation you're reporting on. I don't think [online audience] comments alone on a story quite do it, but if you begin to listen for threads in your community and common patterns, you begin to see reporting opportunities. Through crowdsourcing . . . you can systematize how people can contribute to stories.[12]

ON ASSIGNMENT

Journalists might have an advantage when it comes to using de-biasing techniques discussed in the next section because they are applying them on the job, where their efforts are supported by professional principles, training and education. Once you review the techniques, you may use the tips in Exhibit 10.1 to keep debiasing on your mind while you work.

Cognitive Debiasing Strategies

This mental form of debiasing involves techniques aimed at changing the way people think about a problem. For a journalist, that "prob-

exhibit 10.1   PROMOTING DEBIASING

Two reminders to keep debiasing at the forefront of your thinking:	
TIP #1: **Remember the payoff.**	Adopting a broad-minded, discovery-oriented approach to the world leads to excellent journalism. You'll produce stories and images that are honest and insightful—and that so often the competition doesn't have.
TIP #2: **Make debiasing a habit.**	This happens when we understand what debiasing requires and are intrinsically motivated to do it.[13] If you don't feel all that motivated, review the On Assignment comments by successful working journalists throughout this book. They tell us to trust the truth of Tip 1.

lem" might be the focus of the nut graph or the overall angle on the story. Cognitive strategies help offset merely a handful of cognitive errors, but these few errors are pervasive to how people think.

Consider the opposite

Pausing to think of the ways in which an initial judgment or decision might be wrong can reduce the impact of flawed thinking.[14] Overconfidence in our decision-making abilities, for example, can be cured in part by asking ourselves to *consider the opposite* of our initial judgment: What if the mayor really didn't make those racist comments? What if it's a smear campaign by his opponent? How can I document that?

Some past miscalculations by the news media would have benefitted from the technique of considering the opposite. One memorable instance is the public indictment of security guard Richard Jewell for a deadly bomb attack during the 1996 Summer Olympics in Atlanta, Georgia. Initially portrayed as a hero for saving lives, Jewell became a lead suspect in the case and endured harsh treatment in the media. Another man was eventually found guilty of the crime. Said one commentator:

> Jewell was the security guard at the 1996 Atlanta Olympics who alerted authorities to a suspicious knapsack, hurried people away from it, probably saved a number of lives—and then, for 88 days, found himself not only the prime suspect of the FBI investigation into the bombing but the subject of withering media scrutiny that all but tried and convicted him. . . .

Media coverage of Jewell took on a life of its own, all out of proportion to the facts and evidence of the case. Playing the role of judge, jury and psychologist, the press turned Jewell into a caricature of a "lone bomber," a pudgy guy who lived with his mom and, according to unnamed sources, seemed zealous in performing his security duties and overly eager for a law enforcement career. . . .

In Jewell's case, the media strung together circumstantial scraps of information and shaped them to fit a narrative story line about the type of person the media presumed to be guilty. . . . As it turned out, Jewell's sole connection with the bombing was purely circumstantial: he happened to be there doing his job.[15]

Asking how an initial decision might be wrong can counteract an overly narrow sample of evidence. It forces journalists to explore alternatives and evaluate new information. "Consider the opposite" works because it forces journalists to take into account information they might not otherwise use.[16]

"I covered a story about homeless policy in San Francisco awhile back and I came in with my own set of assumptions. I had an anti-establishment view of it. But in my reporting, I grew to have all sorts of questions about the ways that the homeless advocates appeared to be contributing to the homeless problem themselves because of their own polarizing rhetoric. It literally gave me writer's block. When I finally wrote the story, I heard from both sides after it ran. I was told it was the most balanced story people had read on the homeless issue in San Francisco. That was my most memorable situation where I had to confront my own biases."[17]

LINDA JUE
FOUNDING DIRECTOR AND EXECUTIVE EDITOR,
G. W. WILLIAMS CENTER FOR INDEPENDENT JOURNALISM

Consider alternatives

In addition to considering the opposite, one of the most effective strategies for reducing judgmental biases is to *consider ANY alternative to the judgment made*.[18] Simply thinking of alternative story angles or leads can help reporters and editors counter biases in one direction or another. This takes time and freedom, however. Research shows that the quality of one's decision-making is affected by stress.[19] Not surprisingly, the higher the pressure, the more frantic one's thinking, the less one is able to gather useful evidence. Particularly on complex stories, it's worth filing a bit later in order to provide a news audience with a solid, insightful story.

On quick-hit or less complex stories, do the Two-Minute Brainstorm. Sit down someplace where you won't get interrupted for 120 seconds. Have a piece of paper and pen, no keyboards or keypads. Write every story angle you can think of, however wacky. Allow your mind to unlock closed doors to peek inside at possibilities not yet considered. Even if you come upon a better angle to pursue and have to run the story you have in hand, you can at least remove any words or phrases that imply you aren't aware of broader themes. At this point, you want to file a story that doesn't do damage. Then come back with a story following the better angle.

Training

Formal training in statistics, logic and basic economics helps people develop better reasoning strategies.[20] There is no shortage of training available online, some of it free, through reputable organizations and institutions. Newsroom-based training is sometimes available too. Seek out training in database reporting, probability, newsroom math and how to read scientific studies with sample size in mind; the larger the sample size, the more precise the estimates are and the more credible the study. Such training can help journalists integrate data in daily reporting more comfortably and accurately.

Perspective-taking

Research indicates that the most effective way to avoid stereotyping is to take a positive, outward approach to evaluating someone. That means *not* thinking to oneself, "I will suppress that negative stereotype. I will not think about it." This approach can backfire and lead to the stereotype being more easily brought to mind.[21] Try suppressing a negative stereotype for a day, and you'll see how hard it is. For instance, do you change your stereotype of ill-clad instructors by consciously deciding, "I will *not* think that all professors are poorly dressed nerds"?

Instead, entertain the perspective of someone else. **Perspective-taking** means imagining yourself in the position of the person you often stereotype. It does not mean guessing how the person might feel in this position, but how *you* would feel in a similar situation. Focusing on circumstances and limitations or problems in a *situation* rather than the limitations or problems with a person's *disposition* might reduce the intrusion of stereotypes into decisions as varied as courtroom verdicts or employee promotion, studies show.[22]

Seeing oneself in the same situation capitalizes on our natural egotism and allows us to think about how we would feel and think if we were in that position, especially regarding people in a group to which we do not belong or identify with. For example, if we see more of ourselves in people who are elderly, if we imagine our older selves and attendant circumstances, we will be kinder to them and less likely to stereotype them, research suggests. Our selfish concern for ourselves can lead to positive social consequences. Perspective-taking has been shown to reduce the expression of and even the accessibility in one's mind of stereotypes about others.[23]

Perspective-taking may help reporters understand the behaviors and motivations of sources they interview. It may also encourage them to consider circumstances and not just personality traits when explaining people's actions. But this technique must be used with care—a journalist must also maintain distance and critical thinking about sources. Taking someone's perspective cannot mean slanting coverage in her favor. It is only a tool to better understand a person's motivations for acting, especially when that person is someone toward whom a journalist does not easily relate. Perspective-taking is not an excuse for one-sided or fawning coverage.

Motivational and Technological Debiasing Techniques

Motivational debiasing focuses on incentives or accountability.[24] For example, if a journalist has in the past received complaints from news consumers about blatant stereotyping in his work, he may approach future interactions differently, resulting in stories that depend less on stereotypes and more on individual, personalized information. In another example of motivational debiasing, if a journalist thinks that she will have to explain her decision to others, she will put more effort into making a sound one.

Another strategy is to avoid information that might bias judgment. Some scholars call this *exposure control.*[25] Judges do this when they don't allow juries to hear certain evidence. Wayne Drehs of ESPN.com does this when he's going to profile an athlete; he purposely reads little about his subject *before* meeting him or her so as not to contaminate his thinking with other people's judgments of the athlete. He tries to give the source the benefit of a mind that is "a clean slate."[26]

But preventing so-called "mental contamination" is difficult because often we don't know what may bias us until we've been exposed to the information. However, we can look for patterns; we can look at our reactions over time about a specific person or issue, or at feedback from a variety of sources that suggest the same bias. Or, we can compare our reactions to different groups of people to see whether there is a pattern of judgment that suggests unwanted biases.[27]

Technological debiasing, such as online comments and crowd-sourcing, improves reasoning through electronic tools. Another related tool is **group decision-making.**[28] Groups can serve as an error-checking mechanism during discussion. People with complementary skills interact, and having more people in the conversation dilutes the power of poor thinking. The more people, the more experience, the better the decision. The diversity of perspectives is larger in a group.[29]

In a newsroom setting, a group can be a collection of editors making decisions about what runs on the front page. It can be an investigative reporting team hashing out projects. Listservs and online discussion groups can offer fresh input on possible story topics.

Groups can serve as error-checking systems, and, in more diverse newsrooms, groups can increase the range of experiences available to influence decisions about story coverage or story play, for instance. Group decision-making works best if a news organization not only values and is open to diversity, but also actually *has* a diverse new staff, including diversity of ideology, race and ethnicity, sexual orientation, religious affiliation, geography and socioeconomic status. A newsroom filled with people from similar cultures may more readily deliver narrowly casted news accounts, not inclusive, innovative storytelling.

THE REFLECTIVE JOURNALIST'S MENTAL TOOLBOX

Atheme throughout this book is growing awareness of one's out-ward practices and inward thought processes. Journalists start with a set of skills and knowledge about how to do their jobs. In fact, much of journalism is predictable, involving actions and judgments that are common and routine, like what to include in an obituary or how to lead an inverted-pyramid story on last night's house fire.

Scholar Donald Schön wrote that:

> Many practitioners, locked into a view of themselves as technical experts, find nothing in the world of practice to occasion reflection. They have become too skillful at techniques of selective inattention, junk categories, and situational control, techniques which they use to preserve the constancy of their knowledge-in-practice. For them, uncertainty is a threat; its admission is a sign of weakness.[30]

Schön is describing the technical prowess many professional journalists have learned by experience: how to "write around" a hole in information, how to adeptly manage breaking news situations, how to marginalize a difficult source, what to expect from common scenarios. They never seem uncertain or unsure.

Similarly, students of the craft are taught to become technical experts. Education focuses on building skills, writing a solid lead, memorizing Associated Press style, uploading video and assembling a slideshow. All are essential skills.

But technical skills alone cannot capture and reflect to news audiences the depth, breadth and nuance in our contemporary multicultural society. Pure technical skills don't acknowledge the thinking power needed for excellent journalism. Excellent journalism goes beyond the technical to acknowledge the workings of the mind, both of the journalist and of the source. Excellent journalism comes from knowing that human thinking is efficient and elegant, but also sometimes flawed. There is worth in increasing one's awareness of when and how to correct biases.

Tools for a Career

What has to be present for debiasing to work? Elements helpful in combatting cognitive biases are awareness of what the bias is, its magnitude, motivation to correct it, and the mental control to do so.[31] It is not enough to want to be fair and inclusive; the mind also needs specific tools and techniques to reformat thinking. Exhibit 10.2 recaps many such techniques discussed throughout the book, with a reference to the chapter in which they are discussed in depth.

exhibit 10.2   TWENTY WAYS TO CULTIVATE AN OPEN MIND

1. Nurture the curious attitude, self-awareness and cultural knowledge necessary for effective multicultural reporting. *(Chapter 1)*

2. Be aware of the cultural borders you cross and how your own culture affects your perspective on events. Look for differences among subgroups in a culture. (Review the Maynard Institute's Fault Lines.) *(Chapter 1)*

3. Know your standpoint on the world, the position from which you judge things. This standpoint is influenced by factors such as your age, place of residence, religious beliefs, ethnicity or race, education level, income level and sexual orientation. *(Chapter 2)*

4. Be a reflective practitioner. Find time on a regular basis to pause and reflect on your work. *(Chapter 2)*

5. Use the power of stimulus-driven thinking. This high-effort, intentional thinking helps you consider aspects of a person individually and not as representative of an entire cultural group. *(Chapter 3)*

6. Counterargue your story hypothesis. Explain to someone why your point of view on the story might be wrong in order to entertain other ways of thinking about news happenings. *(Chapter 3)*

7. Look at news events from multiple perspectives to improve recall of details, notice the overlooked and consider information in new ways. *(Chapter 3)*

8. Know yourself. Are you a narrow categorizer or a broad one? Are you uncertainty- or certainty-oriented? What is your orientation toward social groups other than your own? Know your natural tendencies so as to better prevent them from distorting news accounts. *(Chapters 4 and 9)*

9. Replace your negative stereotypes about others with more neutral attitudes. *(Chapters 4 and 10)*

10. Practice Big Umbrella journalism. Think inclusively, not exclusively, so as to broaden your categorization of a news subject. Ask questions from an inclusive, not an exclusive, standpoint. *(Chapter 5)*

(continued)

exhibit 10.2   TWENTY WAYS TO CULTIVATE AN OPEN MIND, *continued*

11. Understand sources' cultural patterns and how they influence basic aspects of life such as work, time and communication. These patterns can help explain behaviors. *(Chapter 5)*

12. Sharpen your attention and fill gaps in observation by developing an eye for what other outlets are ignoring. Look past status quo sources for nontraditional news sources. Question formulaic coverage. *(Chapter 6)*

13. Be accountable to your news audience and your sources. Expect that you will be called upon to justify your work. Is your story factual and fair? *(Chapter 7)*

14. Devote yourself to accuracy. You'll expend more effort on reasoning through issues, pay more attention to relevant information and process it more deeply. *(Chapter 7)*

15. Develop an ear for Blab-speak. Blabs include euphemisms, which are code for offensive and sometimes prejudiced associations. *(Chapter 8)*

16. Challenge sources to clarify their language involving controversial subjects. *(Chapter 8)*

17. Seek the representative anecdote, not the exceptional one. *(Chapter 9)*

18. Train your mind to look for population-based statistics that anchor your story. *(Chapter 9)*

19. Consider the opposite and consider any alternative. This opens your mind to new information or information previously discounted. *(Chapter 10)*

20. Practice empathy. Make the unfamiliar familiar. *(Chapter 10)*

Taking time to reflect and consider how you approach sources, issues and events will improve your journalism. Reflecting on your practice of journalism will serve you throughout your career. Journalists have the rare opportunity to ask strangers about their lives, and amazingly often, the strangers allow us in. Tell the stories of others as you would want your own told—with precision, context and an open mind.

exploration EXERCISES

1. In "Ana's Story," Thomas Curwen of the *Los Angeles Times* strove to use straightforward language in describing Ana Rodarte's appearance. He explains below:

   > As with all stories, honesty—in the use of words and descriptions—was critical. There were small details—identifying neurofibromatosis as a disorder and not a disease—but most critically, I wanted to make sure that I didn't shy away from describing Ana's appearance. While I wanted to be sensitive to her and to her parents, I had to make sure I addressed the readers' concerns and curiosities. If I were too sensitive, I wouldn't be doing my job, and in a way, I would be closeting the disorder.[32]

   a. Access the audio slideshow, text and photo gallery of "Ana's Story" through your newsroom or university news database or online at www.latimes.com/ana.

   b. Look at the photos that accompany Curwen's story. Write your own description of Ana's face. Also, write a few lines about your thoughts when you first looked at the photos.

   c. Compare Curwen's descriptions in the published stories with your own descriptions. What different words are used? How does the tone differ?

   d. Decide whether Curwen struck the balance between sensitivity and honesty in describing Ana's appearance. Share your comments in a one-page reaction paper with specific examples from the article.

2. Put reflective practice to work for you. After a story you produced is aired or published, spend time assessing the work. Mentally backtrack through the key decisions in the story process. Ask yourself the following questions:

   a. What do I particularly like about this story?

   b. What skill did I most use on this piece? (This could be a technical skill, such as a well-written phrase or outstanding video clip. It could be a reporting skill, such as getting an on-the-record quote from a reticent source or asking a particularly insightful question. It might be a processing skill, in that your mind saw a fresh angle or realized a deeper truth at work in the story.)

    c. What do I wish I'd done better? How can I improve in that area? (Identify a strategy. It might be scheduling an interview with a source for background research, enrolling in online training, or reading up on a particular culture.)

    d. Make note of your conclusions. Put them to use when doing your next story.

3. Read, watch or listen to a critical commentary on the U.S. news media's handling of a recent issue involving a cultural group. Brush up on the issue itself. Write a blog posting that addresses these issues:

- Define the issue and provide a link to a reliable news account on the issue.

- Decide whether cognitive bias may be a factor in the reporting of this issue. Identify the bias and show how it applies.

- Summarize the criticism of the news media and link to the source(s) of the criticism.

- Consider the source(s) of the criticism and the viewpoint the source represents.

- Explain whether or not you agree with the criticism and support your answer.

4. After reading all or part of *Overcoming Bias,* make your own list of ways to cultivate an open mind. Include suggestions from throughout the book that particularly resonated with you. Post the list in your work space for reference and reflection.

FOR review

- List some challenges to debiasing one's thinking.
- Identify the elements necessary for debiasing to occur.
- Memorize at least five techniques for more open-minded thinking.

notes

1. Thomas Curwen, "Ana's Story," *Los Angeles Times* (April 4, 2009), http://articles.latimes.com/2009/apr/05/local/me-ana5, p. 2, retrieved January 9, 2011.

2. Thomas Curwen, Interview with author, 2010.

3. Ibid.

4. Society of Professional Journalists, "Code of Ethics" (1996), http://www.spj.org/ethicscode.asp, retrieved January 9, 2011.

5. Irene V. Blair, "The Malleability of Automatic Stereotypes and Prejudice," *Personality and Social Psychology Review 6,* no. 3 (2002).

6. Ibid.

7. John F. Dovidio and Samuel L. Gaertner, "Reducing Prejudice: Combating Intergroup Biases," *Current Directions in Psychological Science* (1999).

8. Edward R. Hirt and Keith D. Markman, "Multiple Explanation: A Consider-an-Alternative Strategy for Debiasing Judgments," *Journal of Personality and Social Psychology 69,* no. 6 (1995); Charles G. Lord, Lee Ross, and Mark R. Lepper, "Biased Assimilation and Attitude Polarization: The Effects of Prior Theories on Subsequently Considered Evidence," *Journal of Personality and Social Psychology 37* (1979); R. Schuette and R. H. Fazio, "Attitude Accessibility and Motivation as Determinants of Biased Processing: A Test of the MODE Model," *Personality and Social Psychology Bulletin 21* (1995).

9. Susan T. Fiske and Shelley E. Taylor, *Social Cognition* (New York: Random House, 1984); C. N. Macrae, A. B. Milne, and G. V. Bodenhausen, "Stereotypes as Energy-Saving Devices: A Peek inside the Cognitive Toolbox," *Journal of Personality and Social Psychology 66* (1984).

10. Richard E. Petty and Duane T. Wegener, "Flexible Correction Processes in Social Judgment: Correcting for Context-Induced Contrast," *Journal of Experimental Social Psychology 29,* no. 2 (1993).

11. Timothy D. Wilson and Nancy Brekke, "Mental Contamination and Mental Correction: Unwanted Influences on Judgments and Evaluations," *Psychological Bulletin 116,* no. 1 (1994).

12. Jan Schaffer, Interview with author, August, 2010.

13. Richard P. Larrick, "Debiasing," in *Blackwell Handbook of Judgment and Decision Making,* ed. Derek J. Koehler and Nigel Harvey (Malden, Mass.: Blackwell, 2004).

14. Ibid.

15. Leonard Steinhorn, "Media Watch: Now's a Good Time to Remember Richard Jewell" (July 5, 2002), George Mason University, http://hnn.us/articles/149.html, retrieved February 4, 2011.

16. Larrick, "Debiasing."

17. Linda Jue, Personal communication, July, 2010.

18. Hirt and Markman, "Multiple Explanation."

19. Jonathan Baron, *Thinking and Deciding,* 4th ed. (Cambridge: Cambridge University Press, 2008).

20. Larrick, "Debiasing."

21. Adam D. Galinsky and Gordon B. Moskowitz, "Perspective-Taking: Decreasing Stereotype Expression, Stereotype Accessibility, and In-Group Favoritism," *Journal of Personal and Social Psychology 78,* no. 4 (2000).

22. Ibid.

23. Ibid.

24. Larrick, "Debiasing."

25. Timothy D. Wilson, David B. Centerbar, and Nancy Brekke, "Mental Contamination and the Debiasing Problem," in *Heuristics and Biases: The Psychology of Intuitive Judgment,* ed. Thomas Gilovich, Dale Griffin, and Daniel Kahneman (Cambridge: Cambridge University Press, 2002).

26. Wayne Drehs, Interview with author, 2010.

27. Wilson, Centerbar, and Brekke, "Mental Contamination and the Debiasing Problem."

28. Larrick, "Debiasing."

29. Ibid.

30. Donald A. Schön, *The Reflective Practitioner: How Professionals Think in Action* (New York: Basic Books, 1983), p. 69.

31. Wilson, Centerbar, and Brekke, "Mental Contamination and the Debiasing Problem."

32. Curwen, Interview with author, 2010.

Story Excerpts

Visit this book's website, www.hhpcommunities.com/overcomingbias, for links to some of these stories.

Chapter 1 Context, Culture and Cognition

Harvesting a Dream—Migrant Workers Sow Sweat, Reap Survival
Chicago Tribune, June 13, 1993
BY SUE ELLEN CHRISTIAN

. . . All the men who work at the sod farm are natives of the village of La Cienaga in the south of Mexico. They know one another's wives. Their children attend the same schools. The common knowledge weaves through their conversations when the dinner dishes are done and there is idle time before sleep.

As at most farms, the men take turns cooking meals. Their kitchen is crowded with three stoves and a battalion of four mismatched refrigerators, one of which is held shut by a rubber trash can fastener.

Most farms quit early on Friday afternoon, when workers pour into the nearest town for the week's groceries. If work has been slow and money is scarce, the migrants can get bags of food from a local church pantry or use vouchers provided by the Illinois Migrant Council.

The sod farm workers say about half of the adult men leave La Cienaga each growing season to work on American farms. Only 5 percent bring their families.

"It costs too much to bring the family," said Emilio Sanchez, 46, who has a wife and six children and has been coming to the farm for six years.

"Plus, you have to fix the papers to bring them."

Chapter 2 Habits of Thought

A Woman's Place: At a Kabul Clinic,
Childbirth Means a Cold Table and a Tireless Doctor
The Washington Post, February 24, 2002
BY TERESA WILTZ

(Author's note: This excerpt refers to Zohra, who is Dr. Zohra Wali, an obstetrician/gynecologist at the 52 Beds Clinic in Kabul, Afghanistan.)

. . . Freedom is relative. At first glance Kabul seems to be a vast metropolis teeming with men and boys, punctuated only by the occasional anonymous blue burqa darting through traffic. Westerners here—relief workers, military personnel, journalists—have dubbed them with a cynical acronym: BMOs, or Blue Moving Objects.

But here, in Zohra's world, a female world, the burqa is more than a potent symbol of her place in society. Rather, it is both prop and shield, handled matter-of-factly, folded away or pushed off the shoulder like a heavy curtain of hair.

Still, for at least one patient, the sight of a man entering the clinic is enough to send her darting for a corner. She turns her face away, wrapping the cobalt fabric of her burqa around her skinny frame like a shroud. It is as if she believes the garment is a magic cloak that will make her invisible.

She is right.

There are no men here, no proud fathers passing out cigars, no birth coaches urging, "Breathe!"

The men wait elsewhere, sometimes for hours or days, anticipating news from their women.

It is the Muslim custom, Zohra explains. It's not good for a man to witness the delivery.

Chapter 4 Story Without Stereotype

Unplanned Parenthood—A Mix of Fear and Ignorance in the Slums
Chicago Tribune, February 1, 1996
BY LAURIE GOERING AND KERRY LUFT

. . . When Somalia arrived in Rio in 1975 life wasn't much easier. She took a job as a live-in maid. By then, her teenage boyfriend, the father of her first child, had abandoned her. He reappeared a year later only to take their son, claiming Somalia was unfit to raise him. She has not seen either of them since.

That same year she met Absolon da Silva, a quiet, barrel-chested furniture delivery man separated from his first wife who was also a migrant from Brazil's parched northeast.

Six months later they bought their first barraca—a wood-and-plastic shack—for $3.

They tried not to have children right away, even though neither of them had heard of modern birth control. They tried techniques passed on by friends—techniques that mostly left both of them sexually frustrated.

Before long, Somalia was pregnant again, this time with Lizandra, her oldest daughter.

Viviane, her third child, came a year and three months later, followed by Milani, Erica, Aline and Jessica.

"They just came," she says, gathering the giggling black-haired girls in her arms. "When I started to understand, the house was already full."

Somalia learned about birth control gradually and without much formal instruction. And, as with many Brazilian women, the results of her sex education were not what she would have hoped.

She had heard from friends in Timbauba about an herb that could be brewed into a contraceptive tea. But after arriving in Rio, Somalia found that the herb wouldn't grow in such a humid climate. The tender seedlings blackened and died on her windowsill.

Chapter 5   Understanding Culture, Understanding Sources

Bringing It Home: U.S. Earnings Mean Better Life for Melgozas in Mexico
Ventura County Star, April 6, 1997
BY M. E. SPRENGELMEYER

Ocotlan, Mexico—For Ana and Jose Luis Melgoza, a dream retirement is finally becoming a reality 1,400 miles south of the border.

After 30 years of building a family and a business in Ventura County, they've settled back here in Ana's hometown . . .

The Melgozas' story has a typical beginning.

Jose Luis Sr. was born in the state of Michoachan and Ana was raised here in Ocotlan, 60 miles south of Guadalajara. Both of their families took them to Ventura County in the 1960s, when they were in their teens.

They started in menial jobs. Jose picked lemons, and Ana worked as a seamstress, stitching together brassieres in a factory.

They met at Our Lady of Guadalupe Church in Santa Paula, married and started a family in Fillmore. Jose took a new job at a factory that made Plexiglas windows. Later, he worked for Mr. Spa in Camarillo, making hot tubs and Jacuzzis.

The family saved money, and when Jose was laid off in the mid-1980s they decided to go into business for themselves. They opened The Melgoza Family Restaurant on Seventh Street near downtown Oxnard and started serving up such Jalisco specialties as birria de chivo, or goat stew.

With the two kids helping in the restaurant, they put away money for a piece of land back in Ocotlan. Slowly, they started building their retirement home. They even bought a fancy Jacuzzi like the ones Jose used to make in Camarillo.

Last summer, they sold the restaurant to a friend and headed south.

Author's note: Readers can access all five parts of Sprengelmeyer's series through the website for the City of Oxnard, Calif., at the following link: www.ci.oxnard.ca.us/Department.aspx?DepartmentID=22&DivisionID=108&ResourceID=527

Chapter 7 Critical Decisions Before Deadline

Homeowners Facing Foreclosure Demand Recourse
The New York Times, October 27, 2010
BY ANDREW MARTIN AND MOTOKO RICH

Ricky Rought paid cash to the Deutsche Bank National Trust Company for a four-room cabin in Michigan with the intention of fixing it up for his daughter. Instead, the bank tried to foreclose on the property and the locks were changed, court records show.

Sonya Robison is facing a foreclosure suit in Colorado after the company handling her mortgage encouraged her to skip a payment, she says, to square up for mistakenly changing the locks on her home, too.

Thomas and Charlotte Sexton, of Kentucky, were successfully foreclosed upon by a mortgage trust that, according to court records, does not exist.

As lenders have reviewed tens of thousands of mortgages for errors in recent weeks, more and more homeowners are stepping forward to say that they were victims of bank mistakes—and in many cases, demanding legal recourse.

Some homeowners say the banks tried to foreclose on a house that did not even have a mortgage. Others say they believed they were negotiating with the bank in good faith. Still others say that even though they are delinquent on their mortgage payments, they deserve the right to due process before being evicted.

Some consumer lawyers say they are now swamped with homeowners saying they have been wronged by slipshod bank practices and want to fight to keep their homes. Joseph deMello, a Massachusetts lawyer who represents Mr. Rought, said the common denominator in many of the cases was an overwhelmed system of foreclosures in which banks relied on subcontractors to do much of the work.

Chapter 8   The Power of Words and Tone

"Greatest Prom" Worth the Wait—Memories of Lifetime Are Weeks in Making
The Washington Post, May 23, 2001
BY CHRISTINA A. SAMUELS

. . . For all the positives of mainstreaming special-needs students into regular schools, Viggiani said, not many of these students would be attending their prom if they were in regular schools.

Erin took a spin on the floor with her father during "My Girl," one of her mother's favorite songs. She danced with Dr. V and with Jasen ("He is great," she said, fanning her face with an exaggerated motion). As one of two students graduating from the school in June, Erin was presented a dozen red roses and a balloon saying "Congratulations."

In two hours, the sandwiches were eaten, the "Moonlight and Roses" sheet cake was gone and the party was over. Parents stacked chairs and folded up tables.

Erin wouldn't leave. Every step forward was followed with two steps back for another hug, another compliment from a teacher, one last picture with a friend.

"This is the greatest prom," Erin said.

"So you'll remember this when you're old and gray?" her father asked.

With exaggerated youthful embarrassment—who thinks about being old and gray on prom night?—Erin laughed like she had been laughing all night. "Oh, great. Thanks for saying that."

Four days later, a little post-prom magic persisted. The balloon was tied to her bookcase, the little pearl pocketbook hung from a dresser drawer knob. Erin admitted that, come graduation, "I'm going to miss my principal. He's great."

Her father has held on to one of the red napkins from the night, printed with "Moonlight and Roses" in silver script.

Chapter 9   Attribution and Editing Without Bias

Cracks Found in War on Drugs—Records of Police Raids Suggest Sloppy Procedure
Columbus Dispatch, December 10, 1989
BY MICHAEL J. BERENS AND ROGER SNELL

Just after dusk, SWAT officers stormed the house at 464 S. Champion Ave., knocking open the front door with a metal battering ram and sweeping through the house, finding lots of crack and bundles of cash.

Donning bulletproof vests, Mayor Dana G. Rinehart and School Superintendent Ronald E. Etheridge tagged along with the media to witness what police called a typical night on Crack Street.

Rinehart and Etheridge later posed inside the house for cameras, holding up clear plastic bags filled with cash and drugs.

By all accounts, the crack raid on Dec. 14, 1988, was considered one of the police narcotics bureau's most successful.

Since then, The Dispatch also has learned that:

Officers never listed on court records the amount of money they seized that night. They simply wrote "cash" on an inventory sheet attached to a search warrant.

Police never mentioned this bust on their official list of crack raids.

A Dispatch computer study of every search warrant obtained by the Columbus narcotics bureau since January 1988 shows police did not record the amount of cash in 79 of 340 crack raids.

Police also claim to have conducted 481 crack raids since January 1988, but the county records account for only 340.

Chapter 10   Journalism and Reflective Practice

A Fate She Didn't Ask For, a Face She'd Like to Change
Los Angeles Times, April 5, 2009
BY THOMAS CURWEN

. . . It is hard to say what my assumptions were when I first saw Ana. The manager of public relations at Scripps Memorial Hospital in San Diego had told me that the hospital and a local doctor were about to treat a young woman with facial tumors similar to the so-called Elephant Man's.

The surgical plan was ambitious, and because the woman and her family could not afford the cost, the hospital and the doctors would donate their services. Would I be interested in such a story?

Certainly I was intrigued. I knew about Joseph Merrick and vividly remembered the 1980 movie about his life, David Lynch's "The Elephant Man."

I made arrangements to meet Ana at Scripps a few days after Christmas in 2005. She was there for a CT scan and an MRI, waiting in a private room, away from the prying eyes of other patients.

We sat across from each other, making small talk, and I initially noticed everything but her face: the studded bell-bottom blue jeans, the baggy, dark-gray sweat shirt that covered a T-shirt emblazoned with "'80s Rock," the pink Hello Kitty purse.

Her curly dark hair was lush and tied back. Her ears were pierced, and she wore small silver studs in them. She had a demure manner, and she turned away from me when she spoke.

I got the impression she wanted all of this—the hospital, the reporter—to go away. Still, I felt provoked by her shyness. I wanted to look at her straight on, but I didn't. I didn't want to make her feel self-conscious, yet I wanted to see evidence of God's meanness.

To be in her company was to feel both pity and curiosity, and as we talked about the complexity of the surgeries that lay ahead, I asked her what she was most afraid of.

B

Surveys and Questionnaires

SOCIAL ATTITUDE SURVEY (Chapter 1)

P lease respond to all items in the survey. Remember there are no right or wrong answers. Please circle the appropriate number to the right.

Strongly Disagree	Disagree	Not Sure	Agree	Strongly Agree
1	2	3	4	5

1. I do think it is more appropriate for the mother of a newborn baby, rather than the father, to stay home with the baby during the first year.   1 2 3 4 5

2. It is as easy for women to succeed in business as it is for men.   1 2 3 4 5

3. I really think affirmative action programs on college campuses constitute reverse discrimination.   1 2 3 4 5

4. I feel I could develop an intimate relationship with someone from a different race.   1 2 3 4 5

5. All Americans should learn to speak two languages.   1 2 3 4 5

6. I look forward to the day when a woman is president of the United States.   1 2 3 4 5

7. Generally speaking, men work harder than women.   1 2 3 4 5

8. My friendship network is very racially mixed.   1 2 3 4 5

9. I am against affirmative action programs in business.   1 2 3 4 5

10. Generally, men seem less concerned with building relationships than do women.   1 2 3 4 5

11. I would feel O.K. about my son or daughter dating someone from a different race. 1 2 3 4 5

12. I was very happy when an African American was elected president of the United States in 2008.* 1 2 3 4 5

13. In the past few years there has been too much attention directed toward multicultural issues in education. 1 2 3 4 5

14. I think feminist perspectives should be an integral part of the higher education curriculum. 1 2 3 4 5

15. Most of my close friends are from my own racial group. 1 2 3 4 5

16. I feel somewhat more secure that a man rather than a woman is currently president of the United States. 1 2 3 4 5

17. I think that it is (or would be) important for my children to attend schools that are racially mixed. 1 2 3 4 5

18. In the past few years there has been too much attention directed towards multicultural issues in business. 1 2 3 4 5

19. Overall, I think racial minorities in America complain too much about racial discrimination. 1 2 3 4 5

20. I feel (or would feel) very comfortable having a woman as my primary physician. 1 2 3 4 5

21. I think the president of the United States should make a concerted effort to appoint more women and racial minorities to the country's Supreme Court. 1 2 3 4 5

22. I think white people's racism toward racial minority groups still constitutes a major problem in America. 1 2 3 4 5

23. I think the school system, from elementary school through college, should encourage minority and immigrant children to learn and fully adopt traditional American values. 1 2 3 4 5

24. If I were to adopt a child, I would be happy to adopt a child of any race. 1 2 3 4 5

25. I think there is as much female physical violence toward men as there is male physical violence toward women. 1 2 3 4 5

26. I think the school system, from elementary school through college, should promote values representative of diverse cultures. 1 2 3 4 5

* Edited to reflect Obama's presidency. The original stated "I look forward to the day when a racial minority person is president of the United States.

27. I believe that reading the autobiography of Malcolm X would   1 2 3 4 5
    be of value.

28. I would enjoy living in a neighborhood consisting of a racially   1 2 3 4 5
    diverse population (e.g., Asians, Blacks, Hispanics, Whites).

29. I think it is better if people marry within their own race.   1 2 3 4 5

30. Women make too big of a deal out of sexual harassment is-   1 2 3 4 5
    sues in the workplace.

Scoring for the Social Attitude Survey

Method One: QDI Total Score

Of the 30 items on the QDI, 15 are worded and scored in a positive direction (high scores indicate high sensitivity to multicultural/gender issues), and 15 are worded and scored in a negative direction (where low scores are indicative of high sensitivity). Naturally, when tallying the Total score response, these latter 15 items need to be *reverse-scored*. Reverse scoring simply means that if a respondent circles a "1" they should get five points, a "2" four points, a "3" three points, a "4" two points, and a "5" one point.

The following QDI items need to be *reversed-scored:*

1, 2, 3, 7, 9, 10, 13, 15, 16, 18, 19, 23, 25, 29, 30.

Score range is 30 to 150, with high scores indicating more awareness, sensitivity, and receptivity to racial diversity and gender equality.

THE SOCIAL DOMINANCE ORIENTATION SCALE   (Chapter 4)

About which of the following concepts or statements do you have a positive or negative feeling? Beside each object or statement, place a number from "1" to "7," which represents the degree of your negative or positive feeling. The scale range is as follows:

Very Negative	Negative	Slightly Negative	Neither Positive nor Negative	Slightly Positive	Positive	Very Positive
1	2	3	4	5	6	7

1. Some groups of people are simply not the equal of others. 1 2 3 4 5 6 7

2. Some people are just more worthy than others. 1 2 3 4 5 6 7

3. This country would be better off if we cared less about how equal all people were. 1 2 3 4 5 6 7

4. Some people are just more deserving than others. 1 2 3 4 5 6 7

5. It is not a problem if some people have more of a chance in life than others. 1 2 3 4 5 6 7

6. Some people are just inferior to others. 1 2 3 4 5 6 7

7. To get ahead in life, it is sometimes necessary to step on others. 1 2 3 4 5 6 7

8. Increased economic equality. 1 2 3 4 5 6 7

9. Increased social equality. 1 2 3 4 5 6 7

10. Equality. 1 2 3 4 5 6 7

11. If people were treated more equally we would have fewer problems in this country. 1 2 3 4 5 6 7

12. In an ideal world, all nations would be equal. 1 2 3 4 5 6 7

13. We should try to treat one another as equals as much as possible. 1 2 3 4 5 6 7

14. It is important that we treat other countries as equals. 1 2 3 4 5 6 7

Scoring Guide for the Social Dominance Orientation Scale

- Items 1–7 are scored as very negative (1) to very positive (7).
- Items 8–14 are scored as very negative (7) to very positive (1).

The higher your score, the more you tend toward a social dominance orientation in relations between different groups of people. See Chapter 4 for more discussion of this orientation.

Source: Felicia Pratto, James Sidanius, Lisa M. Stallworth, and Bertram F. Malle. 1994. Social dominance orientation: A personality variable predicting social and po-

ASSESSING YOUR CATEGORY WIDTH QUESTIONNAIRE   (Chapter 9)

The purpose of this questionnaire is to help you to assess your category width. Respond to each of the statements by indicating the degree to which the statement is true regarding how you typically think about yourself. When you think about yourself, is the statement:

Always False	Usually False	Sometimes True, Sometimes False	Usually True	Always True
1	2	3	4	5

1. I do well on tasks that require integrated information processing.   1 2 3 4 5

2. I do well on tasks that require detailed information processing.   1 2 3 4 5

3. Things can be very dissimilar and share a common quality and I will use the same label to describe them.   1 2 3 4 5

4. I make strong judgments about others.   1 2 3 4 5

5. I do well on tasks that require holistic information processing.   1 2 3 4 5

6. I am confident that I perform well in social situations.   1 2 3 4 5

7. I try to make sure I have sufficient information before judging others.   1 2 3 4 5

8. I do well on tasks that require analytic information processing.   1 2 3 4 5

9. I try to obtain a lot of information before making decisions.   1 2 3 4 5

10. I react strongly to change.   1 2 3 4 5

To find your score, first reverse the responses for the even numbered items (i.e., if you wrote 1, make it a 5; if you wrote 2, make it 4; if you wrote 3, leave it as 3; if you wrote 4, make it 2; if you wrote 5, make it 1). Next, add the numbers. Scores range from 10 to 50. The higher your score, the wider your categories.

Source: Gudykunst, William B. (1998). *Bridging differences: Effective intergroup communication* (3rd ed.). Thousand Oaks, Calif.: Sage, p. 153. Table 5.1.

ASSESSING YOUR UNCERTAINTY
ORIENTATION QUESTIONNAIRE (Chapter 9)

The purpose of this questionnaire is to help you assess your orientation toward uncertainty. Respond to each statement indicating the degree to which it is true regarding the way you typically respond:

Always False	Usually False	Sometimes True, Sometimes False	Usually True	Always True
1	2	3	4	5

1. I do not compare myself with others.   1 2 3 4 5

2. If given a choice, I prefer to go somewhere new rather than somewhere I've been before.   1 2 3 4 5

3. I reject ideas that are different than mine.   1 2 3 4 5

4. I try to resolve inconsistencies in beliefs I hold.   1 2 3 4 5

5. I am not interested in finding out information about myself.   1 2 3 4 5

6. When I obtain new information, I try to integrate it with information I already have.   1 2 3 4 5

7. I hold traditional beliefs.   1 2 3 4 5

8. I evaluate people on their own merit without comparing them to others.   1 2 3 4 5

9. I hold inconsistent views of myself.   1 2 3 4 5

10. If someone suggests an opinion that is different than mine, I do not reject it before I consider it.   1 2 3 4 5

To find your score, first reverse the responses for the odd numbered items (i.e., if you wrote 1, make it 5; if you wrote 2, make it 4; if you wrote 3, leave it as 3; if you wrote 4, make it 2; if you wrote 5, make it 1). Next, add the numbers. Scores range from 10 to 50. The higher your score, the greater your uncertainty orientation.

Source: Gudykunst, William B. (1998). *Bridging differences: Effective intergroup communication* (3rd ed.). Thousand Oaks, Calif.: Sage, pg. 155. Table 5.2.

GLOSSARY

accountability The explicit expectation that one will be called upon to justify one's beliefs, feelings or actions to others.

accuracy of perception Comprises two components: truth and an understanding of the people being covered, meaning a grasp of the beliefs, values and norms that influence a social group's behaviors and decisions.

anchoring heuristic When people base estimates and decisions on "anchors" or familiar positions and then adjust for a final answer.

attribution In cognitive psychology, refers to how people explain the causes of behaviors and events.

availability heuristic A phenomenon in which the more readily we can think of instances of something happening, the more likely we think it will be to happen again.

balance A goal of ethical journalism; requires presenting multiple voices, but not necessarily allotting each viewpoint identical coverage. Journalists must work to discern the most informed, relevant and factual perspectives on issues and offer those to audiences without distortion.

base-rate information Data about the percentage of cases in a population, or the frequency with which an event occurs in a population.

Big Umbrella An inclusive mental placement of groups, both ingroup and outgroup.

category width How broadly a person categorizes things.

certainty-oriented The quality of being uninterested in finding out new information about the world and others; these individuals have a high degree of confidence in their explanations for strangers' behaviors.

cognitive biases Systematic distortions of otherwise correct thinking processes, such as underusing or overusing a particular useful mental function. Automatic, spontaneous and involuntary.

concentric loyalty A model recognizing that membership in and allegiance to two distinct groups can coexist.

confirmation bias   The tendency to seek, interpret and remember information that reinforces one's preconceptions.

conjunction fallacy   When two events that can occur separately are seen as more likely to occur together rather than separately.

connotation   The association a word carries, as opposed to its literal definition.

context   The interrelated conditions in which something exists or occurs.

crowdsourcing   A tool for journalists in seeking and responding to feedback; uses the collaborative information-gathering efforts of news consumers in reporting a news story.

cultural norms   Standards strongly engrained in our lives that offer directions for correct and moral behavior.

culture   A "learned set of shared interpretations about beliefs, values, and norms, which affect the behaviors of a relatively large group of people" (Lustig & Koester, 1999).

debiasing   Techniques to reduce or eliminate distortions or errors in thinking and judgment; these strategies for combatting cognitive error and mental frameworks can be thought of as ways to cultivate a more open mind as a journalist.

denotation   The literal definition of a word.

euphemism   The use of a less direct word or phrase to avoid one that might seem offensive.

event schema   A person's knowledge of the typical sequence of recurring events and regarding standard social occasions; sometimes referred to as a *cognitive script*.

experiential learning   Learning and gaining skills and knowledge by doing, not merely by studying.

explicit stereotypes   The biases that you know you have and knowingly express.

fairness   A goal of ethical journalism; entails considering all relevant perspectives in a news account, and working hard to ensure that the various perspectives are represented clearly and accurately.

framing   The magnifying or shrinking of elements to make them more or less salient, that is, prominent or significant.

fundamental attribution error   The tendency for an observer to overestimate the role of personal, internal factors in affecting behavior and to underestimate the influence of situational factors.

group decision-making   Using groups to provide diversity of perspectives as an error-checking mechanism during discussion.

habits of thought   Common ways of mental processing.

heuristic   A rule of thumb or an aid to problem-solving by trial-and-error. Allows people to make judgments quickly; a mental shortcut.

hindsight bias   Describes how people view something that has happened as being relatively inevitable before it happened.

implicit stereotypes   Subtle biases that affect our attitudes and behavior without our immediate realization.

ingroup members   Those in your own social group, or people with whom you share similar interests and attitudes.

media bias   In general, an intentional and purposeful slanting of the news to a specific viewpoint or ideology.

mental frameworks   The perspective from which one views the world; a viewpoint shaped by background and culture about what is normal or accepted practice and behavior.

metacognition   Thinking about the ways that we think.

motivational debiasing   Focuses on the use of incentives or accountability to reduce cognitive biases.

objectivity   In terms of journalism, according to Michael Bugeja, objectivity means seeing the world as it is, not as the reporter or reader would like it to be. Reporters discern whether they have any biases that might taint a story and, if so, how they might adjust for that when filing a report.

outgroup members   Outsiders, people not in your social group, often viewed as inferior in some way.

perseverance effect   A concept that describes how people's beliefs and schemas persist despite contradictory information.

person schema   A mental file containing your perceptions of a person's traits and goals.

perspective-taking   Imagining yourself in the position of the person you often stereotype; does not refer to guessing how the person might feel in this position, but how you would feel in a similar situation.

Rashomon effect   How individuals remember events differently, but plausibly, from other's remembrances.

reflective practice   Invites professionals to identify and evaluate their automatic perceptions and judgments that have grown up around repeated experience.

representative heuristic   A subjective assessment based on how similar one is in essential characteristics to a parent population; this influences the way people judge probabilities.

role schemas   A person's knowledge about appropriate behaviors attached to social positions; create expectations about people in socially defined categories and can contribute to stereotyping.

schema-driven thinking   Spontaneous and unintentional; low-effort and involving quick judgments based on past experiences.

self-fulfilling prophecy   The tendency for people's expectations to elicit behavior that is consistent with those expectations.

standpoint   The position from which people and things are considered or judged; a point of view or outlook. It determines what we focus on and what we miss; it influences our knowledge of the world.

stereotyping   The application of beliefs about the attributes of a group to judge an individual member of that group.

stimulus-driven thinking   High-effort, controlled thinking that is intentional, conscious, voluntary.

technological debiasing   The use of strategic tools, such as online comments and crowdsourcing, to improve reasoning.

uncertainty-oriented   The quality of being open-minded and evaluating ideas on their own merit, integrating new and old ideas and changing belief systems accordingly.

Allport, Gordon. *The Nature of Prejudice*. Cambridge, Mass.: Addison-Wesley, 1954.

Almond, Louise, Laurence Alison, Marie Eyre, Jonathan Crego, and Alasdair Goodwill. "Heuristics and Biases in Decision-Making." In *Policing Critical Incidents: Leadership and Critical Incident Management*, edited by Laurence Alison and Jonathan Crego, pp. 151–180. Portland, Ore.: Willan, 2008.

Andersen, Kurt. "Rape, Justice, and the 'Times'." *New York Magazine*, Oct. 8, 2006.

Anderson, Craig A. "Inoculation and Counter-Explanation: Debiasing Techniques in the Perseverance of Social Theories." *Social Cognition 1* (1982): 126–39.

Annie E. Casey Foundation. *Kids Count Data Book: Summary of findings*. Baltimore, Md.: Annie E. Casey Foundation, 2011.

Arkes, Hal R. "Costs and Benefits of Judgment Errors: Implications for Debiasing." *Psychological Bulletin 110,* no. 3 (1991): 486–98.

Aronson, Elliot, Timothy D. Wilson, and Robin M. Akert. *Social Psychology* (5th ed.). Upper Saddle River, N.J.: Prentice Hall, 2005.

Banaji, M. R., and A. G. Greenwald. "Implicit Stereotyping and Prejudice." In *The Psychology of Prejudice: The Ontario Symposium, Vol. 7,* edited by M. P. Zanna and J. M. Olson, pp. 55–76. Mahwah, N.J.: Erlbaum, 1994.

Baron, David P. "Persistent Media Bias." *Journal of Public Economics 90* (2006): 1–36.

Baron, Jonathan. *Thinking and Deciding,* 4th ed. Cambridge: Cambridge University Press, 2008.

Bennett, Lisa. "Fifty Years of Prejudice in the Media." *The Gay & Lesbian Review Worldwide 7,* no. 2 (2000).

Berens, Michael J. Interview with author, 2010.

Blair, Irene V. "The Malleability of Automatic Stereotypes and Prejudice." *Personality and Social Psychology Review 6,* no. 3 (2002): 242–61.

Blakley, Jonathan. Personal communication, October 21, 2010.

Boals, Connor. Interview with author, 2010.

Branton, Regina P., and Johanna Dunaway. "Slanted Newspaper Coverage of Immigration: The Importance of Economics and Geography." *Policy Studies Journal 37,* no. 2 (2009): 257–73.

Breslin, Jeffrey W. "Breaking Away from Subtle Biases." In *Negotiation Theory and Practice,* 2nd ed., edited by J. W. Breslin and J. Z. Rubin, pp. 247–50. Cambridge, Mass.: The Program on Negotiation at Harvard Law School, 1993.

Broverman, Aaron, and Kent C. Loftsgard. "Quad Doctors: In or Out?" *New Mobility* (October, 2010), http://www.newmobility.com/articleView.cfm?id=11728.

Brubaker, Rogers, Mara Loveman, and Peter Stamatov. "Ethnicity as Cognition." *Theory and Society 33* (2004): 31–64.

Bugeja, Michael. "Think Like a Journalist: A News Literacy Guide from *NewsTrust.*" *NewsTrust,* http://newstrust.net/guides/think-like-a-journalist.

Chase, Stuart. *The Tyranny of Words.* New York: Harcourt Brace, 1938.

Christian, Sue Ellen. "Harvesting a Dream: Migrant Workers Sow Sweat, Reap Survival." *Chicago Tribune,* June 13, 1993, Metro section, p. 1.

Colon, Aly. "Q & A: Avoiding Bias. Interview with Gelareh Asayesh." Poynter Institute (2002), http://www.poynter.org/content/content_view.asp?id=5852.

Corrigan, Patrick W. "Mental Health Stigma as Social Attribution: Implications for Research Methods and Attitude Change." *Clinical Psychology: Science and Practice 7,* no. 1 (2000): 48–67.

Curwen, Thomas. "Ana's Story." *Los Angeles Times,* April 4, 2009, http://articles.latimes.com/2009/apr/05/local/me-ana5.

Curwen, Thomas. Interview with author, 2010.

D'Agostino, P. R., and R. Fincher-Kiefer. "Need for Cognition and the Correspondence Bias." *Social Cognition 10,* no. 2 (1992): 151–64.

Daily, Catherine, and Dan R. Dalton. "Coverage of Women at the Top: The Press Has a Long Way to Go." *Columbia Journalism Review 39,* no. 2 (2000): 58.

Dang, Alain, and Cabrini Vianney. "Living in the Margins: A National Survey of Lesbian, Gay, Bisexual, and Transgender Asian and Pacific Islander Americans." New York: National Gay and Lesbian Task Force Policy Institute, 2007.

Darley, J. M., and P. H. Gross. "A Hypothesis-Confirming Bias in Labeling Effects." *Journal of Personality and Social Psychology 44,* no. 1 (1983): 20–33.

Dasgupta, Nilanjana. "Implicit Ingroup Favoritism, Outgroup Favoritism, and Their Behavioral Manifestations." *Social Justice Research 17,* no. 2 (2004): 143–69.

Deardorff, Darla K. "Identification and Assessment of Intercultural Competence as a Student Outcome of Internationalization." *Journal of Studies in Intercultural Education 10* (2006): 241–66.

DeLong, Brad, and Susan Rasky. "Twelve Things Economists Need to Remember to Be Helpful to Journalistic Sources." *Nieman Watchdog* (2006).

Detweiler, R. A. "Culture, Category Width, and Attributions." *Journal of Cross-Cultural Psychology 9,* no. 3 (1978): 259–82.

Detweiler, R. A. "On Inferring the Intentions of a Person from Another Culture." *Journal of Personality 43,* no. 4 (1975): 259–84.

Devine, Patricia G. "Stereotypes and Prejudice: Their Automatic and Controlled Components." *Journal of Personality and Social Psychology 56,* no. 1 (1989): 5–18.

Devine, Patricia G., and Lindsay B. Sharp. "Automaticity and Control in Stereotyping and Prejudice." In *Handbook of Prejudice, Stereotyping, and Discrimination,* edited by Todd D. Nelson, pp. 61–88. New York: Psychology Press, 2009.

Dixon, Travis L., and Daniel Linz. "Race and the Misrepresentation of Victimization on Local Television News." *Communication Research 27,* no. 5 (2000): 547–73.

Dovidio, John F., and Samuel L. Gaertner. "Reducing Prejudice: Combating Intergroup Biases." *Current Directions in Psychological Science* (1999): 101–05.

Drehs, Wayne. "Good Deeds Are Warner's Focus," *ESPN.com* (Jan. 29, 2009), http://sports.espn.go.com/nfl/news/story?page=hotread17/kurtwarner.

Drehs, Wayne. Interview with author, 2010.

Duke University Office of News and Communications. "Looking Back at the Duke Lacrosse Case." Duke University, http://today.duke.edu/showcase/lacrosseincident/.

Durkin, Jessica. Interview with author, August, 2010.

Entman, Robert M. "Framing U.S. Coverage of International News: Contrasts in Narratives of the KAL and Iran Air Incidents." *Journal of Communication 41,* no. 4 (1991): 6–27.

Entman, Robert M. "Framing: Toward Clarification of a Fractured Paradigm." *Journal of Communication 43,* no. 4 (1993): 51–58.

Entman, Robert M., and Andrew Rojecki. *The Black Image in the White Mind: Media and Race in America.* Chicago: University of Chicago Press, 2001.

Entman, Robert M., and Kimberly A. Gross. "Race to Judgment: Stereotyping Media and Criminal Defendants." *Law and Contemporary Problems 71* (2008): 93–133.

Fischhoff, Baruch. "Debiasing." In *Judgment under Uncertainty: Heuristics and Biases,* edited by Daniel Kahneman, Paul Slovic, and Amos Tversky, pp. 422–44. Cambridge: Cambridge University Press, 1982.

Fischhoff, Baruch. "For Those Condemned to Study the Past: Heuristics and Biases in Hindsight." In *Judgment under Uncertainty: Heuristics and Biases,* edited by Daniel Kahneman, Paul Slovic, and Amos Tversky. Cambridge: Cambridge University Press, 1982.

Fiske, Susan T. "Social Cognition and the Normality of Prejudgment." In *On the Nature of Prejudice: Fifty Years after Allport,* edited by John F. Dovidio, Peter Glick, and Laurie A. Rudman, pp. 36–53. Malden, Mass.: Blackwell, 2005.

Fiske, Susan T., and Shelley E. Taylor. *Social Cognition.* New York: Random House, 1984.

Fiske, Susan T., and Shelley E. Taylor. *Social Cognition: From Brains to Culture.* Boston: McGraw-Hill, 2008.

Freund, Tallie, Arie W. Kruglanski, and Avint Shpitzajen. "The Freezing and Unfreezing of Impressional Primacy: Effects of the Need for Structure and the Fear of Invalidity." *Personality and Social Psychology Bulletin II*, no. 4 (1985): 479–87.

Fürsich, Elfriede. "How Can Global Journalists Represent 'Other'?" *Journalism 3*, no. 1 (2002): 57–84.

Gaertner, Samuel, and John F. Dovidio. "Categorization, Recategorization, and Intergroup Bias," in *On the Nature of Prejudice: Fifty Years After Allport*, edited by John F. Dovidio, Peter Glick, and Laurie A. Rudman, pp. 71–88. Malden, Mass.: Blackwell, 2005.

Galinsky, Adam D., and Gordon B. Moskowitz. "Perspective-Taking: Decreasing Stereotype Expression, Stereotype Accessibility, and In-Group Favoritism." *Journal of Personal and Social Psychology 78*, no. 4 (2000): 708–24.

Graythen, Chris. Online post, member message board. *SportsShooter.com*, Aug. 31, 2005.

Gudykunst, William B. *Bridging Differences: Effective Intergroup Communication*. Thousand Oaks, Calif.: Sage, 1998.

Gunn, Steve. Interview with author, August, 2010.

Hamill, Ruth, Timothy DeCamp Wilson, and Richard E. Nisbett. "Insensitivity to Sample Bias: Generalizing from Atypical Cases." *Journal of Personality and Social Psychology 39*, no. 4 (1980): 578–89.

Hamilton, James T. *All the News That's Fit to Sell: How the Market Transforms Information into News*. Princeton, N.J.: Princeton University Press, 2004.

Hamm, Benjy. Interview with author, August, 2010.

Hampson, Rick. "Imam's Wife Says, 'We Understand'." *USA Today*, August 22, 2010, p. 1.

Hashtroudi, Shahin, Sharon A. Mutter, Elizabeth A. Cole, and Susan K. Green. "Schema-Consistent and Schema-Inconsistent Information: Processing Demands." *Personality and Social Psychology Bulletin 10*, no. 2 (1984): 269–78.

Hastie, Reid, and Purohit A. Kumar. "Person Memory: Personality Traits as Organizing Principles in Memory for Behaviors." *Journal of Personality and Social Psychology 37*, no. 1 (1979): 25–38.

Heider, Fritz. *The Psychology of Interpersonal Relations*. New York: Wiley, 1958.

Heider, Karl G. "The Rashomon Effect: When Ethnographers Disagree." *American Anthropologist 90*, no. 1 (1988): 73–81.

Hernandez, Macarena. "What Jayson Blair Stole from Me, and Why I Couldn't Ignore It." *Washington Post*, June 1 2003.

Hirsch, Rick. Interview with author, August, 2010.

Hirt, Edward R., and Keith D. Markman. "Multiple Explanation: A Consider-an-Alternative Strategy for Debiasing Judgments." *Journal of Personality and Social Psychology 69* (1995): 1069–86.

Hofstede, Geert. *Cultures and Organizations: Software of the Mind*. New York: McGraw-Hill, 1991.

Holton, B. "Attributional Biases." In *Magill's Encyclopedia of Social Psychology,* edited by N. Piotrowski. Pasadena, Calif.: Salem Press, 2003.

hooks, bell. "Keeping Close to Home: Class and Education." In *Experiencing Race, Class, and Gender in the United States,* 5th ed., edited by Roberta Fiske-Rusciano, 140–47. Boston: McGraw-Hill, 2009.

Howard-Hamilton, Mary F., Brenda J. Richardson, and Bettina Shuford. "Promoting Multicultural Education: A Holistic Approach." *College Student Affairs Journal 18* (1998): 5–17.

Hoyt, Clark. "The Insult Was Extra Large." *New York Times,* August 22, 2009.

Huang, Tom. "Beyond Political Correctness." *Poynter.org* (2011), http://www.poynter.org/how-tos/newsgathering-storytelling/diversity-at-work/23601/beyond-political-correctness/.

Ichheiser, Gustav. "Misunderstandings in Human Relations: A Study in False Social Perception." *American Journal of Sociology 55,* no. 2 (1949).

Irby, Kenneth. "Diversity across the Curriculum Seminar." St. Petersburg, Fla.: Poynter Institute, 2009.

Iyengar, Shanto. "Framing Responsibility for Political Issues: The Case of Poverty." *Political Behavior 12,* no. 1 (1990): 19–40.

Jaschik, Scott. "Anger and Consequences." *Inside Higher Ed* (March 29, 2006), http://www.insidehighered.com/news/2006/03/29/duke.

Jethani, Skye. "An Evangelical Response to the 'Ground Zero Mosque'."(July 30, 2010), http://www.huffingtonpost.com/skye-jethani/an-evangelical-response-t_b_664580.html.

Jost, John T., and David L. Hamilton. "Stereotypes in Our Culture." In *On the Nature of Prejudice: Fifty Years after Allport,* edited by John F. Dovidio, P. Glick and L. A. Rudman, pp. 208–24. Malden, Mass.: Blackwell, 2005.

Jue, Linda. Personal communication, July, 2010.

Kennamer, J. David. "News Values and the Vividness of Information." *Written Communication 5,* no. 1 (1988): 108–23.

Kinney, Aaron. "'Looting' or 'Finding'?" *Salon.com* (2005), http://dir.salon.com/story/news/feature/2005/09/01/photo_controversy/index.html.

Kirtz, Bill. "How Award-Winning Investigative Reporters Earn Readers' Attention, Impress Advertisers." *Poynter.org,* (2011), http://www.poynter.org/how-tos/newsgathering-storytelling/122403/how-award-winning-investigative-reporters-earn-readers-attention-impress-advertisers-work-around-editors/.

Kleider, Heather, Kathy Pezdek, Stephen D. Goldinger, and Alice Kirk. "Schema-Driven Source Misattribution Errors: Remembering the Expected from a Witnessed Event." *Applied Cognitive Psychology 22* (2008): 1–20.

Klosterman, Chuck. "All I Know Is What I Read in the Papers." In *Sex, Drugs, and Cocoa Puffs: A Low Culture Manifesto.* New York: Scribner, 2004.

Koch, T. *The News as Myth: Fact and Context in Journalism.* Westport, Conn.: Greenwood Press, 1990.

Kolb, David A. *Experiential Learning: Experience as the Source of Learning and Development*. Englewood Cliffs, N.J.: Prentice Hall, 1984.

Kruglanski, Arie W., and Tallie Freund. "The Freezing and Unfreezing of Lay-Interferences: Effects on Impressional Primacy, Ethnic Stereotyping, and Numerical Anchoring." *Journal of Experimental Social Psychology 19*, no. 5 (1983): 448–68.

Kunda, Ziven. "The Case for Motivated Reasoning." *Psychological Bulletin 108*, no. 3 (1990): 480–98.

Larrick, Richard P. "Debiasing." In *Blackwell Handbook of Judgment and Decision Making*, edited by Derek J. Koehler and Nigel Harvey. Malden, Mass.: Blackwell, 2004.

Lasorsa, Dominic, and Jia Dai. "When News Reporters Deceive: The Production of Stereotypes." *Journalism and Mass Communication Quarterly 84*, no. 2 (2007): 281–98.

Lerner, Jennifer S., and Philip E. Tetlock. "Accounting for the Effects of Accountability." *Psychological Bulletin 125*, no. 2 (1999): 255–75.

Lester, Paul Martin. "Images and Stereotypes." In *Journalism Ethics: A Reference Handbook*, edited by Elliot D. Cohen and Deni Elliott. Santa Barbara, Calif.: ABC-CLIO, 1997.

Levinson, Martin H. "General Semantics and Media Ethics." *ETC: A Review of General Semantics 64*, no. 3 (2007): 255–60.

Lippmann, Walter. *Public Opinion*. New York: Macmillan, 1922.

Longmore, Andrew. "Death at 90 mph—Was Georgian Really the Only One to Blame for Crash that Killed Him at Winter Games?" *The Sunday Times*, February 14, 2010, pp. 12,13.

Lord, C. G., M. Lepper, and W. C. Thompson. "Inhibiting Biased Assimilation in the Consideration of New Evidence on Social Policy Issues." Paper presented at the American Psychological Association, Montreal, Canada, September, 1980.

Lord, Charles G., Lee Ross, and Mark R. Lepper. "Biased Assimilation and Attitude Polarization: The Effects of Prior Theories on Subsequently Considered Evidence." *Journal of Personality and Social Psychology 37*, no. 11 (1979): 2098–109.

Luft, Kerry. Interview with author, 2010.

Lustig, Myron W., and Jolene Koester. *Intercultural Competence: Interpersonal Communication across Cultures*, 3rd ed. New York: Longman, 1999.

Macrae, C. Neil, and Galen V. Bodenhausen. "Social Cognition: Thinking Categorically about Others." *Annual Review of Psychology 51* (2000): 93–120.

Macrae, C. N., A. B. Milne, and G. V. Bodenhausen. "Stereotypes as Energy-Saving Devices: A Peek inside the Cognitive Toolbox." *Journal of Personality and Social Psychology 66* (1984): 37–47.

Martin, Andrew. Interview with author, November, 2010.

Maynard Institute. "Chapter 6." In *How We See Our Sources, How They See Themselves*. Oakland, Calif.: Maynard Institute, 2011.

Maynard Institute. "Fault Lines." http://www.maynardije.org/faultlines, 2011.

Meadows, Susannah. "Crystal Mangum's Return to Court: A Sad Final Chapter to the Duke Lacrosse Scandal." *Newsweek,* Feb. 22, 2010. http://www.newsweek.com/2010/02/22/crystal-mangum-s-return-to-court.html.

Messaris, Paul, and Linus Abraham. "The Role of Images in Framing News Stories." In *Framing Public Life: Perspectives on Media and Our Understanding of the Social World,* edited by Stephen D. Reese, Oscar H. Gandy, Jr., and August E. Grant, pp. 215–26. Mahwah, N.J.: Lawrence Erlbaum, 2003.

National Association of Hispanic Journalists. "NAHJ Urges News Media to Stop Using the Term 'Illegals' When Covering Immigration," http://www.nahj.org/2009/09/nahj-urges-news-media-to-stop-using-the-term-illegals-when-covering-immigration/, 2009.

National Press Photographers Association. "NPPA Code of Ethics," http://www.nppa.org/about_us/governance/bylaws.html, 2011.

Nelkin, Dorothy. "AIDS and the News Media." *The Milbank Quarterly 69,* no. 2 (1991): 293–307.

Nelson, Thomas E., Rosalee A. Clawson, and Zoe M. Oxley. "Media Framing of a Civil Liberties Conflict and Its Effect on Tolerance." *American Political Science Review 91,* no. 3 (1997): 567–83.

Newsweek. "Should Joseph Stack Be Called a Terrorist?," February 20, 2010, http://www.newsweek.com/2010/02/20/should-joseph-stack-be-called-a-terrorist.html.

Nickerson, Raymond S. "Confirmation Bias: A Ubiquitous Phenomenon in Many Guises." *Review of General Psychology 2,* no. 2 (1998): 175–220.

Nisbett, Richard, and Lee Ross. *Human Inference: Strategies and Shortcomings of Social Judgment,* edited by James J. Jenkins, Walter Mischel, and Willard W. Hartup, Century Psychology Series. Englewood Cliffs, N.J.: Prentice-Hall, 1980.

O'Sullivan, Chris S., and Francis T. Durso. "Effect of Schema-Incongruent Information on Memory for Stereotypical Attributes." *Journal of Personality and Social Psychology 47,* no. 1 (1984): 55–70.

Oliver, Michael. "Disability Definitions: The Politics of Meaning." In *The Meaning of Difference: American Constructions of Race, Sex and Gender, Social Class, Sexual Orientation, and Disability,* edited by Karen E. Rosenbaum and Toni-Michelle C. Travis, pp. 176–79. Boston: McGraw Hill, 2008.

On the Media. "Stop, Drop and Roll." National Public Radio, May, 2009, http://www.onthemedia.org/transcripts/2009/05/01/01.

Oswald, Margit E., and Stefan Grosjean. "Confirmation Bias." In *Cognitive Illusions,* edited by Rüdiger F. Pohl, pp. 79–96. New York: Psychology Press, 2004.

Parsigian, E. K. "News Reporting: Method in the Midst of Chaos." *Journalism Quarterly 64,* no. 4 (1987): 721–30.

Parsons, Christi. Interview with author, 2008.

Payne, Ruby K. *A Framework for Understanding Poverty* 4th ed. Highlands, Tex.: aha! Process, 2005.

Perlmutter, David, and Gretchen L. Wagner. "The Anatomy of a Photojournalistic Icon: Marginalization of Dissent in the Selection and Framing of 'A Death in Genoa.'" *Visual Communication 3*, no. 1 (2004): 91–108.

Pettigrew, Thomas F. "The Measurement and Correlates of Category Width as a Cognitive Variable." *Journal of Personality 26*, no. 4 (1958): 532–544.

Petty, Richard E., and Duane T. Wegener. "Flexible Correction Processes in Social Judgment: Correcting for Context-Induced Contrast." *Journal of Experimental Social Psychology 29*, no. 2 (1993): 137–65.

Pew Forum on Religion and Public Life. "The Future of the Global Muslim Population." Washington, D.C.: Pew Research Center, Jan. 27, 2011.

Pew Hispanic Center. "Country of Origin Profiles." Washington, D.C.: Pew Hispanic Center, April 22, 2010.

Pew Research Center for the People and the Press. "Press Accuracy Rating Hits Two Decade Low," Washington, D.C.: Pew Research Center for the People and the Press, Sept. 13, 2009.

Pew Research Center for the People and the Press. "Death of Bin Laden: More Coverage Than Interest." Washington, D.C.: Pew Research Center for the People and the Press, 2011.

Pew Research Center. "Muslim-Western Tensions Persist." In *Pew Global Attitudes Project*. Washington, D.C.: Pew Research Center, 2011.

Peyser, Andrea. "Mosque Madness at Ground Zero." *New York Post*, May 13, 2010.

Poplin, Kyle. Interview with author, 2010.

Pratto, Felicia, James Sidanius, Lisa M. Stallworth, and Bertram F. Malle. "Social Dominance Orientation: A Personality Variable Predicting Social and Political Attitudes." *Journal of Personality and Social Psychology 67*, no. 4 (1994): 741–63.

Price, Vincent, David Tewksbury, and Elizabeth Powers. "Switching Trains of Thought: The Impact of News Frames on Readers' Cognitive Responses." *Communication Research 24*, no. 5 (1997): 481–507.

Project for Excellence in Journalism. "Principles of Journalism." Washington, D.C.: Pew Research Center, www.journalism.org/resources/principles, 1997.

Project Implicit. "Frequently Asked Questions." IAT Corp, 2007, https://implicit.harvard.edu/implicit/demo/background/faqs.html#faq3.

Puente, Teresa. Interview with author, August, 2010.

Rainville, Raymond E., Al Roberts, and Andrew Sweet. "Recognition of Covert Racial Prejudice." *Journalism Quarterly 55*, no. 2 (1978): 256–59.

Reuters. "Reporting About People." In *Handbook of Journalism*. New York: Thomson Reuters, http://handbook.reuters.com/index.php/Main_Page, 2008.

Rochlin, Martin. "The Heterosexual Questionnaire." In *The Meaning of Difference: American Constructions of Race, Sex and Gender, Social Class, Sexual Orientation, and Disability,* edited by Karen E. Rosenblum and Toni-Michelle C. Travis, p. 175. Boston: McGraw-Hill, 2008.

Roehling, Mark V., Patricia V. Roehling, and L. Maureen Odland. "Investigating the Validity of Stereotypes About Overweight Employees: The Relationship Between Body Weight and Normal Personality Traits." *Group and Organization Management 33,* no. 4 (2008): 392–424.

Ronis, David L., J. Frank Yates, and John P. Kirscht. "Attitudes, Decisions, and Habits as Determinants of Repeated Behavior." In *Attitude Structure and Function,* edited by A. R. Pratkanis, S. J. Breckler and A. G. Greenwald, pp. 213–40. Hillsdale, N.J.: Erlbaum, 1989.

Ross, Lee, and Craig A. Anderson. "Shortcomings in the Attribution Process: On the Origins and Maintenance of Erroneous Social Assessments." In *Judgment under Uncertainty: Heuristics and Biases,* edited by Daniel Kahneman, Paul Slovic and Amos Tversky, 129–52. Cambridge: Cambridge University Press, 1982.

Rudman, Laurie A., Richard D. Ashmore, and Melvin L. Gary. "'Unlearning' Automatic Biases: The Malleability of Implicit Prejudice and Stereotypes." *Journal of Personality and Social Psychology 81,* no. 5 (2001): 856–68.

Samuels, Christina. Interview with author, 2010.

Schaffer, Jan. Interview with author, August, 2010.

Schaller, Mark, and Lucian G. Conway III. "From Cognition to Culture: The Origins of Stereotypes That Really Matter." In *Cognitive Social Psychology: The Princeton Symposium on the Legacy and Future of Social Cognition,* edited by Gordon B. Moskowitz, pp. 163–76. Mahwah, N.J.: Erlbaum, 2001.

Schneider, David J. *The Psychology of Stereotyping.* New York: Guilford Press, 2004.

Schön, Donald A. *The Reflective Practitioner: How Professionals Think in Action.* New York: Basic Books, 1983.

Schuette, R., and R. H. Fazio. "Attitude Accessibility and Motivation as Determinants of Biased Processing: A Test of the MODE Model." *Personality and Social Psychology Bulletin 21* (1995): 704–10.

Shadid, Anthony. "The Iraq Experience Poses Critical Questions for Journalists." *Nieman Reports* (2004), http://www.nieman.harvard.edu/reports/article/100828/The-Iraq-Experience-Poses-Critical-Questions-For-Journalists.aspx.

Shafer, R. "What Minority Journalists Identify as Constraints to Full Newsroom Equality." *Howard Journal of Communications 4,* no. 3 (1993): 195–208.

Shoemaker, Pamela J. "Hardwired for News: Using Biological and Cultural Evolution to Explain the Surveillance Function." *Journal of Communication 46,* no. 3 (1996): 32–47.

Shoemaker, Pamela J. "News and Newsworthiness: A Commentary." *Communications 31* (2006): 105–11.

Shoemaker, Pamela J., and Stephen D. Reese. *Mediating the Message: Theories of Influences on Mass Media Content,* 2nd ed. White Plains, N.Y.: Longman, 1996.

Shoemaker, Pamela J., L. H. Danielian, and N. Brendlinger. "Deviant Acts, Risky Business and U.S. Interests: The Newsworthiness of World Events." *Journalism Quarterly 68,* no. 4 (1991): 781–95.

Shreffler, Annie. Interview with author, June, 2010.

Sledge, Matt. "Just How Far Is the 'Ground Zero Mosque' from Ground Zero?" *The Huffington Post* (July 28, 2010), http://www.huffingtonpost.com/matt-sledge/just-how-far-is-the-groun_b_660585.html.

Snell, Roger, and Michael J. Berens. "Audit Clears Landlord-Police Officer." *The Columbus Dispatch,* March 14 1990.

Society of Professional Journalists. "Code of Ethics." http://www.spj.org/ethicscode.asp, 1996.

Sontag, Susan. "The Double Standard of Aging." *Saturday Review,* Sept. 23, 1972, pp. 29–38.

Sorrentino, Richard M., and Judith-Ann C. Short. "Uncertainty Orientation, Motivation, and Cognition." In *Handbook of Motivation & Cognition: Foundations of Social Behavior,* edited by Richard M. Sorrentino and E. Tory Higgins, pp. 379–403. New York: Guilford Press, 1986.

Spitzberg, Brian H., and Gabrielle Changnon. "Conceptualizing Intercultural Competence." In *The Sage Handbook of Intercultural Competence,* edited by Darla K. Deardorff, p. 11. Thousand Oaks, Calif.: Sage, 2009.

Sprengelmeyer, M. E. "Bringing It Home: U.S. Earnings Mean Better Life for Melgozas in Mexico." *Ventura County Star,* April 6, 1997.

Sprengelmeyer, M. E. Interview with author, 2010.

Stangor, Charles. "The Study of Stereotyping, Prejudice, and Discrimination within Social Psychology." In *Handbook of Prejudice, Stereotyping, and Discrimination,* edited by Todd D. Nelson, pp. 1–22. New York: Psychology Press, 2009.

Steele, Bob. "Ask These 10 Questions to Make Good Ethical Decisions." *Poynter. org* (2002), www.poynter.org/latest-news/everyday-ethics/talk-about-ethics/1750/ask-these-10-questions-to-make-good-ethical-decisions/.

Steinhorn, Leonard. "Media Watch: Now's a Good Time to Remember Richard Jewell." Center for History and New Media at George Mason University (July 5, 2002), http://hnn.us/articles/149.html.

Stocking, S. Holly, and Paget H. Gross. *How Do Journalists Think? A Proposal for the Study of Cognitive Bias in Newsmaking.* Bloomington, Ind.: ERIC Clearinghouse on Reading and Communication Skills, 1989.

Stuart, Heather. "Media Portrayal of Mental Illness and Its Treatments: What Effect Does It Have on People with Mental Illness?" *CNS Drugs: Drug Therapy in Neurology and Psychiatry 20,* no. 2 (2006): 99–106.

Taylor, Jr., Stuart, and K. C. Johnson. *Until Proven Innocent: Political Correctness and the Shameful Injustices of the Duke Lacrosse Rape Case.* New York: St. Martin's Press, 2007.

Tetlock, Philip E., and Richard Boettger. "Accountability: A Social Magnifier of the Dilution Effect." *Journal of Personality and Social Psychology 57,* no. 3 (1989): 388–98.

Tompkins, Al. "Teachapalooza!" In *Let's Get Critical* presentation. St. Petersburg, Fla.: Poynter Institute, 2011.

Trumbo, Craig W., Sharon Dunwoody, and Robert Griffin, J. "Journalists, Cognition, and the Presentation of an Epidemiologic Study." *Science Communication* 19 (1998): 238–365.

Tuller, David. *The Reporting Diversity Manual.* London: Media Diversity Institute, 2004.

Tversky, Amos, and Daniel Kahneman. "Belief in the Law of Small Numbers." In *Judgment under Uncertainty: Heuristics and Biases,* edited by Daniel Kahneman, Paul Slovic, and Amos Tversky, pp. 23–31. Cambridge: Cambridge University Press, 1982.

Tversky, Amos, and Daniel Kahneman. "Judgment under Uncertainty: Heuristics and Biases." In *Judgment Under Uncertainty: Heuristics and Biases,* edited by Daniel Kahneman, Paul Slovic, and Amos Tversky, pp. 3-22. Cambridge: Cambridge University Press, 1982.

Warren, Ellen. "President, Friends Praise Baldrige's Cowboy Spirit." *The Miami Herald,* July 30, 1987.

Warren, Ellen. Interview with author, November, 2010.

Wason, Peter C. "On the Failure to Eliminate Hypothesis in a Conceptual Task." *Quarterly Journal of Experimental Psychology* 14 (1960): 129–40.

Wigboldus, Daniel H. J., Jeffrey W. Sherman, Heather L. Franzese, and H. L. van Knippenberg. "Capacity and Comprehension: Spontaneous Stereotyping under Cognitive Load." *Social Cognition* 22, no. 3 (2004): 292–309.

Wilson, Cintra. "Playing to the Middle." *New York Times,* August 11, 2009.

Wilson, Timothy D., and Nancy Brekke. "Mental Contamination and Mental Correction: Unwanted Influences on Judgments and Evaluations." *Psychological Bulletin 116,* no. 1 (1994): 117–42.

Wilson, Timothy D., David B. Centerbar, and Nancy Brekke. "Mental Contamination and the Debiasing Problem." In *Heuristics and Biases: The Psychology of Intuitive Judgment,* edited by Thomas Gilovich, Dale Griffin, and Daniel Kahneman, pp. 185–200. Cambridge: Cambridge University Press, 2002.

Wiltz, Teresa. Interview with author, 2009.

Woods, Keith. "Diversity across the Curriculum Seminar." St. Petersburg, Fla.: Poynter Institute for Media Studies, 2009.

Woods, Keith. "Diversity Tip Sheets: Is It Something I Said?" *Poynter.org* (Feb. 18, 2008), www2.poynter.org/column.asp?id=58&aid=137948.

INDEX